PC BIOS

Improve & Upgrade Your PC's Computing Power!

Heinz Lange

D1220225

DATA BECKER

Abacus

Copyright © 2000   **Abacus**
5370 52nd Street SE
Grand Rapids, MI 49512
www.abacuspub.com

Copyright © 1999   **Data Becker**
Merosingerstrasse 30
40223 Duesseldorf, Germany

This book is copyrighted. No part of this book may be reproduced, stored in a retrieval system, or transmitted in any form or by any means, electronic, mechanical, photocopying, recording or otherwise without the prior written permission of Abacus Software.
Every effort has been made to ensure complete and accurate information concerning the material presented in this book. However, Abacus Software can neither guarantee nor be held legally responsible for any mistakes in printing or faulty instructions contained in this book. The authors always appreciate receiving notice of any errors or misprints.

This book contains trade names and trademarks of several companies. Any mention of these names or trademarks in this book are not intended to either convey endorsement or other associations with this book.

Printed in the U.S.A.

ISBN 1-55755-364-5

10 9 8 7 6 5 4 3 2 1

Contents

BIOS: Basic Input Output System

Although PC technology has developed quickly in the last few years, it has also become easier and more user friendly. However, this doesn't necessarily apply to the BIOS Setup. It and its mysterious menu items are nearly the same as they've always been. Fortunately, BIOS really is not nearly as complicated as is often portrayed. After looking at the BIOS in this chapter, you'll understand the menu items and their functions. Then you will be able to optimize your computer's memory and hard drive access, the ISA and PCI buses, graphic functions and the interfaces. As a result, your PC will gain in performance and you won't have to spend any additional money.

What is BIOS?

Why does the PC need a BIOS, and what effect do these mysterious Setup settings have? Many users have probably already looked at the Setup menu, but very quickly became intimidated. The user manual from the motherboard manufacturer might describe how to enter the date and time and will possibly discuss some other options very briefly, but there's no information about the rest. Thus, normal users have some definite problems that this book should help solve. This book can't explain all the possible options of the various BIOS versions from all manufacturers, but it will produce a stable computer with a lot of performance.

The schematic structure

BIOS is an acronym for Basic Input Output System. It serves as a standardized communication interface between the computer's hardware and the operating system. BIOS is a small ROM (Read Only Memory) chip on the PC's motherboard. A basic software program containing all BIOS functions is permanently stored in the ROM. This functions as a basic operating system and is responsible for starting the PC. This hardware integrated with software is also referred to as *firmware*.

1. BIOS: Basic Input Output System

Example of BIOS on the motherboard

BIOS history

Intel Corporation developed two sensational microprocessors near the end of the 1970s called the Intel 8086 and the Intel 8088. IBM decided to make an affordable computer system out of the 8088 for commercial and private use. Microsoft created the operating system. This operating system consisted of two parts, one solidly anchored in the BIOS and the other consisting of program files and utilities.

Operating system fundamentals
Old operating systems are based on the BIOS. The BIOS itself is one part of the operating system and the other part consists of the operating system program files. The program files consist of utilities and a kernel that is loaded into the main memory when the computer boots. For example, the kernel of a Microsoft operating system consists of the msdos.sys and io.sys files. The kernel routine msdos.sys controls the keyboard input and the screen output. The IO.SYS kernel routine communicates with the BIOS and contains the actual program code of the operating system and a process control for the hardware.

The program files for starting the PC were scanned into the main memory. This allowed continuous communication with the BIOS. The utilities were for additional system tasks. The operating system was called DOS (Disk Operating System). IBM introduced the complete PC with the operating system in 1981. Many companies became interested in copying ("cloning") this PC. Since parts were freely available, there were no problems in doing so. Also, Microsoft made the operating system itself available to other licensees. Only the BIOS was copyrighted property of IBM, and IBM was not willing to sell licenses. That meant someone had to develop a new BIOS that didn't infringe IBM's copyright.

Compaq Computer Corporation had developed such a BIOS by 1983 in cooperation with an unidentified company. At the same time, they introduced a PC that worked with the same technology as the original IBM PC XT. A short time later Phoenix Technologies released a BIOS package consisting of the source text for IBM-compatible BIOS software and a version of DOS. Popular manufacturers of today, such as AMI, Award and MR-BIOS, followed suit and also developed their own source code for an IBM-compatible BIOS.

The operation is no secret

When you turn on your PC, it requires information to detect its components and to find the operating system on a floppy disk, the hard drive or a CD-ROM. This information is stored in the BIOS. First, the BIOS performs a self test of the PC. This test contains diagnostic routines for initializing the hardware and peripherals, such as the video card, the main memory, the processor, the keyboard, etc., and for checking their functions. You'll see an error message on your screen if an error is detected. If the monitor cannot be addressed due to a hardware error on the motherboard, the BIOS uses *beep codes* that are output by the system loud speaker.

This self test is also called the "POST" (Power On Self Test) since it takes place right after you power up the PC. Next, BIOS looks for additional BIOS memory chips, which could be located on a plug-in card, such as the video card or a SCSI controller. If present, they now run their routines and supplement or replace some functions of the system BIOS. If the components found in the POST no longer match the data stored in the CMOS (as the result of a hardware change, for example) a message appears on the screen prompting you to enter the BIOS Setup.

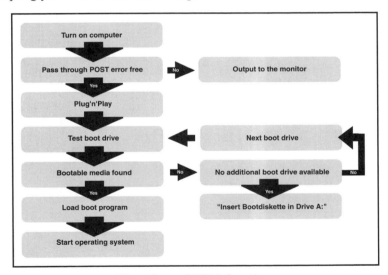

Flow chart of BIOS functions

After all the hardware components have been found and checked, Plug & Play goes to work, provided the BIOS has this option. The interrupts and DMA channels of the plug-in cards in the ISA and PCI buses are queried and distributed. Not until this point is the onboard hardware, which is located directly on the motherboard and in its ISA/PCI slots, configured for operation. After that the BIOS accesses the first sector of the hard drive, also termed the *boot sector*, and starts the "bootstrap loader." This is a small program that knows the file structure of the storage medium and can call the operating system's start routine. Then the operating system kernel is read into the main memory and control of the hardware passes on to the operating system.

An interpreter between two worlds

When the system is running after a successful boot, the BIOS acts as a mediator between the hardware and the software. The operating system can communicate through the BIOS with the hardware and the hardware can communicate with the BIOS. The BIOS works as an interface between the operating system and the hardware.

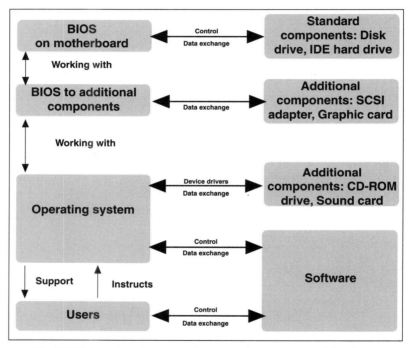

The BIOS interfaces between the operating system and hardware

However, only older operating systems such as MS DOS 6.2 or Novell DOS 7 use this function. The new generation of operating systems, such as Windows 95/98, NT or OS/2, circumvent the BIOS and communicate directly with the hardware through the appropriate drivers.

1. BIOS: Basic Input Output System

CMOS, EPROM and FLASH-ROM

Strictly speaking, the BIOS doesn't just consist of the ROM memory that contains the program, but also includes a RAM module that stores all the settings from the Setup menu and synchronizes them with the programmed data in the ROM. The RAM is designed in CMOS (Complementary Metal Oxide Semiconductor) technology. Because both components form one unit, you'll hear CMOS-RAM. Because the CMOS is a volatile memory, it's not permanent. An additional power source is necessary to ensure that the CMOS saves the data even after you turn off your PC. This power source comes from a battery, similar to that in a watch. This is usually a button cell seated in a retaining clip on the motherboard. This cell typically lasts about four to five years, since the CMOS technology is extremely energy efficient. However, once the battery is removed, the BIOS loses all the settings, and your computer is no longer able to boot. On older motherboards the battery is integrated with the clock chip and can't be removed.

Obsolete BIOS with EPROM

As PROM (Programmable ROM), the first ROM chips were only read-only chips. After they were programmed with their information, they could not be updated or erased. Programming occurred with a special device called the EPROM burner that "burned" the software into the ROM electronically.

Then EPROMs (Erasable Programmable ROM) were developed. EPROM chips could be burned with the same device but could also be erased with an additional device that used a special UV light. Therefore, an erase protection sticker is placed over the light-sensitive memory cell on the top of the programmed EPROM. The opaque erase protection sticker blocks sunlight from the chip. This sticker also displays data from the manufacturer. If a new BIOS is to be used here, the socketed chip must be replaced by hand with a newly programmed chip. This is still the case with many older 486 motherboards.

The current BIOS with FLASH-ROM

An EEPROM (Electrically Erasable Programmable ROM) is usually used today. This is also called FLASH-ROM. The EEPROM can be reburned by applying programming voltage. Only users with an EEPROM chip on the motherboard can update the basic software without additional hardware. The user doesn't even notice this procedure in the EEPROM. The update software from the motherboard manufacturer takes care of everything. FLASH-ROMs have been used since the introduction of the PCI bus. See Chapter 9 to learn how to tell which ROM chip is on your motherboard and how to perform a BIOS update.

1. BIOS: Basic Input Output System

Frequently used EEPROM chips	
Manufacturer	Programming voltage
Intel P28F001	12 Volts
Intel P28F001BX-T	12 Volts
Intel P28F010	12 Volts
CSI CAT28F0101P	12 Volts
MX28F1000PL	12 Volts
MX28F1000PC	5 Volts
SST PH29EE010	5 Volts
Winbond W29EE011	5 Volts

The connection between BIOS-CMOS, BIOS Setup and BIOS chipset

How does the BIOS Setup relate to the motherboard's chipset? The chipset needs a software program for the settings of the internal registers, and this software program is in the BIOS. This program is specially synchronized to the motherboard and its chipset.

A chipset module (TX) on the motherboard

The following table shows the diversity of the current chipsets. Each has its own options in the BIOS Setup menus.

1. BIOS: Basic Input Output System

The model descriptions of the current chipsets		
Manufac	Code Name	Chipset
Intel	Triton	430FX
Intel	Triton 2	430HX
Intel	Triton 3	430VX
Intel	Triton 4	430TX
Intel		440FX, 440LX, 440BX
Intel		450GX, 450KX
ALI	Aladdin 4	M1531
ALI	Aladdin 4+	M1531
ALI	Aladdin 5	M1541
AMD	AMD640	
SIS		5571, 5581/2, 5597/98, 5591
VIA	Apollo VPX/pro	82C585
VIA	Apollo VP2/97	82C595
VIA	Apollo VP3	82C597

The chipset and its registers

BIOS main menu

Chipset Features Setup, Advanced Chipset Setup

The BIOS Setup gives you tremendous influence over the chipset. This program connects the individual components on the motherboard and regulates the data flow between them. How it does this and at what speed is determined by programmable registers, which are evaluated and set by the basic software in the BIOS. Options in the *Chipset Features Setup* or *Advanced Chipset Setup* affect the RAM timing, cache management and the ISA/PCI bus access. Many of these options are set to the safest value by *Auto Configuration*. Although this guarantees that the PC will function 100% in all situations, it also turns your PC into a slow crate.

This is a good starting point for tuning measures that offer up to 15% gain in performance. Depending on the manufacturer of the motherboard, the BIOS doesn't always have all the functions of the registers available. That's also why the menu items in the BIOS Setup of different motherboard manufacturers aren't always the same, despite having the same chipset from the same BIOS manufacturer. However, with a special tool (see Chapter 13) you can make them visible and sometimes even make changes to

1. BIOS: Basic Input Output System

them. So there's another tuning option for your PC. A standard for BIOS menu options isn't likely in the near future, so we may need to experiment a bit.

The Chipset

A motherboard chipset contains several chips that control all the components, including the memory, controller, interfaces and the bus system on the motherboard. As a rule the chips contain a PCI memory cache controller that is responsible for the complete memory management, a system I/O chip for the interfaces and a PCI/ISA bridge that controls the data stream between the ISA bus and the PCI bus. The settings in the BIOS have to be adapted to the hardware that is being used to ensure that the computer functions smoothly.

More Performance, Functionality and Compatibility from BIOS Setup

When you buy a PC, usually the BIOS Setup is automatically configured to the safest, slowest performance settings. The best configuration takes time and effort and has to be recreated each time the hardware components change. That's why most manufacturers are willing to add the parts, but don't want to perform the configuration. You probably don't want to buy a car with 115 horsepower that only delivers 75 horsepower due to poor settings. However, this is exactly what happens with many PCs. So why not get additional performance from your computer at no extra charge through BIOS tuning?

Here's what BIOS Setup has to offer

The BIOS Setup consists of a main menu with several levels that have submenus. The structure is based on system-related areas. However, as we mentioned, there are many different BIOS versions (approximately 1,800) from the manufacturers, all of which have different menu items. To prevent things from getting too cluttered, we'll limit ourselves to the most frequently occurring types from AWARD and AMI.

The AWARD BIOS main menu

Other manufacturers have similar menu options that essentially do the same things. It is only possible to select the menu functions using the keyboard. One exception is the WIN-BIOS version of AMI, which you can operate using the mouse and windows, just as you do Windows itself. See Chapter 3 for instructions on how to get into BIOS Setup.

```
┌─────────────────────────────────────────────────────────────┐
│            BIOS SETUP PROGRAM - BIOS SETUP UTILITIES          │
│    (C) Copyright 1990 American Megatrends, Inc. All Rights Reserved │
├─────────────────────────────────────────────────────────────┤
│                                                               │
│                     STANDARD CMOS SETUP                       │
│                     ADVANCED CMOS SETUP                       │
│                    ADVANCED CHIP SET SETUP                    │
│                  POWER MANAGEMENT BIOS SETUP                  │
│                       PERIPHERAL SETUP                        │
│             AUTO CONFIGURATION WITH BIOS DEFAULTS             │
│            AUTO CONFIGURATION WITH POWER-ON DEFAULTS          │
│                       CHANGE PASSWORD                         │
│                      HARD DISK UTILITY                        │
│                    WRITE TO CMOS AND EXIT                     │
│                  DO NOT WRITE TO CMOS AND EXIT               │
│                                                               │
├─────────────────────────────────────────────────────────────┤
│      Standard CMOS Setup for changing Time, Date, Hard Disk Type, etc. │
└─────────────────────────────────────────────────────────────┘
```

The AMI BIOS main menu

Which BIOS manufacturer?

When you buy a new PC or a new motherboard, it is the quality and equipment of the board that play the deciding role, not the brand of the BIOS. A brand name motherboard will always have a good BIOS. The manufacturer most often used is AWARD. AMI or Phoenix is used only rarely. However, for the most part, they are all identical in function.

Performance

Performance is well hidden in the menus and submenus of the Setup program. The BIOS is not only concerned with the boot procedure of the PC, it also controls the hardware on the motherboard. Access to the hardware is a deciding factor for performance. More than 50% of your hardware performance can be lost due to incorrect settings. The performance disappears into the infinite depths of the system. Your new PC is creeping along and you don't even know why. Not even the hotline can help. That's why it's so important to check the settings in the BIOS and optimize them to enjoy all of your performance potential. While this can sometimes be a lengthy trial of your patience, in the long run it will definitely be worth your while to unleash the complete 100% performance of your PC.

I. BIOS: Basic Input Output System

An overview of the main menu		
AWARD BIOS	AMI BIOS	FUNCTION
!! CPU SOFT MENU !!		CPU voltage and speed (settings are correctly set by PC manufacturer!)
STANDARD CMOS SETUP	STANDARD CMOS SETUP	Date, time, floppy drive and hard drive, video mode
BIOS FEATURES SETUP	ADVANCED CMOS SETUP	Cache areas, Shadow-RAM, typematic rate
CHIPSET FEATURES SETUP	ADVANCED CHIPSET SETUP	All chipset specific components
POWER MANAGEMENT SETUP	POWER MANAGEMENT BIOS SETUP	Energy-saving functions
PNP AND PCI SETUP	PCI / PLUG & PLAY SETUP	Interrupts for ISA and PCI components
INTEGRATED PERIPHERALS	PERIPHERAL SETUP	Interface and controller settings
IDE HDD AUTO DETECTION	AUTO-DETECT HARD DISKS	Automatic hard drive detection and entry in the BIOS
USER PASSWORD	CHANGE USER PASSWORD	Password for boot procedure
SUPERVISOR PASSWORD	CHANGE SUPERVISOR PASSWORD	Password for BIOS settings
LOAD SETUP DEFAULTS	AUTOCONFIGURATION WITH OPTIMAL SETTINGS	Set BIOS options to optimum values (programmed by the motherboard's manufacturer)
LOAD BIOS DEFAULTS	AUTOCONFIGURATION WITH FAIL SAVE SETTINGS	Reset BIOS options to initial values (programmed by the BIOS manufacturer)
SAVE & EXIT SETUP	SAVE SETTINGS AND EXIT	Save settings and exit Setup
EXIT WITHOUT SAVING	EXIT WITHOUT SAVING	Exit Setup without saving

Functionality and Compatibility

The BIOS plays an important role in the compatibility of your system. Hardware development does not stand still. Every day new components that are dependent on the BIOS appear on the market. For example, if your motherboard uses a new processor type that is not correctly detected, the new component won't be able to achieve its ultimate performance or your PC may not even boot up. In such cases, you must update the BIOS to bring the basic software up to date. That's why a Flash BIOS is such an advantage. It can copy the update directly from a diskette to the BIOS. You can get the software from the Internet, a BBS or from the service hotline. The best and fastest way to get the update is from the Internet. The manufacturers also have the most to offer from the Internet. Usually the service hotline of a motherboard manufacturer involves high costs.

1. BIOS: Basic Input Output System

BIOS Suppliers and Special Features

The BIOS market actually consists of only three suppliers. AWARD (http://www.award.com/) dominates about 2/3 of the market, while AMI (http://www.ami.com/) and Phoenix (http://www.ptltd.com/) split the other 1/3. All three suppliers have an almost identical range of functions and possible settings. Many motherboards are equipped with an AWARD BIOS. How did that happen? The motherboard manufacturers decide on a BIOS manufacturer, purchase the basic software and perhaps adapt it to their own product. Thus users have almost no influence in the selection of the system BIOS when they purchase a PC. They have to live with the BIOS installed on their motherboard or else use that of a different manufacturer. The company MR BIOS (http://mrbios.com/) offers a good alternative for almost all common motherboards with an enhanced range of functions, including more than just the default settings and even faster booting.

The BIOS range of functions

The entire range of BIOS functions only becomes visible in the BIOS menus. The more setting options that are available, the more flexibility the user has when it comes to hardware. Then it is possible to adjust the hardware to its optimum performance.

Standard Setup

If you're building a new PC or installing new components to your current PC, you'll have to use the BIOS Setup program. Even if you are only connecting a new printer or a ZIP drive to the parallel port, you may need to change a setting in the BIOS.

How To Access The BIOS

Outwitting BIOS

You have one more possibility if the shortcut keys listed here do not get you into BIOS Setup. Simply unplug the keyboard and restart the computer. Then the POST will detect an error and prompt you to press the shortcut key listed in the message, which starts BIOS Setup. Note the shortcut key and restart the computer with the keyboard connected again. Nothing should go wrong when you press the shortcut key during the memory test.

Each BIOS manufacturer uses a different shortcut key for accessing BIOS Setup. Try the keys listed in the table below. The timing is crucial. It is only possible to call Setup by pressing the key during the execution of the POST memory test that is displayed on the screen. You won't call Setup if you press the key too early or too late. If you do, you'll have to reset the PC and try again. You can also press the keys several times, but do not press and hold them down. This will result in a keyboard error.

Award	AMI	Phoenix
Del	Del	Del
Ctrl + Alt + Esc	F1	Ctrl + Alt + Esc
Ctrl + Alt + S		Ctrl + Alt + S
		F2

Some manufacturers, such as Compaq, Acer and Dell, use different shortcut keys than the ones the BIOS manufacturer provided in the Standard BIOS. If so, all you can do is experiment if you cannot locate the manual. Dell has the setup settings for each computer type for its own BIOS on its web site. The following table lists other possibilities.

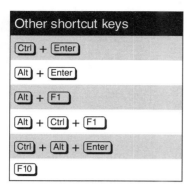

Very old PCs from DEC, Compaq and Olivetti have just a BIOS chip without BIOS Setup. The BIOS Setup software is on a floppy diskette. You will have to run an external program for Setup. Read the manual for the PC or a "Readme file" on the diskette itself.

Getting into BIOS Setup quickly

1. Find the BIOS manufacturer by the company logo that appears on screen right after the PC starts.

2. Find the appropriate shortcut key from the table.

3. Press the shortcut key during the memory test.

4. The main menu of BIOS Setup appears.

Operating the Setup menu

Once you're in BIOS Setup, use the cursor keys to move the cursor. You can call a selection list for specific fields (depending on the manufacturer of the BIOS).

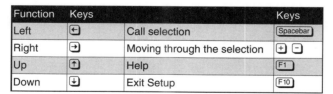

Keyboard operation

The keys and their functions are usually displayed at the bottom of the screen so you won't need to search the manual.

When you exit BIOS Setup, the program automatically prompts you to save the settings *(Write to CMOS and Exit?)* To save the settings to CMOS, press the Y key.

AMI WIN-BIOS is an exception. It works with windows technology that is similar in structure and function to Windows. You can operate this Setup program easily using the mouse or the keyboard.

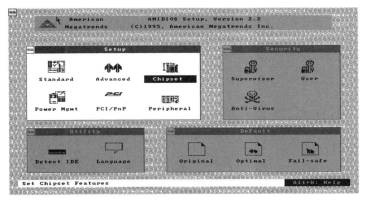

The main menu of the AMI WINBIOS

Keyboard operation

Any changes you make to the BIOS Setup normally will not damage the system. In the worst case, the monitor may stay dark. It's possible for your PC to emit a few beeps. In this case the settings you selected for a component are wrong and it's no longer possible to address the component. Press the [Ins] key when you start your PC to apply the default values for the BIOS. If this doesn't work, your last resort is to reset the BIOS via jumpers (see Chapter 11). Then you can start again with modifying the configuration.

Changing the BIOS Setup colors

You can also customize the colors of the BIOS Setup using the settings with the key functions displayed on the lower screen. Press [Shift] [F2] for the Award BIOS or [F2] for AMI. Press the indicated key(s) to change the color combination.

Online Help

Some BIOS versions have an online Help for the individual menu commands in Setup. Access the Help by pressing the [F1] key. Unfortunately, little help may be available because the EPROM has a maximum of 128K available and the BIOS program and the Help must fit in this small size. Therefore, check the motherboard manual for more information. It should describe some of the menu commands in more detail.

2. Standard Setup

Navigating through the menus

1. Each BIOS has a somewhat different function key layout. First, look at the displayed key layout in the main menu.

2. Select all the menu commands to get an overview of where to find what. Press [Esc] to return to the main menu.

3. Experiment to determine which keys let you change the options in the submenus. Now you see which settings are available.

4. Exit Setup by selecting the *Exit Without Saving* command so no changes are saved.

Enabled and disabled

You'll often see "Enabled" and "Disabled" many times when working through the BIOS menus. Enabled means the particular function is turned on and disabled means that it is turned off.

The default configuration

Whenever you build a new PC, change motherboards or update the BIOS, you must first put the BIOS in a Default configuration. You should see one or two menu commands for this purpose that start a "basic setting" in the BIOS.

Load BIOS defaults

This sets the minimum configuration in the Award BIOS. The BIOS manufacturer sets it so the PC runs. Use it only if you cannot get the PC to run with *Load Setup Defaults*. In the AMI BIOS you can use the *Auto Configuration with Fail Save Settings* option.

Load Setup defaults

This configuration, specified by the motherboard manufacturer, is synchronized with the chipset. It gives you a safe and somewhat powerful setting in the Award BIOS. The PC manufacturer usually enables this setting. The option in AMI BIOS is called *Auto Configuration with Optimal Settings*.

You can't get into the BIOS
❖ Did you press the shortcut key at the right time? You can only call BIOS Setup by pressing a shortcut key when the memory test is running. ❖ Does your motherboard have a BIOS Setup, or only a BIOS chip? Older motherboards, usually 386es and 486es, don't have a BIOS Setup in the BIOS chip. Instead they only have the BIOS chip and a separate Setup program on a floppy diskette. This also suggests how old these are since the BIOS versions are quite old. Therefore, it's not worth the effort because the setting possibilities for an improvement in performance are very slight.

Setting Date, Time and Daylight Savings Time

Setting the time and date

If there is a setting for automatically switching from Daylight Savings Time to normal time and back in the BIOS under *Daylight Saving,* disable it if you are not living in the USA.

It's true that you have more convenient ways to set the date, time and maybe even Daylight Savings Time in any operating system. However, to ensure that these values are already set when you install the operating system, you can also set them in the BIOS. The options are called *Date, Time* or *System Date* and *System Time.* The date format is usually international and ranges from 1/1/1900 and, depending on the date of manufacture for the BIOS, to 12/31/2099. Some BIOS versions also offer a choice between the international (day, month, year) and the US (month, day, year) format.

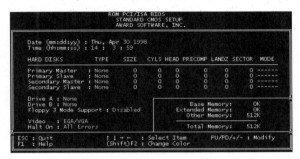

Standard Setup of the Award-BIOS

The RTC

The clock itself, called the RTC (Real-Time-Clock), is on the motherboard. It supplies the date and the time. The RTC uses the same power source as the CMOS to get data when the PC is not running. However, the accuracy is usually poorer compared to a conventional quartz clock due to frequency and temperature-dependent fluctuations.

Therefore, you need to correct the setting regularly. If you need precise time, buy a radio clock module and connect it to the parallel or serial port. It supplies the PC with the current date and time.

2. Standard Setup

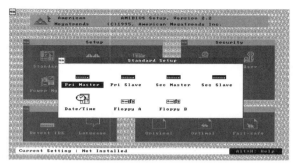

Standard Setup of the AMIBIOS with the selection for date/time and the drive settings

Addressing techniques for hard drives : CHS / LBA and (E)CHS / Large

These terms describe the addressing technique for the translation modes of the hard drive.

Modes	Size up to
CHS	528 Meg
LBA (old)	2.1 GB
LBA (new)	8.4 GB
(E)CHS / Large	8.4 GB

The addressing technique

Picture the addressing technique like you would the post addressing on a letter or a package. A letter or package has the name, the street and the city but with a hard drive, it's the cylinders, heads and the sectors. The data are addressed similar to a letter sent by mail, and are delivered to the appropriate area on the hard drive.

The flood of technical terms

Since CHS, LBA, (E)CHS and Large deal with the hard drive, we'll need to start by briefly explaining the function of the hard drive. This will help you understand terms such as cylinders, heads and sectors. You can skip this information if you're already familiar with hard drives.

Hard drive operation

A hard drive has several parts. Its data carrier usually consists of several aluminum plates on top of each other. These plates are coated with an extremely thin magnetic layer. They rotate at 3,600 rpm (revolutions per minute) with old hard drives and 10,000 rpm with current models. The read/write heads are above them and float on a cushion of air above the plate. This cushion of air results from the rotation

18

and is important because direct contact with the plate surface would damage the extremely thin magnetic coating. This floating on a cushion of air lets the read/write heads move in the right position above the data carrier. The controller board governs access to the read/write heads and transfers the data to the interface.

The internals of a hard drive

Recording technology

To make it possible to write and read data to and from the hard drive, a physical partitioning must occur. This physical partitioning is specified in *cylinders* and *sectors*. The sector is a memory block in a track that runs like a circle around the entire disk surface. One way to imagine this is to consider the hard drive as a pie that is cut into individual pieces. Each individual piece is a sector. The cylinder is the concentric tracks of the individual platters. The read/write heads are positioned so precisely that they can store the data in the memory blocks and retrieve it again.

2. Standard Setup

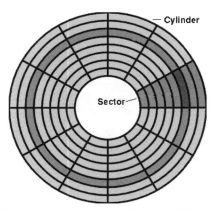

The physical structure of the hard drives

Old IDE hard drives use CHS mode (Cylinders-Heads-Sectors). It addresses the hard drive through cylinders, heads and sectors and therefore cannot manage more than 528 Meg. It works only with up to 1024 cylinder, 16 heads and 63 sectors (see Chapter 3).

Parameter	BIOS	LBA/(E)CHS	IDE max.
Sectors	63	63	255
Heads	16	255	16
Cylinders	1024	1024	65536
Capacity	528 Meg	8.4 GB	136.9 GB

Changing the mode

If you wish to change translation mode, make certain to back up your data first. Because the modes are not compatible with each other, you'll likely lose data. After the change, you have to format and partition the hard drive. Only then can you restore the backup data.

This is the limit for CHS mode. Although completely outdated, it's still called the **Normal** mode in BIOS because a larger hard drive above 528 Meg is addressed with a translation. The BIOS manages the data blocks with LBA (logical block addressing) or ECHS (**E**xtended-**CHS**). Through a translation, or more accurately, a conversion, the drive is partitioned into blocks that are numbered consecutively. The physical specification of the hard drive is translated into a logical specification.

LBA is the newer mode. ECHS or XCHS, also called **Large** in BIOS, is the older and less used mode. It also only functions with DOS as the operating system. If the hard drive is larger than 528 Meg and it doesn't support LBA mode, which is rare, use Large mode. If the hard drive is linked in the BIOS by *IDE AUTO DETECTION,* the possible modes are available for selection. If the hard drive is larger than 528 Meg and LBA is available, this setting is to be preferred over the others. This setting is also the most current.

Use the correct mode

If your hard drive is smaller than 528 Meg use normal mode, but if your hard drive is larger than 528 Meg, use LBA mode. If this mode is unavailable in your BIOS, use a hard drive manager. Only by using these two options can you address the larger memory.

If you only work with DOS and there is no LBA mode in the BIOS and no hard drive manager, you can also use Large mode. This applies in very rare cases for hard drives that are larger than 528 Meg and don't support LBA mode.

LBA translation
The POST routine creates a special hard drive parameter table called the EDPT (Enhanced-Drive-Parameter-Table). This table contains two records with the information of the cylinders, heads and sectors. The BIOS passes one record directly to the control system and the hard drive creates the other one. The hard drive creates the second record upon a command of the BIOS when LBA mode is selected. Each installed hard drive is entered in the EDPT and the corresponding mode of the hard drive is assigned through a flag.

Automatic Detection for EIDE Drives

Entering the parameters of the hard drive correctly into the BIOS was a big problem a few years ago. This was especially true when there wasn't any label with the values on the drive and the manual was useless or not available. The values were occasionally printed on the antistatic bag in which the drive was delivered. Unfortunately, this bag was usually discarded after installation and configuration. Then you might have trouble getting these values again from the manufacturer.

2. Standard Setup

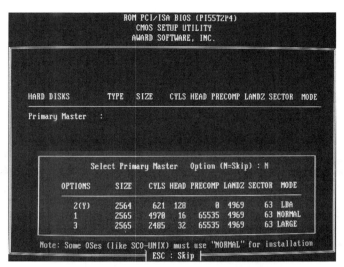

Automatic detection in the AWARD-BIOS

Automatic detection using MR-BIOS

If you use MR-BIOS, you can simply specify a question mark in the Size and Type box. Then the values will be automatically detected and entered.

Automatic detection and CD-ROM

You don't have to register a CD-ROM drive like a hard drive. Furthermore, it won't be detected by Auto Detection.

Fortunately, such work is now history. Thanks to the automatic detection of hard drives in today's BIOS Setup, which occurs using *IDE HDD AUTO DETECTION*, *Auto-Detect Hard Disc*, *Autotype Fixed Disk* or simply *Type*, it's almost automatic. The system BIOS reads out the values of the sectors, heads and cylinders and displays them with the possible operating modes (*LBA, LARGE, NORMAL*) in the selection menu. If the selection is confirmed, the values are displayed in the standard CMOS Setup and later written into the CMOS when you exit using *SAVE & EXIT* or *Save Settings and Exit*. The individual BIOS versions have different properties in using automatic detection. The menu command with Award and AMI is simply selected. The parameters are soon displayed. In MR-BIOS, the setting *Auto* is selected and with Phoenix the hard drives are detected by pressing (Enter) in the *Autotype Fixed Disk* field.

The SAVE & EXIT menu from the AWARD-BIOS

The operating system cannot address the hard drive until after it has been entered in the BIOS. If you install a new hard drive, you must first partition and format it before the operating system can work with it.

Other hard drive functions, which we'll talk about in the following chapters, will also make fine tuning of the hard drive possible. Don't make any changes to them in the BIOS Setup until after successfully restarting the PC.

Automatic is always good

Make certain to use automatic detection for hard drives if it's available in your BIOS. This ensures that the parameters of the hard drive are detected correctly.

CD-ROMs and other devices on the EIDE port have no influence on automatic detection.

2. *Standard Setup*

Automatic detection of the hard drive doesn't work

❖ Are the connection cables connected properly and in good order?
  Pin1of the controller has to match with Pin1 of the hard drive. The marked conductor on the 40-pin connection cable is used to mark Pin1 (it should also point at it). A torn, pinched cable or a cable coming loose on the plug can also be the cause.

❖ Are the master and slave correctly jumpered?
  Make certain t verify the configuration of master and slave or only master (without slave) for a hard drive. Check the jumper positions using the manual or imprint on the hard drive.

❖ Are the primary and secondary ports enabled in the BIOS or by jumper?
  The port to which the hard drives are connected must be enabled in the BIOS Setup (Integrated Peripherals) or on the controller (jumper). If the port is disabled, the connected hard drive(s) cannot be detected.

❖ Is the hard drive larger than 2.1 GB with an old BIOS version on the board?
  If incorrect values or no values are displayed for a hard drive larger than 2.1 GB, it means you have an outdated BIOS version produced before October 1996 on your motherboard. In this case, the only solution is to update the BIOS for the automatic detection to work. However, you might be able to use a hard drive manager, but read the instructions in the manual carefully when installing it.

❖ Do you have SCSI hard drives installed in your system instead of EIDE hard drives?
  It's possible that you have one or more SCSI hard drives installed in your system. They are automatically detected by their own controller and cannot be entered in the BIOS Setup.

❖ Very old IDE hard drives are often not detected, despite correct installation.
  If you are using an IDE hard drive from 1992 or earlier, it's possible that the system BIOS cannot correctly read out the drive information. You'll have to enter the values of the hard drive manually.

Manual entry of the hard drives

It's possible that automatic detection doesn't work. This could be caused by very old IDE hard drives or by two hard drives on one port that are not 100% compatible with each other. The two hard drives will only be found during automatic detection if one of the two is alone on the port as the master. They won't be detected with each other as master and slave. If there's no secondary port available to separate the hard drives from each other, many combinations will work. You'll have to enter the drive(s) manually in the standard CMOS Setup. A dialog box is available for this purpose. It's similar to a table where you enter the values of the hard drive.

Switch the master and the slave

Replace the master and slave settings with each other. While this is not always practical as far as drive properties are concerned, if the new combination runs without force, you usually get better performance.

Backing up hard drive parameters

Depending on which hard drive parameters your hard drive is registered in the BIOS, you must enter this setting again exactly so the data is not lost. If you didn't write down the settings or back them up in some other way, you won't be able to access the data on your hard drive. You can enter and even format EIDE hard drives with different parameters. Let's say that instead of entering 1002 cylinders, you only enter 980 cylinders in the BIOS Setup. Your hard drive would still function after formatting but with less disk space.

The following is an example. You have an older PC with a BIOS that doesn't have automatic hard drive detection. Someone entered the parameters manually in setup. Now you get a new motherboard for the PC and have the automatic detection enter the hard drive. After restarting, the PC no longer boots up as expected from the drive. Instead, the following message appears: *No System or Drive Error, Change and Press Key*. This means that the hard drive was not registered correctly before and you can no longer access your data.

```
HARD DISKS         TYPE    SIZE   CYLS HEAD PRECOMP LANDZ SECTOR  MODE
Primary Master   : None      0      0    0       0     0      0   ------
Primary Slave    : None      0      0    0       0     0      0   ------
Secondary Master : None      0      0    0       0     0      0   ------
Secondary Slave  : None      0      0    0       0     0      0   ------
```

The boxes for manual entry in the Award BIOS

The Type

The Type box has specifications for very old hard drive types up to 152 Meg included in a type numbering from 1 - 46. It's safe to ignore this for today's hard drives by selecting the setting *User* or even *Type 47*. Then you can enter values in the other boxes for Cylinders, Heads and Sectors. Newer BIOS versions also support the *"Auto"* setting. With this setting, each time you start the PC the values of the hard drive are read again and entered in the BIOS. This is a big advantage for users of removable hard drives of different sizes. If only SCSI hard drives are used, or there is no EIDE controller installed in the system, you have to enable the *None* or *Not Installed* settings.

Removable hard drives of different sizes

If you used removable hard drives of different sizes in your system, then you've probably realized the amount f work involved in entering of parameters in BIOS Setup when you switch hard drives. Fortunately, it doesn't have to be that way. If your BIOS supports the Auto option the parameters will be automatically read after each change.

2. *Standard Setup*

The Size

The *Size* box specifies the size of the hard drive by cylinders, heads and sectors, that the BIOS calculates itself. This entry is only for informational purposes and doesn't always have to be correct, especially with older hard drives. Therefore, no change is planned.

The Cylinders (Cyls)

In the *Cyls, Cyln, Cyl* or *Type* box you enter the number of cylinders. It varies, depending on the BIOS version and manufacturer, from 1024 to 16384 cylinders. In EIDE mode a maximum of 65536 cylinders would be possible.

The Heads (Head)

The heads of the hard drive are entered in the *Head, Heads, Hd* or *Hds* box. The number ranges from 1 - 16 heads.

The Precompensation (Precomp)

Enter the cylinder number for the Write Precompensation here. This box could be called *Write Precomp, WPComp* or *Precomp*. You can probably ignore it because it's only required for the truly old hard drives. Modern hard drives manage such hard drive internal affairs themselves. Leave this box set to *"0"*.

The Landing zone (Landz)

In the *LandZone, Lzone, Parking Cylinder* or *Park Cyl* box you define the track of the landing zone on which the hard drive heads can land after parking the hard drive motor. Use this only for old hard drive types that may be in the type list. Today's hard drives have a built-in parking mechanism for the heads built by the manufacturer that is activated when you shut off the PC.

The Sectors (Sector)

The number of sectors per track is entered in the *Sect, Sectors, Sct* or *Sectors/Track* box. Up to 63 sectors, or 64 with Phoenix, are supported. If the manufacturers used the maximum number of sectors, 255 sectors would be possible.

The Mode (Mode)

The settings determine the translation mode for LBA or Large. They are selected in the following listed boxes. The current hard drives all use LBA Mode if it is supported. However, this mode was not available in the BIOS versions until April 1994. In these versions the *Mode, IDE LBA Mode, Translate, IDE LBA Control* or *Large Disk Access Mode* option is available. For older BIOSes either an update or a hard drive manager is necessary so that hard drives larger than 528 Meg can be used completely.

Manual is inconvenient

If your BIOS does not have automatic detection built-in, you will have to enter the parameters manually.

Use the parameters that are specified on the hard drive, the packaging or in the manual for this purpose. Incorrect parameters either will not work at all or won't let you use the complete size of the hard drive.

Selecting floppy drives

You must also enter the floppy drives in the BIOS Setup. Some BIOSes can manage up to four drives. However, this also requires a controller card for four drives. A standard controller only manages two floppy drives. Enter the values of drive A or B through the selection list in the appropriate box. Floppy drives are defined in the following manner:

Size	Format
5.25"	360K
3.5"	720K
5.25"	1.2 Meg
3.5"	1.44 Meg
3.5"	2.88 Meg

Problems with 2.88 Meg floppy drives

If you install a 2.88 Meg drive and the BIOS does not support this format, you must use an appropriate driver from the drive manufacturer. Otherwise, the drive cannot be correctly addressed. Never use the driver and the BIOS support simultaneously.

Floppy 3 Mode support

In some BIOS versions you will find a setting option for *Floppy 3 Mode.* However, this mode is only used in Japan. In this case a 1.2 Meg format is used on the 3.5-inch floppy. For 3.5-inch floppy drives with 1.44 Meg or 720K, set it to *Disabled.*

Operating Your PC with Two Video Cards/Monitors

It's sometimes necessary to install a second video card when working with CAD, graphic design and image processing software. A dual video system results from a color video card and a monochrome video card. One reason this makes work easier is because the drawing tools appear on one monitor and the graphic itself appears on the other monitor but without the toolbar.

This type of system requires a program that also supports two video cards, such as Windows 98. However, the MDS (Multiple Display System) also has some problems. Not all video cards are supported as a second PCI or AGP video card in the system. You have to have a VGA part that can be disabled, either manually by jumper or automatically (currently some ATI models, Cirrus chip 5436, 7548 and 5446, the ET 6000, and a few with Trident and S3 chips are available).

2. Standard Setup

Before making any purchases, be sure to ask the manufacturer whether the card can be used as a secondary card in Windows 98, and whether it will work with your existing video card. The primary card is usually the one in the PCI slot with the smallest number, since it is detected first by the PnP system. If you have a video card onboard, it will automatically be used as the secondary card.

BIOS will automatically detect the existing video cards in the system. Therefore, automode is always active and as the default setting, no video card is provided. If only one video card is normally installed in the system, only this detected card will be displayed in *Primary Video*. On the other hand, if two video cards are installed, the user will specify one as the primary card and the BIOS automatically registers the other one as a secondary card. A secondary option cannot be changed. The boxes are named *Primary Display - Secondary Display, Video, Primary Video - Secondary Video* or *Video System*. The corresponding card is entered in the *Primary Video* box. This is the card that is to be controlled by the operating system. The *Secondary Video* box is automatically set to the other card. The primary video card is always active and the secondary card, enabled by the graphics software, is in standby mode.

The BIOS manufacturers also let you work without a video card in the system. This is important for a file or print server connected to a network. To using this power-saving measure, set the *Not installed* or *None* option in the *Primary Video* box. Exit BIOS Setup and save the setting. Now you can remove the video card from the system and restart the computer.

Installing the video cards

1. Plug both video cards into their slots on the motherboard.

2. Use the *Primary Video* option to select the video card that is to serve as the primary. The secondary video card will automatically be assigned.

All Settings Using CPU-SOFT-MENU

CPU-SOFT-MENU is a useful program because you won't have to work with jumpers to configure the processor. The CPU (Central Processing Unit, or simply the processor) can be set in BIOS Setup according to the manufacturer's specifications. Unfortunately, few motherboard manufacturers have yet to use this simple method.

```
              ROM PCI/ISA BIOS (2A59IA1B)
                  !! CPU SOFT MENU !!
                 AWARD SOFTWARE, INC.

 CPU Name Is : Intel Pentium II MMX

 CPU Operating Speed : User Define
 - Turbo Frequency   : Disabled
 - External Clock     : 66MHz
 - Multiplier Factor  : x3.5
 - Speed Error Hold   : Disabled




                              ESC : Quit        ↑↓→← : Select Item
                              F1  : Help        PU/PD/+/- : Modify
                              F5  : Old Values  <Shift>F2 : Color
                              F6  : Load BIOS   Defaults
                              F7  : Load Setup Defaults
```

The CPU-SOFT-MENU in the Award BIOS

All the settings for the processor occur in the *CPU-SOFT-MENU*. The CPU speed is determined by the internal and external clock. This clock must be selected exactly according to manufacturer specifications.

External and internal clock

The external clock is generated on the motherboard in a PLL frequency generator with a quartz crystal and electronic equipment. It makes the external clock available for the processor, the system and PCI bus as well as the ports. The processor has separate PLL chips integrated for the internal clock that are set by the multiplication factor.

The BIOS detects some processors automatically by the specification code and displays the type of CPU, the manufacturer and the processor family in the *CPU Name/Type* option. It cannot be modified.

BIOS option
CPU Operating Speed

You can enter the "real" processor clock directly here. The BIOS then automatically sets the *External Clock* and *Multiplier Factor* option to the correct values. For example, if you enter 166, 66 MHz appears in the *External Clock* option and 2.5X appears as the *Multiplier Factor*. If you wish to determine the values for *External Clock* and *Multiplier Factor* yourself, you have to select *User Defined*.

BIOS option
External Clock

The *External Clock* option determines the external clock. Depending on the motherboard, up to 83 MHz are available here.

BIOS option
Multiplier Factor

2. Standard Setup

The *Multiplier Factor* option determines the internal clock. Depending on the motherboard, an internal factor of up to 5.5X is available.

How to calculate the processor clock

If you multiply the two values times each other it results in the processor clock of most CPUs. Therefore, for a 166 MHz processor the external clock (External Clock) is set to 66 MHz and the internal clock (Multiplier Factor) is set to 2.5X (66 x 2.5 = 166). The manual for the motherboard usually includes a table with the processor types and the clock rates to be set. If your processor is not included, ask your dealer for the appropriate settings.

Although automatic detection is supposed to do this for you, the manufacturer refers to a manual entry of the values, since the detection is designed for processor models of the future. The following table contains some examples for setting the clock setting.

External Clock	Multiplier Factor	Processor
66	3.5	233
66	4	266
66	4.5	300

(Speed = external clock x internal clock)

This type of processor configuration is especially interesting for tuning enthusiasts who want to boost the processor to the next performance level. The technical term for this is *overclocking*. Without having to open the PC case for a different jumper configuration, you can switch between the possible performance levels in the BIOS Setup. For secure working in the office environment you use the "normal" setting and for games or multimedia you can use the "hot" setting. For a thorough description of how to do this, see Chapter 5. Note that using overclocking is dangerous. If the processor is used beyond its specifications, the result can be a system crash, data loss or destroyed hardware. Therefore, overclocking is only for advanced BIOS pros.

BIOS option
Turbo Frequency

A better option than overclocking, and one with less risk of damaging the processor, is called *Turbo-Frequency. It*'s an option in BIOS Setup. You'll see it displayed if the external clock of your CPU supports Turbo mode. It accelerates the external clock by 2.5%. However, as with overclocking, most motherboard manufacturers advise against using Turbo mode. The CPU could operate beyond the manufacturer specifications and eventually be damaged.

If you ever replace your processor for a different type, first set the speed to the minimum. The automatic detection doesn't always work correctly. If you forget that, you might not be able to boot your PC and you won't be able to get into *CPU-SOFT-MENU*. Then you'll either have to reinstall the old processor or reset by jumpers. However, by resetting, you delete the complete BIOS settings and you'll have to reconfigure everything.

BIOS option
CPU Power Plane

This option lets you determine the voltages for the processor. The following table describes the three possible setting options.

Options	Description
Single Voltage	For processor models (without MMX) that only require one voltage. Only the Plane Voltage option is enabled.
Dual Voltage	For processor models (with MMX) that require two voltages. The I/O Plane Voltage and Core Plane Voltage options are enabled.
Via CPU Marking	With this option the voltage is automatically set in the processor by the specifications code. The BIOS reads out the five-digit code (e.g. SY016) and can, as a result, determine the processor and the necessary voltage(s) for it. All other options are then disabled.

The *Via CPU Marking* option does not function with all processor types. The reason is that new types are constantly coming out on the market and their specification codes are not yet stored in the BIOS. In such cases, you must make the selection manually by the processor specifications.

BIOS option
Plane Voltage

Plane Voltage sets the processor voltage. This option is only active when the setting is at *Single Voltage* in the *CPU Power Plane* option so only one processor voltage is required (for example, older CPUs without MMX).

BIOS option
I/O Plane Voltage

I/O Plane Voltage sets the external I/O voltage of the processor. It's only active when the setting in the *CPU Power Plane* option is at *Dual Voltage*.

BIOS option
Core Plane Voltage

Core Plane Voltage sets the internal voltage of the processor. It is only active when the setting in the *CPU Power Plane* option is at *Dual Voltage*.

2. Standard Setup

Protect the processor from incorrect settings

Consider assigning a password in your BIOS setup since incorrect settings can destroy the processor.

When manually setting the voltage, be sure to follow the specifications of the manufacturer in the manual. Many processors also have the voltages printed on the case.

Warning!!
An incorrectly set voltage can result in unstable system behavior or destruction of the processor.

Configuring the processor

1. Install the processor according to the instructions of the motherboard manufacturer.

2. You still have to set the voltage for the processor on some motherboards with a jumper. Other motherboards offer this option in CPU-SOFT-MENU.

3. Set the external and internal clock in the corresponding BIOS options to match the processor.

4. You can also enable the Turbo Frequency option for some processors. Turn it on if the option is displayed.

Onboard Components

Modern motherboards have all the ports such as the EIDE, SCSI, parallel and serial, infrared, USB or Firewire integrated, or onboard.

The Onboard connections on a motherboard

Not only can you configure them directly in the BIOS Setup, but you can also enable and disable them. This allows you to distribute the resources optimally. Set their options along with them at the beginning.

Then modern operating systems can properly initialize the ports at installation and set them up with the appropriate drivers.

The Memory Modules

BIOS option
AUTO CONFIGURATION

The memory of the PC is also onboard, although in modules that make it possible to specify the size of the memory. You can set the memory to safe values in the BIOS by switching on *AUTO CONFIGURATION,* which also allows the PC to boot up correctly.

What else is happening in Standard Setup

BIOS option
Halt on

HALT ON in the Award BIOS

The *HALT ON* menu in the Award BIOS specifies which errors will cause the BIOS to halt the computer in the test routine. The *All Errors, No Errors, All But Keyboard, All But Diskette* and *All But Disk/Key* options are available. It's best if you select the *All But Keyboard* option.

Options	Description
All Errors	All errors
No Errors	No errors
All But Keyboard	All errors except keyboard errors (start without keyboard possible)
All But Diskette	All errors except diskette errors
All But Disk/Key	All errors except keyboard and diskette errors

Then you're assured that the hardware of the computer is working correctly (except for the keyboard). The reason to exclude the keyboard is that an error message, such as *"Press any key to continue",* cannot be confirmed and you're locked out of your PC. Your only resort then is to reset the CMOS using jumpers.

Detecting errors

See Chapter 11 if specific errors occurred during the BIOS configuration. This chapter describe most common errors and screen messages.

3

Important EIDE and SCSI Basics

Most complete systems have an EIDE hard drive installed, since the necessary controller for it is also already integrated on most motherboards. This is also called an *onboard controller*. An additional SCSI controller as a plug-in card or a motherboard with an onboard SCSI controller is not needed. The hard drives themselves are also more reasonably priced than a SCSI model.

Each generation of hard drives, regardless of whether EIDE or SCSI, is more powerful. Therefore, a suitable controller is necessary for each standard to take advantage of the full performance of the hard drive. The same also applies for CD-ROM drives. The standards and protocols lately have been undergoing such a tremendous increase that it's easy to get lost in the jungle of standards.

IDE, EIDE and ATAPI – The Standard and the options

While the suppliers always use the designations IDE, EIDE and ATAPI, these designations tell us very little about the actual performance and compatibility. They are only term derivations that developed from the confusing standards of ATA, ATA-2, ATA-3 and ATAPI. The basic terms for users are EIDE and ATAPI. Users actually only know these terms, go into the nearest store and ask for an EIDE hard drive or an ATAPI CD-ROM. While these devices will run with the correct setting in the BIOS or an appropriate driver, they'll only get maximum performance through a proper controller.

EIDE
Advantages
❖ The controller is already integrated on the motherboard
❖ Reasonably priced components are available
Disadvantages
❖ Connection for only four components
❖ Each component needs a driver
❖ Each port occupies an interrupt
❖ Low data transfer rate
❖ Laborious configuration

3. Important EIDE and SCSI Basics

IDE comes with everything

IDE is an acronym for Integrated Drive Electronics. Because it's directly integrated in the hard drives, CD-ROM, CD-ROM burner and ZIP drives, it gives manufacturers the option of adapting the controller to the specifics of their drives. This in turn, is reflected in a performance plus and a favorable price. The controller on the motherboard is not a true controller. It is instead an adapter that establishes a connection of the IDE component to the system bus on the motherboard. It only has a primary port to which a maximum of 2 drives can be connected with a 40-pin flat ribbon cable. However, the hard drive capacity is restricted with values that can only be set to 63 sectors, 16 heads and 1024 cylinders in the BIOS to 528 Meg. All BIOS versions until about mid-1995 were designed this way. A data transfer rate up to 2.1 Mbyte/S was possible. With only 2 drives and a maximum hard drive size of only 1 GB, you soon reach the limits of the system. The speed, especially for multimedia applications, leaves something to be desired. A new standard with more options was needed.

Switching from IDE to EIDE

If you want to switch from IDE to EIDE, buy a new motherboard at the same time, but do not buy an EIDE controller to plug into the ISA bus. The ISA bus severely diminishes the performance of EIDE, and you are actually saving money in the wrong area.

The (E)nhanced IDE Standard

EIDE (Enhanced Integrated Drive Electronics) functions like IDE but with enhanced functions. These consist essentially of a primary and a secondary port to which two drives each can be connected. Therefore, the horizon has already expanded to a total of four drives on two independent ports. However, each port requires its own interrupt, which isn't usually available. The CHS/LBA conversion eliminates the 528 Meg limit. About 8 GB per drive are now addressable. The possible data transfer rate increases to a considerable 16.6 MByte/s through PIO mode.

The EIDE ports on the motherboard

Ultra DMA/33 for more power

Even with EIDE, we still haven't reached "the end of the flagpole." The new Ultra DMA/33 protocol promises even more power. The data transfer rate was doubled from 16.6 MByte/s to a whopping 33 MByte/s. Unfortunately, this is only a theoretical value because hard drives have yet to reach this level.

Ultra DMA/33
Advantages
❖ The controller is already integrated on the motherboard
❖ It can also be installed later as a separate controller
❖ Reasonably priced components are available
❖ Higher data transfer rate than ATA3
Disadvantages
❖ Connection only for four components
❖ Each component needs a driver
❖ Each port occupies an interrupt
❖ Laborious configuration

ATAPI and the CD-ROM drive

IDE controllers under the ATA standard were only planned for hard drives. CD-ROMs had their own controller as a plug-in card in the ISA bus. This was even an advantage in an IDE system, the CD-ROM didn't occupy either of the two connection options and they could both be used for connecting hard drives (the original intent). The CD-ROM drive manufacturers, following the EIDE standard, also started considering using it for their drives. After all, four were available, and few users ever consider

3. Important EIDE and SCSI Basics

connecting four hard drives. Therefore, they developed the ATAPI (Advanced Technology Attachment Packetized Interface) standard for the CD-ROM drive. However, this requires a driver for the EIDE controller. Thus, the BIOS cannot work together directly with the ATAPI standard. It is the driver that finally registers the device on the EIDE port and in the BIOS. Even manufacturers of other peripherals, such as the ZIP drive from Iomega, use this interface. It saves the cost of a separate controller and doesn't eventually occupy all the expansion slots on the motherboard when three connections might still be free on the EIDE controller.

ATAPI CD-ROM

Advantages
❖ The controller is already integrated on the motherboard
❖ Reasonably priced components are available in large selection

Disadvantages
❖ Data transfer rate is not as high as with SCSI
❖ Laborious configuration through drivers

Connecting an ATAPI drive

1. Set the jumper for master or slave operation.

2. Insert the device into the bay and secure it with the appropriate screws. If you use different screws than the ones provided by the manufacturer, make sure they are not too long.

3. Plug the connecting cables for the data and power into the device. Make sure they are correctly aligned.

4. Install the necessary drivers for the device otherwise it will not operate.

Setting jumpers

Before installing a hard drive or CD-ROM drive in its bay, determine whether the drive will be the master or the slave. We've listed the best recommendations for configuration on page 39. The jumpers will then be set accordingly. Once the drive is installed you will have either a very hard time getting at the jumpers or you won't be able to do it at all. Then you'll have to remove the drive.

Last resort

You want to install a second hard drive and don't know what the setting for master and slave is on your first hard drive because you don't have the manual. Remove the drive. The jumper settings for Single, Master or Slave are often printed on the top of the hard drive when it is on the rear connector side. If the jumpers are on the board side you may see a label such as MS or SL.

3. Important EIDE and SCSI Basics

Master and Slave

There is also a hierarchy in the system with EIDE devices. The controller has to know which drive is the first one (master) and which one is the second (slave) one on the port for addressing purposes. The master learns that it has a slave and the slave finds out that it has a master. You make this setting using jumpers on the drives.

The hard drives are not detected

If *IDE AUTO DETECTION* or *Auto-Detect Hard Disk* in the BIOS Setup doesn't detect any of the hard drives, it means the two drives are not compatible. Try switching the master and the slave. Sometimes that works.

Primary and Secondary

The EIDE controller has a primary (the first) and a secondary (the second) port. You can connect two drives to a port with a shared cable. However, each port requires an interrupt. The primary port occupies IRQ 14 and the secondary port takes IRQ 15. You can enable or disable the two ports in BIOS Setup under *Integrated Peripherals*. The options are called *On-Chip Primary IDE* or *On-Chip Secondary IDE*. For this purpose, an external controller as a plug-in card uses a jumper. If a port is not used, the IRQ can be enabled for other devices.

```
Onboard PCI IDE Enable    : Both
IDE Ultra DMA Mode        : Disable
IDE0 Master PIO/DMA Mode  : Auto
IDE0 Slave  PIO/DMA Mode  : Auto
IDE1 Master PIO/DMA Mode  : Auto
IDE1 Slave  PIO/DMA Mode  : Auto
```

With the Onboard PCI IDE Enable option you can enable or disable the ports.

Allocating the connections properly

Different solutions are possible for connecting several EIDE components to the ports. Components that are connected in the wrong sequence can adversely effect the performance of the entire system.

Configuration	Primary / Master	Primary / Slave	Secondary / Master	Secondary / Slave
1 Hard drive	Hard drive 1			
1 Hard drive, 1 CD-ROM	Hard drive 1		CD-ROM 1	
2 Hard drives, 1 CD-ROM	Hard drive 1	Hard drive 2	CD-ROM 1	
3 Hard drives, 1 CD-ROM	Hard drive 1	Hard drive 2	Hard drive 3	CD-ROM 1
2 Hard drives, 2 CD-ROM	Hard drive 1	Hard drive 2	CD-ROM 1	CD-ROM 2

3. Important EIDE and SCSI Basics

Quick overview of the configurations

1. You only want to connect one EIDE hard drive. Then the correct solution is to connect the hard drive to the primary port as the master.

2. You want to connect one EIDE hard drive and one ATAPI CD-ROM. The correct solution is to connect the hard drive to the primary port as the master and the CD-ROM to the secondary port as the master. The CD-ROM would definitely slow down the hard drive in a master/slave combination on the secondary port. However, this is often what happens with complete systems because it allows the manufacturer to save a cable.

3. You only want to connect two EIDE hard drives. You'll need to determine whether to connect both hard drives as masters to the primary and secondary ports or to use a master/slave combination on the primary port. The second option is a better solution because the processor load is lower by using only one port. You don't have to juggle with two IRQs and port addresses for the CPU. There are even more advantages for you if PIO mode can be set separately for both hard drives.

CD-ROM is not detected

At CD-ROM on the secondary port with the correct setting as the master may not be detected. If so, try setting it to slave.

4. You want to connect two EIDE hard drives and one ATAPI CD-ROM. The correct solution is to use a master/slave combination of the hard drives on the primary port and the ATAPI CD-ROM on the secondary port as the master. Doing this prevents the hard drives from being slowed by the slower CD-ROM. Here again, you have an advantage if PIO mode can be set separately for both hard drives.

5. You want to connect three EIDE hard drives and one ATAPI CD-ROM. The correct solution is a master/slave combination of the hard drives on the primary port and a master/slave combination for the hard drive and the ATAPI CD-ROM on the secondary port. Use the hard drive on the secondary port as the master and the CD-ROM as the slave. However, because the slower CD-ROM will slow down the hard drive, use the old hard drive for this position.

6. You want to connect two EIDE hard drives and two ATAPI CD-ROMs. In this case, you probably have already figured out the correct solution. Put the two EIDE hard drives together in a master/slave combination on the primary port and put the two ATAPI CD-ROMs together in a master/slave combination on the secondary port.

3. Important EIDE and SCSI Basics

Connecting cable

The 40-pin flat-ribbon cable has three plugs that are lined up in varying distances. The two plugs that are closer together go to the drives and the other one goes to the controller. The red conductor is important. It marks Pin 1 on the cable and connects to Pin 1 of the controller and the drives. To do this, use the terminal assignment in the manual of the corresponding device. Pin 1 is usually on the side next to the voltage connector with hard drives and CD-ROM drives. You cannot plug it in wrong since the plug has a key and therefore fits only in one direction. It's designed this way because plugging it in wrong could immediately destroy the electronics of the drive, the controller and perhaps even the power supply when you turn on the PC.

The drive LED stays on

If the LED of the hard drive stays on continuously during the POST (see page XXX) and the computer locks up, it means the 40-pin connection cable is incorrectly attached. Pin 1 and 40 are reversed compared to the controller. This does not harm the components.

IDE and the 528 Meg limit

A few years ago a 528 Meg hard drive was considered huge but today it's barely enough for Windows and a few applications. Therefore, many users are connecting a new, larger hard drive to the old IDE controller. However, the controller can only provide 528 Meg through the limited parameters in the BIOS. The rest of the drive space is simply ignored. The BIOS can only manage 63 sectors, 16 heads and 1024 cylinders. If you multiply the values and the result again by 512 (DOS manages 512 bytes per sector), the result is 528,482,304 bytes. After partitioning the drive, you have only 504 Meg left. The only way to get around the problem is with a hard drive manager or an additional EIDE controller with its own BIOS.

Fooling the BIOS

To save yourself the trouble of installing a hard drive manager, try "tricking" the BIOS. Convert the original parameters of the hard drive and enter them in the BIOS manually. Double the number of heads and halve the values of the cylinders. The number of cylinders cannot exceed 1024. For example, let's say you have a hard drive with 850 Meg that has 1652 cylinders, 16 heads and 63 sectors. Then use 826 cylinders, 32 heads and 63 sectors. Although this won't work with all hard drive types, it is worth giving a try.

Hard drive managers are slow and dangerous

Many hard drive manufacturers supply an appropriate hard drive manager such as EZDrive or Ontrack with their hard drives. However, OEM (Original Equipment Manufacturer) hard drives may not include a hard drive manager so you may have to buy one in this case. It's structured similar to a driver, which lodges in the MBR (Master Boot Record) of the hard drive and acts as a translator between the hard drive and the operating system. Hard drive operations no longer occur by hardware through the BIOS, but instead, occur with software through the driver.

3. Important EIDE and SCSI Basics

Manufacturer-dependent hard drive managers

The hard drive managers that are packaged with hard drives only work with the manufacturer's drive, of which at least one has to be installed. The hard drive managers usually won't accept another brand. One exception is the hard drive manager from Western Digital. It can be used for all drives and is available free on the Internet.

Everything runs smoothly with an operating system such as DOS. On the other hand, if you use Windows 95 you'll have to install the latest 32 bit drivers; the operating system is incompatible with older versions. The performance of the new hard drive is naturally also slowed considerably by the driver. You won't need to worry about this if you use Windows NT or Linux.

Removing the hard drive manager

You can remove the driver of the hard drive manager by using the startup disk. This, disk should include the FDISK.EXE file. Boot from the disk and then enter the following at the DOS prompt: fdisk /mbr This rewrites the Masterboot-Record and the hard drive manager is gone. However, due to the now missing driver, all the data on the hard drive is also gone.

There are also other problems in using the complete memory size. For example, if your system crashes, you can no longer access the data of the hard drive with a conventional startup disk because the driver is not loaded in the MBR. Therefore, make certain to create a new startup disk with the tools of the hard drive manager.

2.1 GB limit through BIOS or FDISK

This problem is similar to the one with an IDE controller and the 528 Meg Limit. Now, you have an EIDE controller on the motherboard and there is an LBA option in the BIOS. You believe everything is great, but appearances can be deceiving. If the BIOS was produced between mid-1995 and late 1996, probably only 4,096 cylinders can be managed, which gives you about 2.1 GB. You now need to make a decision. If you install a larger drive, either you won't be able to get into the BIOS any more or the automatic hard drive detection will report meaningless values. Sometimes the drive won't even be found. However, there's a way to use the drive in full capacity with EZDrive or Ontrack. To do this, set the values of a 504 Meg hard drive in the BIOS manually. That way the drive can be addressed and you can install a hard drive manager.

BIOS Setup refuses

If you cannot get into the BIOS because the PC locks up after powering up due to the large drive, your only resort is to unplug the drive, boot up the PC, enter the values manually, plug the drive back in and reboot.

The second obstacle is that with FDISK from DOS 6.2 or Windows 95A, only one partition can be generated with 2 GB. This is because of the cluster management of the FAT16 (File Allocation Table). The only solution here is to divide the drive into several partitions or to use the FAT32 with Windows 95B/OSR2. Dividing the drive into several partitions is more favorable since large clusters can waste memory. Small data such as a text file with just a single letter for content also occupies an entire cluster, and the remainder is still free. The larger the cluster, the larger the unused remainder.

Partition size	Cluster size
Up to 128 Meg	2K
128 up to 255 Meg	4K
256 up to 511 Meg	8K
512 up to 1023 Meg	16K
Up to 2 GByte	32K

8.4 GB Limit

At the moment we have the 8.4 GB hurdle. It is caused by the limit to 16,383 cylinders, 16 heads and 63 sectors in the BIOS. You can solve this problem by working with a hard drive manager. Another option, which does not make the entire memory available, is the limiting jumper that some manufacturers of hard drives offer. It degrades the drive to only 2.1 GB.

If you install a drive larger than 8.4 GB, there are two ways to use all the memory. You can either get a BIOS update for your motherboard or a hard drive manager. The BIOS update is the better solution, but it is not available for every motherboard. It must have the enhanced INT 13 interface so the BIOS can communicate with the hard drive. This makes it possible to address up to 136.9 GB.

These BIOS versions already have the 8.4 GB support:

Manufacturer	Revision date/Version
Award	October 1997
AMI	01.01.1998
Phoenix	Version4, Revision6

Even this boundary will be passed someday. Hard drives with 250 GByte should be available and even larger hard drives (to 5 Terrabytes, or 5,000 Gbytes) are being planned.

3. Important EIDE and SCSI Basics

The mathematical size of the hard drive is always smaller

The mathematical hard drive size is determined differently than the size that the dealer mentions. You'll see 1 Meg often to mean 1,000,000 bytes. However, 1 Meg is actually 1,048,576 bytes (1K consists of 1024 bytes). This may not apparent until you partition the hard drive using FDISK. FDISK calculates correctly, with 1024 bytes.

Example: You have a 100 Meg hard drive and want to calculate the final memory.

100 Meg = 100,000,000 bytes / 1,048,576 bytes = 95,367,431 bytes, that is, 95.36 Meg that can be used as memory.

Sound card with ATAPI port is an emergency solution

Most sound cards are also equipped with a port for CD-ROM drives. Users who still have an older motherboard with only one IDE controller for two drives in their PC with both already occupied by hard drives can consider themselves lucky with such a sound card. A secondary port is now available for the CD-ROM that you enable either by software or jumpers on the sound card. On the other hand, if your motherboard has an EIDE controller installed on it, use it for the CD-ROM since it is clearly faster. If the port on the sound card is enabled, you have to disable the secondary port for the other controller in the BIOS Setup under *Integrated Peripherals or Peripheral Setup*, otherwise a device conflict will occur. If you're using a separate EIDE controller as a plug-in card, disable the secondary card with a jumper.

EIDE controller on the sound card

44

Hard drive utilities in the BIOS are killer!

BIOS main menu
Hard Disk Utility, HDD Low Level Format

If you still have an older motherboard with a BIOS produced before 1994 in your PC, the BIOS probably has an option for testing and low-level formatting the hard drive in the main menu under *Hard Disk Utility* or *HDD Low Level Format*. As its name suggests, a low-level format not only formats a hard drive but also determines the interleave factor and marks defective sectors as unusable. It was designed for the predecessor models of the EIDE hard drive, for example, only for MFM, RLL, ARLL and ESDI types. In the transition phase the option remained in the BIOS, even if an IDE drive had been installed in the PC for the longest time.

Check your manual to be absolutely certain that you don't have an IDE drive installed. Alternatively, open the case of your PC and look at the connection cable of the hard drive to the controller. If it's a 40-pin cable, it is definitely an EIDE drive. If it is a different type of connection - one with 34-pin and the other a 20-pin - you have old hard drive technology designed for low-level format.

Each new EIDE hard drive is treated by the manufacturer during production with a special low-level formatting synchronized to the drive. If it's formatted with the wrong low-level format for the old hard drive technology from the BIOS utilities, the drive is unusable. The only way to repair the drive is the expensive method of having the manufacturer reformat it. Therefore, avoid the hard drive utilities that are no longer used.

IDE-PIO/DMA and UDMA Modes

The standardized transfer norm for EIDE hard drives is called ATA. It specifies the complete port in its form with modes and transfer rates.

ATA, Fast ATA, Fast ATA2 and Ultra ATA

In the beginning only the ATA-Standard could provide PIO mode (Programmed Input/Output) 0, 1 and 2. It was replaced rather quickly by the Fast-ATA standard.

Waitstates for DMA
You may find an option called DMA CAS Timing Delay in some BIOS versions of AMI that grants some wait states to DMA access. If possible, set this to disabled werden so that the DMA runs at full speed. However, if read/write errors occur with either the floppy drive or hard drive, enable it again. The same also applies for problems with a CD-ROM/burner, ZIP, scanner or other devices that use DMA.

3. Important EIDE and SCSI Basics

Fast-ATA essentially consists of 2 options: PIO Mode 3 and DMA Mode 1. The additionally integrated standard called DMA (Direct Memory Access) causes the data from the hard drive to be transported to the main memory without burdening the CPU. As a result, not only is data transfer accelerated, but also the speed of the entire system is faster.

As the storage media became more powerful, it became necessary to create a new standard. Fast-ATA2 consists of PIO Mode 4 and DMA Mode 1. Data transfer rates are being achieved with this today that are sufficient for a home or office PC.

However, this is not the end of the story. The Fast-ATA2 standard was modified once more with the release of Ultra-ATA. It boasts a data transfer rate of 33 MByte/s, which no peripheral had been able to deliver. A good hard drive currently supplies about 12 MBytes/s in linear reading and writing. The entire ATA standard is downwardly compatible. That's why a Fast-ATA2 hard drive can be connected to a Fast ATA controller or to an ATA controller. Naturally, the data transfer rate sinks to that of the existing controller.

PIO Mode

PIO (Programmed Input/Output) mode is an industry standard and specifies the data transfer method between controller and hard drive. The following table shows the data transfer rates :

Mode	Transfer rate
PIO 0	3.33 MByte/s
PIO 1	5.22 MByte/s
PIO 2	8.33 MByte/s
PIO 3	11.11 MByte/s
PIO 4	16.66 MByte/s

PIO Auto-Mode

Auto mode for detecting PIO mode doesn't always function properly. You will see which PIO mode the BIOS detected during the boot procedure in the boot table. Depending on the BIOS version, the PIO modes for the corresponding device will be displayed after the primary and secondary ports, except for the hard drive size.

Errors in the file system

If ScanDisk regularly finds errors in the file system, it can be caused by a PIO mode that has been set too high. Continue to lower the setting until the errors disappear.

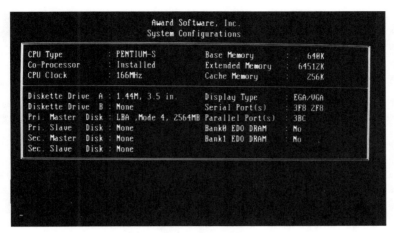

The boot table in the BIOS

Above all, older controllers with a hard drive and a CD-ROM drive on the primary port lead to incorrect interpretations of the mode. For example, the slower PIO from the CD-ROM will also be used for the hard drive, which actually supports PIO 3. The CD-ROM slows your hard drive. Disable auto mode and make the correct setting manually. You'll find it in the BIOS Setup under *Integrated Peripherals* or *Peripheral Setup*. You have the following options: *Auto, 0, 1, 2, 3* and 4.

Setting PIO mode

Either use the automatic detection or set the correct mode manually.

You will find the correct mode for the device in the user manual. A mode that is set too high can cause problems.

The jumpers for master or master/slave have to be correctly set according to the devices on the port. For example, if both are configured as the master on the same port, neither device will function.

3. Important EIDE and SCSI Basics

When EIDE doesn't work

❖ Are the primary and secondary ports activated in the BIOS?
  The primary or the secondary port for the connected device must also be enabled in the BIOS under Integrated Peripherals or Peripheral Setup.

❖ Are the hard drive parameters entered in the BIOS?
  The values of the hard drive(s) also have to be correctly entered in the BIOS Setup. It's best to have automatic detection enter them for you.

❖ Are the jumpers for the master and slave set correctly?
  The jumpers for master or master/slave have to be correctly set according to the devices on the port. For example, if both are configured as the master on the same port, neither device will function.

❖ Is the connection cable properly poled at the controller and connected at the drive?
  Pin 1 of the controller must match with pin 1 of the hard drive. The marked conductor on the 40-pin connection cable is used to mark pin 1 and is supposed to point at it.

❖ Is the 4-pin cable for the operating voltages plugged in?
  Don't forget the cable for the operating voltage!

❖ A hard drive must be partitioned with the DOS FDISK utility and formatted with FORMAT. The hard drive has to be prepared to store data. It gets one or more partitions using FDISK. The partitions can then be formatted using the Format command, similar to a floppy.

Busmastering with DMA

Besides PIO mode, many EIDE hard drives also support DMA mode (direct memory access). We have already briefly mentioned this. In DMA mode, data is transported from the hard drive to RAM without burdening the CPU. The system performance increases because the CPU can also accomplish other tasks during the data transfer. This has an especially favorable effect in the multimedia area. However, DMA mode is not supported directly by the BIOS but rather by the chipset on the motherboard and the operating system. This technique is called *busmastering*. This requires a busmaster chip-dependent "busmaster driver" for the operating system being used. The motherboard manufacturer should supply this driver along with installation guidelines. Check the manuals of the operating systems for information. Some reference sources for the current chipsets are also available on the Internet. Motherboard manufacturers also make them available there.

The CD-ROM at the secondary EIDE port is gone

You installed the busmaster driver in Windows 95 but after rebooting, the CD-ROM drive has disappeared from the secondary EIDE port. The busmaster chip is not being properly detected and Windows is disabling the secondary port. You have only one option here. Delete the driver using the manufacturer's uninstall program (if one is available).

However, this all sounds better than it actually is because busmaster drivers also cause some problems. The driver allocates IRQ15, even if you don't need the secondary port. If you're uncertain whether your hard drive supports DMA, do not enable DMA support under any circumstances. Otherwise you could lose data or equipment may not work right (a CD-ROM burner can suddenly only read, but can no longer write with an installed busmaster driver, for example). Busmaster drivers still have a few bugs with some hardware. It may work well with some components, but it will cause errors with most components. Therefore, we don't recommend installing the busmaster driver. Instead, go for more performance with the Ultra DMA/33 standard (see below).

Ultra DMA/33 Mode

The new chipset generations since the 430TX from Intel, also known as Triton3, support Ultra DMA/33 mode in addition to the older PIO and DMA modes. Other chipset manufacturers such as ALI, VIA or SIS have also already adopted the standard. It also has a new protocol with automatic error correction. In addition, the connectors of the connection cables are protected by resistors. As a result, the bus runs just as stable as with a lower data transfer rate.

```
Onboard PCI IDE Enable    : Both
IDE Ultra DMA Mode        : Disable
IDE0 Master PIO/DMA Mode  : Auto
IDE0 Slave  PIO/DMA Mode  : Auto
IDE1 Master PIO/DMA Mode  : Auto
IDE1 Slave  PIO/DMA Mode  : Auto
```

Ultra DMA Mode in the BIOS

Mode	Transfer rate
DMA 0	4.16 MByte/s
DMA 1	13.33 MByte/s
DMA 2	16.66 MByte/s
Ultra DMA 0	16.66 MByte/s
Ultra DMA 1	25.00 MBytes/s
Ultra DMA 2	33.33 MByte/s

Using EIDE and SCSI Together

Many users have a PC with EIDE components but would like to upgrade the system with a SCSI bus (**S**mall **C**omputer **S**ystem **I**nterface). While this can be done easily, you still need to be careful in some cases.

3. Important EIDE and SCSI Basics

How SCSI works

SCSI is a professional standard that has had most of its success in UNIX and Apple systems. A PC with SCSI components is more expensive than its EIDE counterpart but is also more powerful and flexible. The speed advantage alone in transferring larger data blocks, such as in the multimedia field, is significant. Also, other components such as a CD-ROM drive don't slow down data transfers with SCSI anywhere near the way they do with EIDE.

The SCSI Host Adapter

A SCSI system always consists of a host adapter (SCSI controller) to which the devices are connected. Similar to EIDE, the controller is just an adapter. The control is in the peripheral. There are bootable models with their own BIOS and non-bootable without a BIOS that are mainly used for scanners, tape backups and CD-ROM burners.

You can buy adapters for the ISA or the PCI bus. If you have both in your system, be sure to get the PCI adapter. It's more powerful and is easier to install because it's Plug&Play. The intelligence of the SCSI system is always in the peripheral device itself. Depending on the standard, up to 15 devices can be connected to the host adapter in any sequence you like. There is no master/slave configuration here because all devices on the bus are equivalent. You simply set an identification number on the peripheral and enable or place a terminator on the last device. The host adapter is linked to the operating system through the driver.

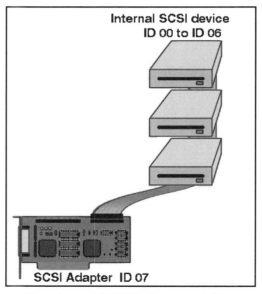

Flow chart with SCSI adapter and drives

3. Important EIDE and SCSI Basics

SCSI CD-ROM

Advantages
- ❖ High data transfer rate
- ❖ Easy connection to one cable
- ❖ Up to 15 devices on one controller possible
- ❖ Devices can also be operated externally

Disadvantages
- ❖ Components are more expensive than EIDE
- ❖ SCSI controller costs more
- ❖ Wide SCSI components not compatible with SCSI
- ❖ Greater heat build-up

SCSI 1

SCSI 1 is outdated and is no longer even used.

SCSI 2, also called Fast SCSI

SCSI 2 is the typical standard with which everyone is familiar. It operates seven devices at 8 bit data width and a data transfer rate of up to 10 MByte/s. The bus is robust and quite insensitive to interference. Termination can occur with resistance decades. The plug-in cards are available in ISA or PCI models. This standard is satisfactory for normal users.

SCSI 3 or Ultra-SCSI

Ultra SCSI is a variant of fast SCSI. It can achieve a data transfer rate of 20 Mbytes/s by doubling the bus clock. Here too, the bus works at 8 bit data width. Doubling the clock requires an active termination for disturbance-free operation. Select good quality cables for an external connection. Such cables have a ground cable internally for each single conductor "twisted pair" in the entire cable. A good exterior shield is also important. While this makes the cables extremely thick and not very flexible, they are also very secure from interference that disturbs the entire bus. Their length is restricted to a maximum of 1.5 meters.

Wide SCSI

Wide SCSI is an adaptation of the SCSI 1 and SCSI 2 standards and is now called Fast-Wide and Ultra-Wide. The bus was upgraded to 16 bit data width. That means a data transfer rate of 20 MByte/s for Fast-Wide and 40 MByte/s for Ultra-Wide. The number of devices that can be connected has also been increased. Wide SCSI uses 68-pin connection cables, while all other SCSI standards use 50-pin cables. The same thing we said earlier applies for the quality of the external connection cable.

3. Important EIDE and SCSI Basics

SCSI Host Adapter

Standard	Data transfer rate	Num. Devices	Cable
SCSI	5 MByte/s	7	50-pin
Fast-SCSI	10 MByte/s	7	50-pin
Ultra-SCSI	20 MByte	7	50-pin
Wide-SCSI	20 MByte	15	68-pin
Ultra-Wide-SCSI	40 MByte	15	68-pin

Selecting a SCSI-ID

So the host adapter can tell the individual components apart and address them, each peripheral has its own ID - including the adapter. The SCSI ID (identification) is determined through numbering. The numbers 0 – 7 are available for SCSI and the numbers 0 – 15 are available for Wide-SCSI. Set them for internal devices with 3 jumpers and use DIP or rotary switches for external devices. Keep in mind that you can assign each ID only once. ID 7 is usually reserved for the host adapter. Some adapters can only boot from ID 0 or ID 1. Therefore, these numbers are usually used for the hard drives. This also concerns the priority of the components. The ID is queried for the access of the adapter in ascending order. Therefore, the C: drive is normally the lowest ID, 0, the second hard drive (D:) is ID 1, the CD-ROM drive (E:) ID 2 and components that are not addressed very often have the higher ID numbers, for example, ID 6.

3. Important EIDE and SCSI Basics

Jumpers for the SCSI-ID setting

Termination

The SCSI bus is open in front and in back on the connection cable. To prevent the data from being reflected at the ends, you need a terminator, consisting of resistance decades. This terminator destroys signals in the connection cable that want to run back to the last device. The first and last device in a SCSI chain always need a terminator. The host adapter itself has an automatic terminator. If it has an interface for external devices, it's not always the last member of the chain. Depending on whether an external device is currently plugged in, the terminator is switched on or off. Any problems in the SCSI bus can usually be traced to a defective terminator. Active terminators are used with Ultra SCSI and higher. Active terminators consist of a circuit that keeps the bus voltage at a constant 3.6 volts. Passive terminators allow too much fluctuation that affect the sensitive high performance bus.

Plugs for the termination of external devices

Installing a SCSI device

1. Set the SCSI ID on the device (be certain the ID you wish to assign is still free). Boot the PC before assigning the ID and look at the table of SCSI devices. This shows all the SCSI IDs being used for the devices.

2. If the device to be installed is the last device in the chain, it must be terminated. The terminator of the next to last device must then be removed.

3. Insert the device into the bay and attach it using the appropriate screws. Make sure the screws aren't too long if you're not using the screws supplied by the manufacturer.

4. Plug the connection cable for the data and power into the device.

Symbioslogic Host Adapter

One reasonably priced alternative is the Symbios Logic adapter (previously called the NCR adapter). It is now equipped with the sym810-SCSI chip and meets the Fast SCSI standard for the PCI bus. The advantage about it is that it doesn't have its own ROM-BIOS, instead it uses the system BIOS on the motherboard. Some manufacturers support this option directly or through a BIOS update.

When SCSI doesn't work

❖ Did the host adapter get a free IRQ?
   The host adapter requires a free IRQ. If it is not Plug&Play capable, the IRQ is set by jumper. Make sure the IRQ you are using isn't double allocated.

❖ Is the connection cable plugged in properly to the controller and the drive?
   Pin1of the controller must match pin1 of the hard drives. The marked conductor on the 50 or 68-pin connection cable is used to mark pin1 and needs to be pointing to it.

❖ Is the SCSI ID correctly set?
   The same SCSI ID on the device may not be assigned twice. ID 7 is usually reserved for the host adapter. Watch out! Some adapters can only boot from ID 0 or ID 1. That's why you normally need to use these for the hard drives.

❖ Are the last drive and the host adapter correctly terminated?
   The first and last device must always be terminated. If an external device is connected to the external port, it must also have a terminator. The controller is, in this case, no longer the last device and may not be terminated. If the controller does not have an automatic terminator, a jumper has to be set. From Ultra SCSI always use an active terminator!

❖ Is the 4-pin cable for the operating voltage plugged in?
   Don't forget the cable for the operating voltage!

❖ A hard drive has to be partitioned with the FDISK DOS utility and formatted with FORMAT before you can use it.
   The hard drive has to be prepared for the storage of data. With FDISK you divide it into one or more partitions and then format them with Format, similar to the way you format floppies.

3. Important EIDE and SCSI Basics

Using EIDE and SCSI together in one system is usually possible. You may have to install a SCSI controller in your existing EIDE system for specific hardware components. Many scanner manufacturers supply a SCSI adapter as a basis for connection. Iomega also supplies an 8 bit ISA SCSI host adapter for its internal ZIP drive. CD-ROM burner kits also use such a simple SCSI adapter.

You may already have installed one of these hidden SCSI adapters in your EIDE system without realizing it. To see if this is true, load the Windows 95/98 Device Manager by selecting *Control Panel/ System* and clicking on the *Device Manager* tab. Then you can even locate an "unintentionally" installed SCSI host adapter. If the SCSI controller icon is available, click the [+] in front of it and you'll see the SCSI adapter.

If you want to boot from your EIDE hard drives, a better host adapter without its own BIOS can replace the one included with the devices. Host adapters without their own BIOS are much cheaper. Then you have internal and external connections on the adapter and can use, for example, the scanner, the ZIP drive and the CD-ROM burner on the same adapter. You can also address a hard drive through a driver, like the other devices. The only thing you won't be able to do is boot from the hard drive.

The EIDE slowdown for CD-ROMs

If you are running a CD-ROM as the only EIDE device on the primary port (only SCSI hard drives are being used) the BIOS won't enable 32 bit access the way it does for hard drives. As a result, the CD-ROM will only be controlled in 16 bit mode, thus suffering significant losses in performance. In the worst case scenario, the system may not even be able to find the drive and won't be able to address it. Here all you can do is add a pseudo hard drive to the primary port.

You can also install a bootable SCSI host adapter into an existing EIDE system. However, in this case the EIDE hard drive entered in the BIOS will take precedence over the SCSI hard drive for booting. If your motherboard has a newer system BIOS, you can give priority to the SCSI through the *Boot Sequence* command in the BIOS *FEATURES SETUP*. Normally, both EIDE ports and SCSI can be fully used. On the other hand, if only the primary EIDE port is used for hard drives or a CD-ROM drive, we recommend disabling the secondary port in the BIOS and using the free interrupt for the SCSI host adapter

4

Using Tricky Options in the BIOS

BIOS contains many options that not only enhance performance but also provide security and practical features. It includes a BIOS virus detection that is very effective for many viruses. The cache storage areas are also important features. If they're present but not enabled, you'll lose a costly 50% of performance. The accelerated hard drive accesses provided by Block-Mode and 32-Bit-Mode are also important; they contribute to the positive performance of the entire system. The Shadow-RAM function is a secret tip for users who still work with DOS. It works like a turbo switch, especially with graphic-intensive applications such as CAD and computer games. The option of booting almost any drive in the system opens new and very useful possibilities.

Although many BIOS functions increase system speed, it's sometimes better to disable others since they decrease speed unnecessarily. These include outdated options for initializing devices and a triple storage test of the BIOS that the operating system repeats one more time. By disabling such "brakes" on the system, you can reduce booting time by as much as ten seconds.

Virus Detection by BIOS – Background information

BIOS Options
Virus Warning , Anti-Virus

Computer viruses have been a much-feared enemy of PCs for many years. This is especially true today with millions of people using the Internet and buying shareware software. The tricks of the enemy range from obvious error messages to total system-crashes. They often cause irreparable damage to the sensitive files on the hard drive. It's very difficult to remove a virus once it infects a computer. In the worst case, you must format the disk and reinstall everything - including the operating system. Weeks of configuration and fine-tuning of the operating system may be lost. Because new viruses appear regularly, we cannot discuss viruses and the specific methods used to block them. Instead, we'll talk about BIOS virus protection.

4. Using Tricky Options in the BIOS

Data security and anti-virus program

Virus protection in the BIOS is limited to viruses that attack the boot sector. It cannot detect other types of viruses. Therefore, use a virus checker program and back up your data regularly.

Over 10,000 computer viruses have been identified. These viruses have attacked the boot sector, partition tables, files or file systems. The types of viruses are sometimes classified as companion, TSR, stealth or polymorph viruses. An exhaustive account of viruses would require a separate, technical book. Therefore, we will briefly discuss only the boot sector viruses that the BIOS can block.

EIDE

Advantages
- ❖ Blockage of boot sector viruses
- ❖ Free virus monitoring

Disadvantages
- ❖ Uncertain
- ❖ Detects only boot sector viruses
- ❖ Can cause problems with boot managers or force you to reinstall the operating system

Boot sector viruses nest in the boot sector and use it as their host. The virus code is activated as the PC boots and then begins its individual destructive work on the files. The BIOS virus detection prevents only this pest. It is activated by the command *Virus Warning* or *Anti-Virus* and blocks every write command to the boot sector. You'll see a warning if a virus or any other program attempts to write to the boot sector. In the Award BIOS the warning is: *"Warning: Disk boot sector is to be modified. Type "Y" to accept write, or "N" to abort write."* In the AMI BIOS the warning is: *"Boot sector write!!! Possible VIRUS: Continue (Y/N)?"* The write to the boot sector can proceed only when you press the Ⓨ key.

The warning can also occur when hard drive tools or optimization utilities are used, when you install a new operating system or when the boot manager activates two operating systems, such as OS/2 and DOS.

Virus attack on the BIOS

The BIOS is powerless when faced with a virus attack against itself. Some viruses (for example, CMOSDeath, CMOS.3622, CMOSDense.807) extinguish or alter the CMOS. If a PC fails to boot from the hard drive, either a low CMOS-battery or a virus could be the reason.

New virus strain deletes basic software

The CIH-Virus from Taiwan that has been circulating since August, 1998 is a very serious virus. The virus is activated on the 26th of every month and deletes a small portion of the basic software in the

BIOS (the boot code). This renders the hardware (especially the motherboard) useless since the PC can not be started if the BIOS is defective.

Protect the BIOS

Make sure the "write-protection jumper" of the BIOS is in the correct position. The virus is powerless if there is no "write voltage." Increasingly, however, motherboards are produced without this jumper because of the additional cost. In that case, you must depend on an up-to-date virus scanner that removes the virus before it inflicts damage. A substitute BIOS can save you a trip to the PC repair shop.

The 1K virus is resident in memory and then moves into the program area of .exe files when they are opened in Windows. It progressively infects all programs using this route. On the 26th of every month it begins its attack on the Flash-BIOS and overwrites the boot code with a couple of commands. In this way the BIOS is lost. Even if you have protected the original BIOS file with a Flasher you cannot retrieve it since the PC can no longer be booted to run the Flash program.

Since the boot code has been destroyed, nothing will make the BIOS work again. You're only alternative is a new BIOS or motherboard. Users who have a motherboard with a permanently programmed BIOS (EPROM) are fortunate. The virus is powerless against that type of BIOS. However, even this BIOS isn't 100% safe because the virus has an additional ability. It also overwrites the first 2,048 sectors of the hard drive that contain all the information concerning files. In this way, the files are also hopelessly lost. The disk will then have to be partitioned again and formatted.

That is the first virus that can attack a Flash-RAM and destroy the files on it. But, how will this development of virus programming proceed? Other BIOSes are present in a PC. It's possible that viruses in the future could infect video cards, SCSI host adapters, CD burners, network cards and even modems.

Active virus monitor prevents Windows 95/98 installation

Installing Windows 95/98 with virus detection enabled is particularly tricky. The installation program locks up for no apparent reason and the warning signal, which would immediately clarify the situation, does not appear. You should always disable virus detection before installing a new operating system. However, this is not possible in many versions of Award BIOS. Therefore, you'll need to set a software switch in the installation that prevents a write to the boot sector. After installation the system files must be copied from the boot diskette to the hard drive using the command *SYS C:*.

Setup and virus protection

If you cannot disable the virus detection for Windows 95 Setup in the BIOS, use the /ir switch to prevent access to the boot sector. Start the installation-routine with Setup /ir.

4. Using Tricky Options in the BIOS

The later virus detection is pointless under Windows 95/98 and NT. It circumvents the BIOS routines for hard drive access. Such access is managed from the operating system using corresponding drivers, and it contains its own warning if a program attempts to write to the boot sector.

When virus detection in the BIOS is worthwhile

Virus detection is therefore useful only in certain circumstances. These include when an older operating system is being used (DOS or Novell DOS and PTS DOS) that have no internal protection mechanisms, or if you frequently boot from a diskette, for example, with DOS games.

Caches in the PC

If you don't keep oil in your car engine, it will soon stop working. Similarly, if there is no cache in a PC or if the BIOS is not enabled, the system cannot perform. (The word cache comes from the French and means "hidden." The concept "hidden" was apparently used because the cache performs its function unnoticed and its files are therefore hidden in the cache storage. It releases its individual files only by special request from the processor.)

Cache memory
The cache storage consists of two areas called L1 cache and L2 cache. The L1 is in the processor and the L2 is on the motherboard. Both caches are in the processor in the Pentium Pro and the Pentium II. It works as an intermediate storage between the fast processor core and the slow main storage. If no cache were available, the processor would undergo many waiting cycles to prevent the RAM elements from being overloaded with files. However, with cache available, the processor undergoes only few waiting cycles. Also, when the processor retrieves files from the main storage without recourse to the cache, it takes much longer than when the cache is used. The L1 cache is always present in the Pentium processor. If the L2 cache is missing, as with the Pentium II C or on the motherboard of Socket 7 processors, the system is significantly restrained.

High performance through the cache

BIOS Options
CPU internal Cache, External Cache

If the L1 and L2 cache (also 2nd level cache) are present in the BIOS Setup, they should always be enabled. The options are called *CPU Internal Cache* and *External Cache*. Depending on the benchmark test being used, the increase in performance is 20% if the L1 cache is enabled and an additional 25% if the L2 cache is enabled.

4. Using Tricky Options in the BIOS

L1 Cache with Cyrix 6x86

On many older motherboards with a Cyrix 6x86 processor, if the L1 cache is enabled in Windows 95, memory problems occur. These problems are reflected in frequent violations of the protection. In that case you will have to disable the L1 cache again.

More power with L1 and L2 cache

The option for internal and external cache is available in your BIOS. In the *BIOS FEATURE SETUP*, enable both options: *CPU Internal Cache* and *External Cache*. This will yield up to 45% more performance in your PC without risking your files.

Mode matters

1. 486 motherboards have another setting for the cache memory called "Write Through" and "Write Back Mode" for the L1 and L2 cache, which is combined with the *CPU Internal Cache* and *External Cache* settings.

2. Not every processor can use write back mode. So, write back mode can be separate or set only for the L2 cache. If the processor can use write back mode, enable it. Unlike write through mode, it can buffer the write-accesses of the CPU and then asynchronically transfer them to RAM. That operation proceeds about 5% faster than unbuffered transfer.

3. The Pentium generation automatically uses the Write Back mode, so the BIOS Setup no longer contains settings for this feature.

Cache memory

Advantages
* ❖ Increases system performance considerably
* ❖ Up to 45% more performance
* ❖ Available in all BIOS versions

Disadvantages
* ❖ None

RAM and Cache

BIOS Options
Above 16 MByte Cacheable

Only a few BIOS versions can determine the amount of storage to be cached. AMI offers an option if the machine has only 16 Meg or less of RAM; in this way the smaller amount of storage is accessed more rapidly. If you have more than 16 Meg, always enable the *Above 16 MByte Cacheable* option.

4. Using Tricky Options in the BIOS

Even more settings

The L2 cache on current motherboards always works in Pipelined-Burst-Mode; but the timing can usually not be altered in the BIOS. Therefore several tools that let you change the settings are available. Such tools, also available as shareware, include AMI-Setup and TweakBIOS. These burst-accesses depend on the size and the manner of operation of the cache storage.

BIOS Options
CPU Fast String Move

The Pentium Pro and the Pentium II support a String Move Command mode that can be enabled in some BIOS versions with *CPU Fast String Move*. You should always enable it because it influences the performance of the L1 cache in the processor.

BIOS Options
Video RAM Cacheable

The *Video RAM Cacheable* option caches the frame buffers on the video card. This slightly increases performance during graphic generation, but is scarcely worth mention and hardly measurable with a benchmark. The option works well with more recent video cards; but problems can occur with older cards.

BIOS Options
Video RAM Cache Methode, Write Combining

This determines the method for caching the frame buffer. This option is available only on Pentium Pro and Pentium II motherboards since only these processors support the more rapid access method. It should be on Enabled or USWC (Uncacheable Speculative Write Combining).

A cache for the BIOS too?

BIOS Options
Video BIOS Cacheable, Video BIOS Cache, System BIOS Cacheable, System BIOS Cache.

Video BIOS Cacheable, Video BIOS Cache, System BIOS Cacheable or *System BIOS Cache*. More options are available for the cache that caches the Video BIOS and the system BIOS. However, the system BIOS and the video BIOS are cached only if the *Video BIOS Shadow* and *System BIOS Shadow* options are enabled. DOS users, especially those who frequently use computer games, need to enable these functions if they're present in the BIOS. This does not apply to Windows 95/98, however. In these cases you should disable both options since they can decrease system performance by about 1%. In summary, the options afford only a slight boost in performance, and only for DOS users

4. Using Tricky Options in the BIOS

Quick start: Cache

❖ L1 and L2 Cache enabled?
   Be sure to enable the L1 and L2 cache; it gives you a huge boost in performance of the processor.

❖ Is the right mode set?
   If possible, set the cache mode to Write Back for even better performance.

❖ L1 Cache option for Pentium II
   If the String Move Option for L1 Cache is available, enable it.

Booting faster saves time

No one likes to wait while the operating system starts up. Fortunately, there are options to accelerate the boot process when they are not enabled. For example, the system memory is first tested by the BIOS and then again by the operating system. If you're confident your PC is in good condition, you can disable both options and have the memory tested only once by the POST. Furthermore, you usually won't use a floppy drive so it probably doesn't need to be initialized. Nevertheless, these tests are often included as standard settings in the various BIOS versions.

Switch off the memory test in the "himem.sys"

The /testmem:off switch can turn off the memory test that is conducted in DOS and Windows 95 through the memory manager "himem.sys" in config.sys. The line in config.sys of DOS and Windows 95 should then read device=himemsys/testmem:off.

The memory test

BIOS Options
Quick Power On Self Test, Memory Test Above 1 MB, Memory Test, Memory Priming

First shut off the unnecessary, intensive memory test that occupies the BIOS three times as long as the normal test. In Award BIOS use *Enable* in the option *Quick Power On Self Test* to shut off the repeated memory test; as a result the test will run only one time.

4. Using Tricky Options in the BIOS

```
 Award Modular BIOS v4.51PG, An Energy Star Ally
 Copyright (C) 1984-95, Award Software, Inc.

#401A0-0105

PENTIUM-S CPU at 166MHz
Memory Test :  65536K OK
```

The memory test of the Award BIOS

Other BIOS manufacturers use similar options, such as *Memory Test Above 1 MB, Memory Test* or *Memory Priming*. You can also increase the speed of the memory test considerably by using abbreviated test routines.

Disk drives are time-consuming

BIOS Options

Boot Up Sequence, Boot up Floppy Seek, Swap Floppy Drive

You might save some time by resetting the options for disk drive settings in the BIOS Features Setup.

Reset the boot priority

1. Go to the *Boot Up Sequence* option. This option determines on which drive the machine will first seek a bootable disk. The normal sequence is *A, C*.

2. Choose the setting *C, A*. This will prevent your PC from searching the disk drive for a bootable disk. This saves time since the search no longer occurs. Furthermore, it avoids an error message when a non-bootable diskette is left in the drive. That is particularly irritating if you turn on the PC and leave to do something else during the booting process. When you return to the PC, the diskette must first be removed and the error message confirmed.

```
                    ROM PCI/ISA BIOS
                   BIOS FEATURES SETUP
                  AWARD SOFTWARE, INC.

 Virus Warning           : Enabled    Video  ROM BIOS   Shadow  : Disabled
 CPU Internal Cache      : Disabled   C8000  -  CBFFF   Shadow  : Disabled
 External Cache          : Disabled   CC000  -  CFFFF   Shadow  : Disabled
 Quick Power On Self Test: Disabled   D0000  -  D3FFF   Shadow  : Disabled
 HDD Sequence SCSI/IDE First: SCSI    D4000  -  D7FFF   Shadow  : Disabled
 Boot Sequence           : A,C        D8000  -  DBFFF   Shadow  : Disabled
 Boot Up Floppy Seek     : Disabled   DC000  -  DFFFF   Shadow  : Disabled
 Floppy Disk Access Control : R/W
 IDE HDD Block Mode Sectors : Disabled Boot Up NumLock Status    : Off
 Security Option         : Setup      Typematic Rate Setting    : Disabled
 PS/2 Mouse Function Control: Enabled Typematic Rate (Chars/Sec): 6
 PCI/VGA Palette Snoop   : Disabled   Typematic Delay (Msec)    : 250
 OS/2 Onboard Memory > 64M : Disabled

                                      ESC : Quit        ↑↓→← : Select Item
                                      F1  : Help         PU/PD/+/-  : Modify
                                      F5  : Old Values   (Shift)F2 : Color
                                      F6  : Load BIOS  Defaults
                                      F7  : Load Setup Defaults
```

BIOS Features Setup

4. Using Tricky Options in the BIOS

Switch off initialization

1. Go to the *Boot up Floppy Seek* option. This option is intended for initialization, whether it is a 40 track or an 80 track drive, and functions as a considerable brake during boot up. It is also entirely unnecessary, since the disk drive is normally correctly indicated in the *STANDARD CMOS SETUP*. Also, the movement of the read/write head makes considerable noise, particularly when there is no diskette in the drive. This may even cause problems for the mechanical parts if the write/read head engages with excessive force.

2. So, always set this setting to *Disabled*. This will not affect the function of the drives. Only if an old 5.25-inch drive with 40 tracks (360 KB) is run as an 80 track (1.2 Meg) drive, the warning signal will fail, since it is no longer tested.

Replacement is only rarely necessary

Currently, one such unnecessary option is exchanging drive A: with B:. If a cable is used to connect a 3.5 inch drive as drive A: and a 5.25-inch drive as drive B:, the 3.5 floppy may be considered as B: and the 5.25-inch floppy may be considered as A:. That makes sense only in certain circumstances, for example, if a boot diskette has the format of drive B:, or if an installation program with the format of drive B: can only be started on drive A:. This is only rarely the case, however. Therefore, disabling this option will not affect the function of the drives.

1. Go to the *Swap Floppy Drive* option.

2. Move the setting to *Disabled*.

You can, if you ever should need to, avoid rearranging the cable on the floppy drives. Only the drive on the outer end of the cable is drive A:. Fortunately, most PCs today have only one floppy drive so this option is now obsolete.

Old hard drives need time

BIOS Options
Delay for SCSI/HDD, Cold Boot Delay

If you're still using an old IDE or SCSI hard drive in a High-Tech-System, rapid booting can overtax their capabilities. The hard drive cannot be entirely initialized and an error message occurs. If the processor is then started with a Reset, it will suddenly work.

Time for initialization
If you do not have any of the options in the BIOS Setup, it is helpful to enable the intensive memory test as described in this chapter. In this way the slow hard drive gains sufficient time to get up to speed.

4. Using Tricky Options in the BIOS

That is typical for this error. The slow hard drive has only gradually attained its full rpms. Several BIOS versions have an option for delaying the POST during the hard drive routine, and allowing the drive a set time for initializing. The *Delay for SCSI/HDD* or *Cold Boot Delay* options are used for this purpose. You can either disable this option or set the delay time from 1 to 30 seconds.

Disabling automatic PIO and hard drive detection

BIOS main menu
Integrated Peripherals, Peripheral Setup

A modern BIOS automatically detects the parameters and the PIO modes of the connected hard drives. However; when this automatic recognition is switched on, it requires up to five seconds of time since the BIOS must first ascertain the values and then register them. Enter these values permanently in the BIOS Setup in the corresponding option (*Primary Master, Primary Master PIO*, etc.) if you don't use removable drives.

Booting faster
❖ Did you press the shortcut key at the right time?
❖ Reduce the memory test Allow the memory test in the BIOS to be executed only in its abbreviated routine.
❖ Disable the useless options for disk drives You can disable the many time-consuming options for the disk drives for most PCs that have only one drive.
❖ Watch the options for old hard drives The Cold Boot Delay or Delay for SCSI/HDD options can prolong the boot process considerably when they are not used.
❖ Enter PIO mode by hand If the PIO mode is still on Auto, be sure to enter the values by hand.

Variable booting from SCSI, CD-ROM, ZIP or the network

The possibilities in current BIOS versions for choosing the boot drive are already considerable and more are still being added. You could previously only boot the PC from a diskette or the hard drive; now you can boot from virtually any storage medium.

4. Using Tricky Options in the BIOS

Specifying the boot sequence

BIOS Options
Boot Sequence, System Boot Up Sequence

In the BIOS Setup under the *BIOS FUTURES SETUP* menu item you can use the *Boot Sequence* or *System Boot Sequence* option to determine the sequence in which the system will search the drives for a bootable medium. The menu then determines the sequence. If no bootable disk is found in the first drive, the next drive is searched. If no bootable disk is found in any drive, the PC will display an error message such as *Disk Boot Failure, insert system disk and press Enter*, *No Boot Device Available*.

The various BIOS versions offer different options for determining which drives will be available for selection. At a minimum this will be *A; C;* or *C; A;*. A larger selection is available with the more current BIOS versions that were produced with the TX chip. Available possibilities are listed in the following table.

Boot sequence
A, C, SCSI
C, A, SCSI
C, CD-ROM, A
CD-ROM, C, A
D, A, SCSI
E, A, SCSI
F, A, SCSI
SCSI, A, C,
SCSI, C, A
A, SCSI, C
LS/ZIP, C

Build your own boot manager

If you use FDISK to make a second hard drive bootable, an error message occurs. That is logical since only one drive can boot. If two drives were bootable the system would not know which one to boot from. However, MR-BIOS switches the drive letters of the hard drives in the Screen Prompt option. If you choose drive D: as the boot drive, it is changed automatically to C:. If no bootable operating system was installed on drive D:, the BIOS returns automatically to the Screen Prompt. Boot from a diskette and call up FDISK. Now you have outwitted it and drive C:, originally D:, can be designated bootable. Install your operating system. In the future you can choose from the Screen Prompt which drive should be used for starting.

MR-BIOS offers the following options: *A: 1st, C: 1st, Screen Prompt* and *Auto-Search*. *Auto Search* begins by searching the disk drives for a bootable drive and proceeds to start the operating system.

4. Using Tricky Options in the BIOS

Screen Prompt offers a menu that lets you select between the disk drive and hard drive. You can then determine the drive letter from A: to F:. The disk drive that is used for booting is then designated as A: and the hard drive is always C: since MR-BIOS always makes those designations. Remember this feature, otherwise you may quickly become frustrated by the changing drive letters.

The features of (E)IDE / SCSI hard drives

BIOS Options

HDD Sequence SCSI/IDE First, 1st Boot Device

BIOS Setup has many possibilities here. However, this is not all. If you select SCSI, A, C, or SCSI, C, A (depending on the SCSI host adapter model you use) you can also determine through software configuration the SCSI drive that will be used to boot up. This, of course, applies only if more than one are installed. Some Award BIOS versions also have the *HDD Sequence SCSI/IDE First* option. If you set this option to *Enabled*, SCSI will boot up before IDE. The option in AMI BIOS is called *1st Boot Device*. You can choose from *SCSI, CDROM, IDE-0, IDE-1, IDE-2* and *IDE-3*. That is the case when the option *SCSI, A, C* does not occur in the selections under *Boot Sequence*. Unfortunately, older BIOS versions do not have either of these last two possibilities. In those cases you can boot from the (E)IDE only if a drive is attached to the port.

Booting from CD-ROM

If you can set *CD-ROM, C, A* in the BIOS or, as in the previous paragraph, if you can set the option *CD-ROM* in *1st Boot Device*, you can also boot from CD-ROM. However, this is only possible with a special operating system CD-ROM that was burned to be bootable. Not all programs for the CD burner support the necessary "El Torito" file format. If necessary, however, you can generate a boot sector manually. Phoenix offers a good set of instructions for doing this on its Internet site.

The trusty old ZIP drive

You can also boot from ZIP drives. There are two means of access to these drives if they are internal: the SCSI or the most recent (E)IDE. If the drive depends on a SCSI Controller, a software setup of the controller can designate the ZIP drive as the boot drive or, correspondingly, it can be designated as the bootable drive using the (E)IDE and the BIOS Setup. Of course, in this case the BIOS must support ZIP drives, according to the information given in the manual for the motherboard or available from the manufacturer.

Problems with booting

Some BIOS versions that supposedly support the ZIP drive cause problems for booting on that drive. In that case it helps to remove the 3.5-inch disk drive from the BIOS.

The Zip drive is variable

The LS-120 can also boot

The most recent BIOS versions also offer a boot procedure for an LS-120 drive. The LS-120, from O. R. Technology, is a 3.5-inch disk drive for 120 Meg diskettes. Beause it is also downwardly compatible, you can also use 3.5 inch diskettes with 1.44 Meg or 720K. If your BIOS does not yet support the LS-120, you can still use it but you cannot boot with it unless you use an optional controller card.

The LS 120 is already built in some PCs as a replacement for the 1.44 Meg drive

You can also do it from the network server

You can also boot from a network. This requires a network card with its own ROM-BIOS that transfers control of the system to the network server. To do this, the BIOS of the network card must intercept interrupt 18h of the system BIOS. Otherwise, it would block the system by outputting an error message when it could not find a bootable medium. Then interrupt 18h is routed to the network by a "no boot routine," and the boot then occurs from the network.

When you use network cards without their own BIOS, only PCs with their own bootable drives can be connected and exchange data. However, you can add a BIOS from the manufacturer to the card at any

4. Using Tricky Options in the BIOS

time to make it capable of supporting a boot. This requires only that a BIOS chip be placed in the present edition and possibly that a jumper be set.

Network card without its own BIOS

Variable booting
❖ Hard drive, CD-ROM, ZIP & Co.   Simply select the most favorable boot sequence for your purposes from the menu.
❖ Booting from the network   A network card that has its own BIOS makes it possible to boot from the network as well.

Making the keyboard faster

BIOS Option:
Typematic Rate, Keyboard Typematic Speed

The default keyboard setting works well with the "one finger hunt and peck system," but it is too slow for ten-finger typists. This can get on your nerves when rapid keystrokes are simply lost. That's why the *Typematic Rate* or *Keyboard Typematic Speed* option is available; it specifies the possible keyboard input per second. The default value of 15 is often too slow and can be increased to 30 with no concerns.

BIOS Option:
Typematic Delay, Typematic Rate Delay, Delay Before Keys Repeat, Keyboard Auto Repeat Delay

The second keyboard option that can be set is *Typematic Delay, Typematic Rate Delay, Delay Before Keys Repeat* or *Keyboard Auto Repeat Delay*. This option specifies the delay time in milliseconds between two keystrokes. The default value of *250 msec* is just right.

4. Using Tricky Options in the BIOS

BIOS Option:
Typmatic Rate Settings, Typmatic Rate Programming

First, however, the *Typematic Rate Settings* option in the Award BIOS and the *Typematic Rate Programming* option in AMI must be set to *Enabled*, or you cannot change the values.

The Number Lock key

BIOS Option:
Boot Up NumLock Status, NumLock State at Bootup, NumLock

The numeric keypad has a Number Lock (Num Lock) key that toggles the keys between cursor operation and number entry. This (Num Lock) key can be *Enabled* or *Disabled* in the BIOS. Accordingly, the NumLock function is either enabled or disabled after boot up. This setting is important for users who wish to work exclusively with either cursor control or number entry. The desired setting can be enabled and users do not have to enter it manually each time they boot up.

What's Gate A20?

BIOS Option:
Fast Gate A20 Option, Gate A20 Option, Force A20-Gate Always On

This function has a long history that began with the 8088 processors. Since it is important only for the old 286 processors, we won't go into detail. The A20 signal switches the processor from "Real Mode," which uses the memory area up to 1,024 K, to "Protect Mode," which uses the memory above 1,024K. The BIOS controls this action.

In the case of the 286 processor, the switching was done by using the slow keyboard controller. Only gradually has the function been incorporated into a chipset, so that toggling can occur more rapidly. Several programs and operating systems such as Windows and OS/2 switch back and forth automatically between Real Mode and Protect Mode. The keyboard controller was simply to slow for this.

4. Using Tricky Options in the BIOS

The keyboard controller (above, left) on the motherboard

However, the address line 20 of the processor is responsible for the toggling itself. Only now, depending on the setting in the BIOS, it is either combined with the slow keyboard controller or with the fast chipset. For this reason, always enable *Fast Gate A20 Option*, *Gate A20 Option* or *Force A20-Gate Always On*.

Another option for the keyboard

BIOS Option:	
Fast Reset Emulation, Keyboard Reset Control	

You are surely acquainted with Ctrl + Alt + Del for resetting the processor. The reset button on the computer case accomplishes the same thing, but the keystroke combination is faster and simpler. To avoid data loss, you can disable this function in some BIOS versions. Set the *Fast Reset Emulation* or the *Keyboard Reset Control* option to *Enabled* or *Disabled*.

4. Using Tricky Options in the BIOS

Accelerate the keystroke

❖ The Typematic Rate option prevents lost key strokes.
   Simply increase the rate and the problem is solved.

❖ The Number Lock function
   You can specify your selection for cursor control or number entry at bootup.

❖ Enable Gate A20
   If it's available, always enable the Gate A20 option. This allows
   programs to toggle back and forth more quickly between Real mode
   and Protect mode.

❖ Block reset
   Prevent accidental resets.

Speeding up hard drive accesses with Block mode and 32-bit mode

Block mode and 32-bit mode insure that your hard drive gets real power and doesn't merely limp along. These lessen the burden on both the hard drive and the processor, since the files are transferred in a "packet." Otherwise the processor would have to address every bit individually. That would require both time and performance that can better be used elsewhere. Especially in DOS and Windows 3.x, data transfer is greatly accelerated. Windows 95/98 circumvent these BIOS functions and use their own drivers to access the hard drive. Accordingly, the option is irrelevant for these programs.

Block mode brings real power

BIOS Option:
IDE HDD Block Mode, Multi Sector Transfer, IDE Block Mode Transfer, Multiple Sector Settings

Block mode enables the hard drive to transfer its data to and from the EIDE controller in blocks rather than as individual bytes. Several large, 512-byte blocks can be transferred simultaneously. The actual number of blocks depends on the hard drive and ranges from 2 to 32. To find out the maximum number your hard drive will support, consult the manual or look on the Internet for the technical information of your hard drive. For some BIOS versions it is necessary to specify the maximum number of blocks. However, most versions do that for the user automatically and unnoticed. In that case there is a setting for *Enable* and *Auto* or *HDD Max*. The options for Block mode are variously called *IDE HDD Block Mode, Multi-sector Transfer, IDE Block Mode Transfer,* or *Multiple Sector Settings.*

4. Using Tricky Options in the BIOS

Estimate the blocks

If you don't know how many blocks your hard drive supports, perform a test. Run Scandisk or a similar program with which you can test the drive for errors; if any occur, you will naturally have to eliminate them. Now enter 16 in the BIOS as the number of blocks and copy a large quantity of unimportant files into a new folder on the drive. Run Scandisk. If no errors occur, the number of blocks can be increased; if errors occur, reduce the number of blocks until no more errors occur.

Problems with Block mode

Block mode can also cause problems with Windows 3.x and CD burners. This occurs especially with hard drives that are more than a few years old. In Windows 3.x, only disabling the 32-bit disk support using software at the system level or using Block mode in the BIOS can alleviate this. If a "Buffer Underrun" occurs when burning CD-ROMs or if transfer errors occur during data transfer using a modem, Block mode can be the cause of the failure. Disable it and try again; this may obviate the error.

Block Mode

Advantages
❖ Speeds up system performance
❖ Available in many BIOS versions

Disadvantages
❖ Can cause errors burning CDs or through double support in Windows 3.x
❖ Can only be used under DOS

Tremendous performance increase through Block mode

❖ If your hard drive supports Block mode, by all means enable it. Block mode can increase data transfer speed by up to 50%.

❖ On the other hand, if errors occur with Block mode enabled, as described above, disable it to see if there is a difference.

Enabling 32-bit mode

CD-ROM not up to speed

If BIOS automatically enables 32-bit mode, interruptions in data transfer can occur with 24x (and faster) CD-ROM drives if they are alone on a port. In that case, support for 32-bit mode will neither be detected nor enabled. The data will only be transferred in 16-bit mode. In this case the only solution is to attach a hard drive to the same port.

4. Using Tricky Options in the BIOS

BIOS Option:
IDE 32-bit Transfer Mode, Xfer Mode

32-bit mode

Advantages
- ❖ Speeds up hard drive operations
- ❖ Available in almost all BIOS versions
- ❖ In some cases automatically supported operations

Disadvantages
- ❖ Can only be used under DOS

With 32-bit mode, data with a 32-bit bandwidth is transferred from the EIDE controller to the hard drive. If the option is switched off, a much slower 16-bit transfer occurs. Current motherboards no longer have this option integrated in the BIOS Setup. It is automatically enabled if a hard drive with a 32-bit compatible command set is connected to the EIDE controller port. If you find the *IDE 32-bit Transfer Mode* or *Xfer Mode* options in the BIOS Setup, you need to enable them.

Quick Check: Hard drive accesses

- ❖ Enable block mode
  If an option for block mode is available, enable it for better system performance. Data will be transferred more rapidly and the load on the processor will be lessened.

- ❖ Enable 32-bit mode
  The same applies here as for block mode. Hard drive operations will speed up considerably.

Shadow RAM - DOS Turbo

Shadow RAM

Advantages
- ❖ Accelerates graphic output
- ❖ Available in all BIOS versions
- ❖ Up to 30% more performance
- ❖ Other BIOSes can also be shadowed

Disadvantages
- ❖ Can only be used under DOS

4. Using Tricky Options in the BIOS

Shadow RAM is gradually becoming obsolete. Modern operating systems such as Windows 95/98, NT and OS/2 manage most BIOS options through their own drivers. This also applies to Shadow RAM. Even Windows 3.x had this capability. Therefore, it is still relevant only for DOS. Certain computer game manufacturers have integrated their own drivers even for DOS. Normal DOS programs (and some still exist) run as though driven by a turbo.

The function of Shadow RAM

Shadow RAM simply shadows the system ROM and the video ROM of the BIOS. Why is that necessary? The reason is simple: Both the system and the video ROM work only with 8-bit data width and are therefore comparatively slow. This is particularly disadvantageous for programs that must access the ROM frequently. This occurs especially when DOS games perform numerous functions, especially producing graphics through video ROM.

Switching on turbo

BIOS Option:
Video ROM Shadow, Video BIOS Shadow, System ROM Shadow, System BIOS Shadow

The options to activate turbo are called *Video ROM Shadow, Video BIOS Shadow, System ROM Shadow* and *System BIOS Shadow*. You can find them in the BIOS Features Setup or in another menu.

```
Video  ROM BIOS  Shadow  : Disabled
C8000  -  CBFFF  Shadow  : Disabled
CC000  -  CFFFF  Shadow  : Disabled
D0000  -  D3FFF  Shadow  : Disabled
D4000  -  D7FFF  Shadow  : Disabled
D8000  -  DBFFF  Shadow  : Disabled
DC000  -  DFFFF  Shadow  : Disabled
```

Shadow RAM options in the BIOS

ROM brought into RAM

How does this work to produce such a considerable advantage in speed? The answer is simple. Both the system ROM and the video ROM are copied to the same address in the adapter segment of RAM. Picture it to yourself as a mirror image in the RAM memory between 640 and 1,024K (the adapter segment). This segment is normally equipped with 32-bit SIMMs (Single Inline Memory Module) with an access time of 60 ns (nanoseconds) or 64-bit DIMMs (Dual Inline Memory Module) with an access time of 10 ns. In comparison, the BIOS has an access time of 170 ns. Thus the access time in RAM is considerably shorter, and the access speed is greater. That makes this a very effective method.

Speeding up other ROMs

The adapter segment could also mirror other ROMs, such as those on a network card. To do this, you have to know the exact memory segment of the ROM. Then you can usually enable it in the BIOS Futures Setup. The hardware presently on the market usually includes drivers that assume this function in the BIOS without being enabled. Therefore, always consult the manual of the card to see whether drivers are used, or malfunctions may occur.

The shadow function is not suitable for use with the ROM of a SCSI host adapter, since it also writes in the I/O area. However, the BIOS mirrors this area in RAM, thus blocking the write access. This can lead to a fatal error with data loss. In case of doubt, consult the user manual to see whether shadowing is possible.

5

Power Tuning in the Depths of the PC

In this chapter we'll discuss tuning options for the BIOS. They will need to be tested for the best results and although this will take time, the effort is worth it. Optimizing the memory timing alone can yield up to 15% more performance. The ISA/PCI accesses are critical for good overall system performance. If you have a BIOS with *CPU-SOFT-MENU*, then you also have overclocking. This is the technical term for running the CPU up to the next performance level. The result is 15% more speed.

Note that safety and reliability when tuning are written in CAPITAL LETTERS in this chapter. There are a few simple steps for avoiding optimizing your BIOS to death. So now let's jump into the heart of the BIOS and exploit all the potential performance you've already paid for.

Before and after - Printing out BIOS settings

Imagine you've just spent several hours optimizing and your PC is running great. Just one more setting, you say, and then it will be perfect. However, you've forgotten which setting was the last one optimized and problems have developed. Now, all those hours of work are lost and you have to revert to the default settings.

Do things in order

Never change multiple settings at one time. Instead, use a benchmark after each change to check the PC's performance. If the result is positive, you can go to the next step. Don't forget a printed log, otherwise it may be difficult or impossible to restore a previous configuration.

This is why it's important to print any given screen page from the BIOS menu. To do this, simply press the `Print Screen` key and you'll have a hardcopy of the current settings. A few printers may not respond to the `Print Screen` key. If so, the printer probably has a control button for this purpose. The print quality may not be perfect, but you have a copy of the settings in case of problems.

Correcting the log

Before you make the changes, print a log of the menu and enter the new values by hand next to the old ones.

5. Power Tuning in the Depths of the PC

1. First print all the BIOS setup menus so you will have a comparison for later of the previous settings.

2. Always change just one setting at a time, and check the results (use an appropriate benchmark program if possible).

3. Always print a log or make a note of the corresponding menu first so it will be easy to restore the default setting. It's possible problems may occur that won't let you get back into the BIOS. If so, your only recourse is to recreate the default values. At least you have your printed log, and with it you can restore all the values except for the one which caused the problem.

Print out the log again when finished

Once you have finished your BIOS tuning, and are completely satisfied with the results, print all the menus. This gives you a written confirmation of the configuration. Now in case the BIOS crashes due, for example to a dead battery, you know exactly how to proceed.

4. There is another way to save the BIOS settings. Software is available which saves the complete contents of the BIOS and can also write it back.

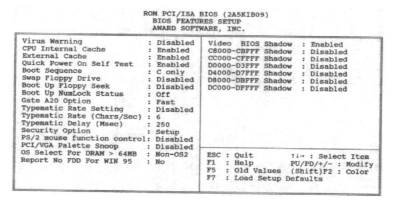

A hardcopy of BIOS-FEATURES-SETUP

Important basics on memory accessing - EDO/FPM & Co. timing

Memory modules have undergone drastic changes over the past 4 years. Normal 30-pin SIMMs (**S**ingle **I**nline **M**emory **M**odule) in 8-bit configuration with 70 or even 80ns access time were first. Then 72-pin PS/2 SIMMs with 60ns access in 32-bit configuration and FP mode (**F**ast **P**age) appeared. They were quickly replaced by EDO mode (**E**nhanced **D**ata **O**utput). Now we have 178-pin DIMMs (**D**ual **I**nline **M**emory **M**odule) with an access time of 10-15ns and 64 bits. As you can guess, this includes

5. Power Tuning in the Depths of the PC

many technical terms and contradictions. To give you a better overview, let's first look at how the modules still being used function.

FP module

The SIMM module is actually the origin of today's RAM technologies. Before that SIP modules (**S**ingle **I**nline **P**ackage) were used. They resemble SIMMs but have an additional small pin soldered to the contacts. The basic difference is only that the socket for mounting is different. Since the little pins are easy to bend and the socket can present contact problems of its own, only SIMMs with clamp contact mounting were used.

The SIMM module itself consists of several numbers of DRAM chips (Dynamic RAM). Most examples have nine chips on the 30 or 72-pin module. It consists of a 2-dimensional, matrix-like structure made of memory cells arranged in rows and columns like a spreadsheet table. This is exactly how they are used. The two values give the exact memory address (page).

The memory controller that controls the process reads the row first and then the column address. To do this, it uses the RAS (Row Address Strobe) and the CAS (Column Address Strobe) signal. To hold the data in the memory cells, it also regularly uses a refresh signal. Although the refresh cycle slows the module's working speed, this is unavoidable. The refresh techniques have greatly improved so the interruption is short.

Unlike a normal RAM module, the FP module uses a special technique for faster addressing of the memory cells. Fast page mode cuts down on address cycles to retrieve information from one general area, based on the fact that the second access to a memory location on the same page takes around half the time as the first. The page address is noted, and if the next data is in the same area, a second address cycle is eliminated as only the line and column address need to be sent.

Most motherboards automatically support FP mode if such modules are used. In older 486 boards however, you may find the menus *Fast DRAM* or *Fast Page Mode DRAM*. Then they must be *enabled*. Nearly all PS/2 RAM modules support this mode, increasing performance by around 20%.

In addition, some motherboard manufacturers use an additional means of shortening the time-stealing refresh cycle, dividing memory into two or four memory banks that process data alternately. While one is getting a refresh, the other can be accessed for data. This technique is called interleaving. It has been used for many years for screen imaging in monitors and for accessing hard drives. Modules that use interleaving have a considerable speed advantage over those that don't.

The EDO module

The EDO module works similar to the FP module. The differences are that the EDO module can hold data longer and the refresh cycle is extended. The longer cycle eliminates the need for interleaving. In addition, the data is made available longer for the processor by using a form of cache effect so that new data can be written. This special read cycle has a speed advantage of around 5-10% over FP modules. The appearance of an EDO module can't be distinguished from the 72-pin FP modules. Note that the chipset must be able to support EDO otherwise there is no advantage to these modules which can also be used without EDO support.

Externally there is no difference between an EDO and an FP module.

The BEDO module

BEDO modules (Burst EDO) modules were on the market briefly. The reason for their brief appearance is that they are only supported by the Natoma chipset.

The DIMM module

The DIMM module consists of different RAM chips than their predecessors, specifically SDRAM chips (**Synchronous DRAM**). They run directly off the external system bus clock and remain stable up to 100 MHz. They also feature a substantial, internal 2K cache for longer data retention. This also makes short access times of 10-15ns possible. Lower costs have allowed most PCs now to be equipped with DIMM modules.

SIMM and DIMM mixed
If SIMMs and DIMMs are combined in your system, set Auto Configuration to Enabled. Reducing the values is extremely critical with modules so different as these.

5. Power Tuning in the Depths of the PC

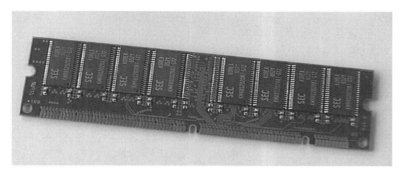

A DIMM module

Computer hangs while booting

If your computer locks up while booting, this could be caused by an enabled parity. Check if your memory modules are not equipped with a parity bit. Simply turn off this option in the BIOS.

Memory parity

BIOS options
Memory Parity Check, Memory Parity Error Check

All memory chips come with and without a parity bit. The parity bit acts as an error detector for the RAM, and is used for the checksum during the memory test. In the BIOS setup it is set to *Enabled* or *Disabled* using the option *Memory Parity Check* or *Memory Parity Error Check*. If it is not correct, an error message such as *Memory Parity Error At …* is output. Many RAM manufacturers have dropped this function since the chips were so good and errors almost never occurred. The cost was another factor; without the parity bit, modules could be made much cheaper.

Automatic error correction in the module

BIOS options
Memory parity SERR# (NMI)

In the meantime, SDRAMs with ECC (**E**rror **C**orrection **C**ode) have reached the market. They not only report an error during booting, but also perform correction of memory errors while the system is running. The chipset must support this function, otherwise it can't be activated in the BIOS under *Memory parity SERR# (NMI)* and then has no purpose.

Which modules are in your PC

BIOS options
Auto-Configuration

5. Power Tuning in the Depths of the PC

Now you've had the overview of different ways in which RAM functions in your PC. However, you're probably asking yourself, which ones are actually installed in my PC. You can answer that by looking in the boot table right after the POST. It tells you which modules the banks contain. If *Auto-Configuration* is turned on in *Chipset Features Setup*, then only the options for the corresponding memory type (DRAM or SDRAM) are filled in with parameters or are *Enabled*.

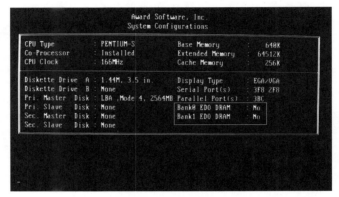

The memory type is displayed in the boot table (here showing FP modules)

If there are no EDO modules, but rather FP modules installed, *Bank0 (1) EDO DRAM: No* is displayed. If EDO modules are present, a *Yes* appears here. You can also have EDO modules in one bank and FP modules in another.

Power or Stability —Auto-Configuration

Whether you want your system to have power or stability depends on what you do with your PC. You'll either need a reliable and secure working compuer (such as for business and personal home use) or you'll use it for games or entertainment, where a system crash isn't so serious. This is were you decide whether to run the PC at its limits or let *Auto Configuration* in *Chipset Features Setup* take control at a somewhat slower but more reliable pace.

For advanced users only

Any setting you change with Auto Configuration turned off carries a risk, including data loss. Therefore, seriously consider whether some awkward reconfiguration of the memory parameters is really worthwhile.

Some RAMs are faster

If you're using good quality 70ns RAMs, you can use the 60ns setting. Then you have automatic tuning and don't have to worry about the individual values under Options.

5. Power Tuning in the Depths of the PC

BIOS options
Auto-Configuration / Disable, Enable, 50ns, 60ns and 70ns

Auto Configuration essentially affects the timing values for the RAMs. Depending on the BIOS version, you can select from the *Disable, Enable, 50ns, 60ns and 70ns* options. The standard setting is *Enabled* or *70ns*.

Using Auto Configuration

If you're planning to use *Auto Configuration*, set to *Enabled* or the value for your actual RAMs. If you don't know exactly which modules are installed, and *Enabled* isn't an available selection, set to *70ns*. A setting of *70ns* is only relevant for old 30-pin SIMMs in a 486. PS/2 modules will work with 60ns. You can change the values yourself only by selecting *Disable*.

Unknown BIOS settings

BIOS main menu
Load BIOS Default, Load Setup Default

Are there options in your BIOS that are not self-explanatory and not covered in the user's manual? Would you like to know whether more performance can be gained with *Enable, Disable* or by setting some parameter higher or lower? To accomplish this, you can misuse the *Load BIOS Default* and *Load Setup Default* options. *Load BIOS Default* sets the minimal configuration of the BIOS manufacturer so the PC at least runs. *Load Setup Default* contains the configuration of the motherboard manufacturer with the "best possible" settings for the chipset. Now you can compare the set values in the unknown BIOS settings to easily determine which value provides the best performance. There is a catch of course: some of the settings remain identical.

DRAM timing, refresh, burst, ...

Now we'll squeeze the last drop out of the RAMs. The timing settings are extremely important, but very complicated to figure out. In particular there are many combinations possible with the various options that, when changed, keep resulting in a different performance picture. Depending on the manufacturer's Auto Configuration, you can look for a gain of 5-10% of more power. The most productive changes are to be found in the options for burst access, in the wait states and the refresh settings. The full range of setting options can always be found in *Chipset Features Setup*. Before you make any changes, perform a benchmark test with your computer as described in this chapter. Afterwards you will be able to determine what the result of your tuning was. However, first do a backup of your CMOS data, preferably using a utility so that if needed you can restore the original settings.

5. Power Tuning in the Depths of the PC

Setting options in Award's Chipset Features Setup

Test and retest

If you are using a benchmark program to determine the best performance values, don't run it only under DOS. Step the process occasionally to run some memory-intensive Windows programs, such as a graphics program. The system may work flawlessly in the benchmark program under DOS and still give you protection faults suddenly under Windows. In that case, always restore the last change to its previous value.

Faster by the block

BIOS options
DRAM R/W Burst Timing, DRAM Read Burst Timing, DRAM Write Burst Timing

FP and EDO modules

If you have a mixture of FP and EDO modules in a PC manufactured before mid-1996, you cannot set the values as low as with EDO components alone. The EDO modules adapt themselves to the slower FP modules. Only after mid-1996, were motherboards used that could consider EDO and FP modules independently.

Auto Configuration pre-selects

Turn on Enabled in Auto Configuration, and look at the pre-selected values. These are the most reliable values for the installed memory modules that the BIOS had determined. You have a reference point. Switch to Disabled and proceed, one value after the other.

5. Power Tuning in the Depths of the PC

Burst mode

In burst mode, a large amount of data is sent in a block. This saves time and resources in addressing. This access mode is used for the L2 cache and the RAM. In the case of RAM, the values for the read and write cycles can be adapted to the chips. Slower chips also need a slower cycle to avoid losing data. The faster the cycle, the faster the system runs. You may need to experiment to determine what clock rate the chips can handle.

There are many possibilities for various BIOS versions and memory types. The read and write cycles are either set together or in various options. If the read/write cycle is set together in the *DRAM R/W Burst Timing* option, the first value represents read cycle and the second value represents the write cycle (X444/X333). DRAM R/W Leadoff Timing is also such an option (8/7). Here the first value represents the number of processor cycles for the read cycle and the second for the write cycle. If the values are set individually, the options are *DRAM Read Burst Timing* and *DRAM Write Burst Timing* (X222). There are extra options for the read cycle with FP and EDO modules. The timing here is determined for the read cycle. There are BIOSes with very simple settings. These are defined by the values that are called *DRAM Speed* or something similar and has options like *Fastest, Fast, Slowest, Slower*. Try the *Fastest* option first. Then reduce step-by-step if you get any errors.

Speculating like in the stock market

BIOS options
DRAM Speculative Read, SDRAM Speculative Read or DRAM Speculative Leadoff, SDRAM Speculative Leadoff

Some versions also offer *DRAM Speculative Read, SDRAM Speculative Read* or *DRAM Speculative Leadoff and SDRAM Speculative Leadoff*. This means the first part of the burst access can be accelerated if it is set to *Enabled*. However, under some conditions this can cost you some performance. This is because the addressing commands are executed speculatively, based on assumption, and may miss the target. Because these options do not represent an additional tuning factor, they should be *Disabled*.

More power with RAM turbo

BIOS options
DRAM Turbo Read Leadoff, Fast EDO Leadoff

If your BIOS version has *DRAM Turbo Read Leadoff* or *Fast EDO Leadoff*, definitely enable it. This determines how many clock cycles the memory modules use for the burst when at the first access (XYYY). Use this option for EDO modules without a second thought for a considerable performance gain. FP modules, on the other hand, don't always work with these options. So, system crashes and protection faults usually result. The only advice is to try it and see whether the system runs stably.

5. Power Tuning in the Depths of the PC

Recuperation not desired

BIOS options
DRAM Read WS, DRAM Read Wait States

Wait states
Since the processor and the system bus usually work faster than the DRAMs can react, the processor always has to run wait cycles - ticks of the system clock - while it's waiting for the memory to catch up. The more wait cycles the processor has to perform, the slower the whole system.

Some of the many options you'll find here include names such as *DRAM Read WS, DRAM Read Wait States* or similar. They provide settings from *0 WS* to *4 WS*. The lower the value, the faster the system. Page-mode memory and interleaved memory, as discussed earlier, are some ways of avoiding wait states.

For FP modules only

BIOS options
Turn Around Insertion

The *Turn Around Insertion* option inserts a single wait cycle between successive memory accesses if it is *Enabled*. This really only applies to old 70ns FP modules. All other memory modules are considerably slowed by this option. So, if you don't have an old FP module on a newer motherboard, which supports this BIOS option, leave this one *Disabled*.

Ideal for tuning freaks
If you're experimenting with a higher bus clock and your EDO modules are giving out, set the option to Enabled. This will give your memory some additional recuperation time.

Delay in the memory matrix

BIOS options
RAS-to-CAS Delay or RAS-To-CAS Delay Time

Wait states are also active in the RAM, because there must be a certain time between the RAS (Row Access Strobe) Signal and the CAS (Column Access Strobe) Signal. This time is determined by the RAS-to-CAS Delay or RAS-to-CAS Delay Time. Here again, a lower value means more performance.

5. Power Tuning in the Depths of the PC

Pre-charge

BIOS Options

RAS Pre-charge Time, RAS Pre-charge Period, RAS to CAS Pre-charge/Refresh, CAS Pre-charge, CAS Pre-charge in CLKS, DRAM CAS Pre-charge, Refresh RAS Assertion

The refresh

DRAMs consist of capacitors that eventually lose their charge. This means they need a short refresh in order to hold their information. The refresh itself is a quick current pulse that can recharge the capacitors in the module within a few microseconds. The manufacturers of RAM chips are constantly creating new ways to lengthen the refresh times. These are called concurrent, hidden, self, burst and slow refresh.

The names for refresh options depend on the BIOS version and the manufacturer. Typical names include *RAS Pre-charge Time, RAS Pre-charge Period, RAS-to-CAS Pre-charge/Refresh, CAS Pre-charge, CAS Pre-charge in CLKS, DRAM CAS Pre-charge, Refresh RAS Assertion* and many more. Although they have many names, the function is always the same. The options determine the time span (pre-charge time) for the refresh between memory accesses. It is measured in processor clocks (1T, 2T) or time values (1CCLK). The time period for such repetitive accesses between a RAS (line) or CAS (column) access needs to be kept as short as possible. Therefore, try for small values in the options.

Timing is everything

The timing of the burst, the wait states and the refresh must be mutually compatible. It's not possible to state precisely which values are optimum for which module. Once again, it's a case of experimenting and testing.

It's always hard at the beginning

Preferably start with the two options DRAM Read Burst Timing and DRAM Write Burst Timing. It's usually harmless to drop them by a value of 1 lower than set in Auto Configuration. It becomes more difficult with RAS options ito reduce the values.

The settings for SDRAMs

BIOS options

SDRAM RAS-to-CAS Delay, SDRAM RAS Pre-charge Time SDRAM CAS Latency Time

The same applies to SDRAMs as to DRAMs: coordinating the possible values such as *SDRAM RAS-to-CAS Delay, SDRAM RAS Pre-charge Time,* and *SDRAM CAS Latency Time* while keeping them as small as possible.

Keep in mind that if your system crashes due to over-optimizing, and you have to restart Windows or OS/2, any speed advantages you already gained are lost.

5. Power Tuning in the Depths of the PC

How to optimize RAM speed

1. Set the *Auto Configuration* option to *Disabled*.

2. Change the *DRAM Read Burst Timing* and the *DRAM Write Burst Timing*. Smaller numbers represent faster read/write speeds of the RAM.

3. Decrement the value for DRAM RAS to CAS by one step at a time. The shorter the wait state between RAS and CAS, the faster the modules are.

4. The same applies to the DRAM R/W Leadoff Timing. Here the number of processor cycles for the read and write cycle are determined. Its default setting is often too high.

5. Once you get to DRAM RAS Pre-charge Time, it becomes more difficult to extract any more out of the system. However, sometimes there's a little something to be gained. If the time span for the refresh is too short, the RAM will lose all its information.

Quick overview of the options	
Option	Value
DRAM Read Burst Timing	X333
DRAM Write Burst Timing	X222
DRAM RAS to CAS	3
DRAM RAS Pre-charge Time	3
DRAM R/W Leadoff Timing	6/5

Checking your tuning success

Use a fast benchmark program like Wintune or PC-Checkup to verify the RAM performance immediately. This is very important because the results won't necessarily show an improvement after reducing the values, they may even get much worse if the timing response is incorrect.

Checking with Wintune

Wintune is particularly suited for checking RAM settings, since many values are obtained and displayed at one time. On our test computer, the following settings existed as determined by *Auto Configuration:*

Option	Previous value
DRAM Read Burst Timing	X333
DRAM Write Burst Timing	X333

5. Power Tuning in the Depths of the PC

1. Start the program and run the complete test routine by clicking on *Analyze now*.

2. Save the displayed results in the program under *File, Save Current Results* or print out the test report under *File, Print*.

3. Run the BIOS Setup and change the settings.

We changed the values on the test computer as follows:

Option	New value
DRAM Read Burst Timing	X222
DRAM Write Burst Timing	X222

4. Run the program again and compare the results with each other by saving the values under a different name or printing the report again.

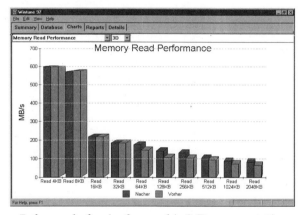

Before and after in the graphic 3-D representation

5. Keep the settings if the results are positive. Otherwise, if the results are negative, change the settings back.

The Wintune comparison

On our test machine we recorded the change, illustrated above, with Wintune. In the right column of the graphic are the values for the original settings, saved as "Before". In the left column are the values for the optimized settings, saved as "After".

5. Power Tuning in the Depths of the PC

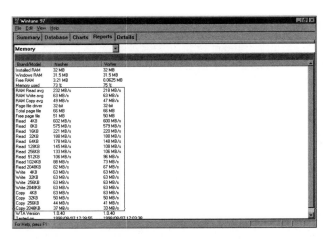

You can see exactly how the memory throughput and thereby the performance was significantly increased by changing just two settings. Next, we move to *DRAM RAS to CAS*. On the test machine, *Auto Configuration* had set this to a value of 3.

Option	Before	After
DRAM RAS to CAS	3	2

Give the setting a value of 2 by repeating steps 1-5.

Option	Before	After
DRAM RAS Pre-charge Time	4	3

Proceed in the same manner for *DRAM RAS Pre-charge Time* or *DRAM R/W Leadoff Timing*.

Checking with PC-Checkup

1. Start the program and run the test routine by clicking on Performance Data.

2. Save the displayed values in the program under File, PC Comparison List, Save or print the test report by clicking on the [Test Report] button.

3. Open the BIOS Setup and change the settings just as described for Wintune. The process of making a change in the BIOS and the testing tools is usually the same.

4. Start the program again and compare the obtained results by clicking on the [Analyze] button.

5. Select the User-defined Selection option . The currently saved values are already selected in the comparison. Now double-click the previously saved PC name in the *Reference Devices* window. Now it is also displayed in the left window.

5. Power Tuning in the Depths of the PC

6. Click on the *Memory Throughput* tab. Now you can see before and after as a graphic.

7. Keep the settings if the results are positive. Otherwise, if the results are negative, change the settings back.

Once you have completed a point, check your settings again for stability by running a few application programs. If you notice errors, restore the default configuration. The chips apparently can't handle the faster timing. Use this same test procedure for checking all the other settings.

More memory options

How did that hole in my memory get there?

BIOS options
Memory Hole At 15M - 16M

Using the *Memory Hole At 15MB-16MB* option means address memory is blocked off at between 15 and 16 Meg. This is intended only for very old ISA video cards with frame buffers. If the option is *Enabled*, Windows 95/98 cannot address a memory above 15 MB. Your system is then running with a "parking brake" on. Always *Disable* this and enable it again only if you have problems with the above-mentioned card.

OS/2 and more than 64 MB RAM

BIOS options
OS Select For DRAM > 64 MB

You're running under OS/2 and have more than 64 Meg of RAM: set the *OS Select For DRAM >64 MB* option to *OS2*. Now the accessing is done specially for this operating system.

AGP and the RAM

BIOS options
AGP Aperture Size (MB)

Another current option is *AGP Aperture Size (MB)*. This is used to reserve a memory address window in RAM for the AGP (**A**ccelerated **G**raphics **P**ort) video card. The aperture is part of the PCI memory address range dedicated for graphics memory address space. Host cycles that hit the aperture range are sent to the AGP without any translation. The value ranges from 4 to 256 MB and can remain at its default setting of 8 MB.

1K missing from low memory

BIOS options
Hard Disk Type 47 RAM Area

5. Power Tuning in the Depths of the PC

You only have 639K instead of 640K. This is caused by the hard drive data that are in the DOS memory BIOS reserves. In the Advanced CMOS Setup of AMI BIOS you'll find the setting *DOS, 1KB* selected in the option, *Hard Disk Type 47 RAM Area*. Use *0:300* here because then the BIOS will use a sector in the adapter area with the I/O address 300h instead of the DOS memory. However, first you have to verify that no other device is also using this area (sound card, network card, etc.), otherwise you may lose some data. If one of your devices uses address 300h, you can certainly reconfigure it to a different address and gain 1K of memory in the lower area at the same time.

RAM options

❖ Are the burst accesses optimized?
First, set DRAM Read Burst and DRAM Write Burst lower by one value. Then try to reduce the wait states.

❖ Have you reduced the wait states?
Lower the DRAM Read Wait States by just one value each at a time. Then do a thorough test, preferably by starting all your applications. If everything is still working, lower them again by a single increment.

❖ Are the refresh values still enough?
The RAS Pre-charge Time option is often critical and is quick to create memory errors when set too low. You may be able to squeeze out some here.

❖ Is the function timing correct?
Once you feel that all the options are optimally set, try working with all the programs installed in your machine to be sure that you don't get any system hangs or protection faults. Then you can run a benchmark test of before and after to compare the values.

Different clocking

If your motherboard has an Award BIOS with *CPU-SOFT-MENU*, then it's relatively easy to overclock the processor and gain up to 15% more hardware performance.

What's overclocking?

Wouldn't you rather have a Pentium 300 than a P266? After all, your PC's performance would improve noticeably. The answer may be *overclocking*. This is the technical term for taking the processor to the next clock frequency. The higher the clock, the more speed and performance your system can deliver. This is why overclocking the processor (CPU) is the most effective method of performance gain without purchasing new hardware.

Motherboard manufacturers advise against this. However if you don't overdo it and try to turn a P233 into a P300, you probably won't destroy your hardware. In the worst-case scenario, you'll have to reset

5. Power Tuning in the Depths of the PC

the BIOS, if due to an overclocking error in the processor you can't get back into BIOS Setup and the screen stays dark. The processor can not keep up with any overclocking.

In extreme cases, hardware damage could result. The processor might overheat to the point of melting a socket or burning some circuit board traces. This would destroy the motherboard. As we said, don't expect to turn a 133MHz processor into a 200, or a 233 into a 300. The manufacturing tolerances are simply too large for this. There is always a slight risk here and damage cannot be completely ruled out.

How overclocking works

The clock on the motherboard feeds 66 MHz to a Pentium 233. This is the external clock of the processor. The clock frequency of 66 MHz is multiplied by 3.5 internally. That increases the processors speed to 233 MHz. This is the correct setting for a Pentium 233 that runs at 233 MHz.

However if the clock frequency of 66 MHz is multiplied by 4 to produce 266 MHz, you will get the same performance from the 233 MHz processor as from a 266 MHz chip. It is possible to raise the performance level of almost any processor by one level. Increasing the clock frequency is done with the CPU-SOFT-MENU. It works with several processors without using jumpers. Overclocking can also be done in BIOS without CPU-SOFT-MENU, but then requires moving jumpers on the motherboard. The software approach is generally preferred since you don't have to worry about hardware.

Settings in the CPU-SOFT-MENU

BIOS options
External Clock, Multiplier Factor

The external clock is entered in the *External Clock* field. New motherboards currently use up to an 83 MHz clock with an internal multiplier of 3.5. Multiplying these two values gives you the processor speed of most CPUs. If you use SDRAM on your motherboard, a 75 or 83 MHz external clock can be used. This also accelerates any components coupled to the system bus, increasing overall performance instead of just processor speed. So depending on your motherboard, it may well be that possibility #3 (see table), which yields a 250 MHz processor clock, is faster than possibility #1 which results in a 266 MHz frequency.

Possibilities	External Clock	Multiplier Factor	Processor speed
Original	66	3.5	233
1	66	4	266
2	75	3.5	266
3	83	3.5	250

5. Power Tuning in the Depths of the PC

Safety vs. power - changing the processor clock in BIOS Setup

If the processor is run outside of its specifications, the result can be a system crash and data loss. Therefore, for reliable operation in the office environment it is best to run the processor only at the settings that the manufacturer intended.

Have your values ready
Write down the settings on a Post-It note and stick it to your monitor. This way you will always have them accessible and don't have to go through piles or file folders to find them again should you want to change from the manufacturer's values to the overclocking values or vice-versa.

If you use the same PC also for games or other power-intensive applications, simply change the settings recommended by the manufacturer to the overclocking settings in the *CPU-SOFT-MENU*. This lets you switch from power settings to safety settings.

Decent yet legal acceleration

BIOS options
Turbo-Frequency

There is a small performance boost built into the BIOS Setup that you can use without any worries. This option is called *Turbo-Frequency* and is displayed if the external clock for your CPU supports turbo mode. It accelerates the external clock by 2.5%. The motherboard manufacturers naturally advise against it, since the CPU is then running outside the recommended specifications and could eventually be damaged.

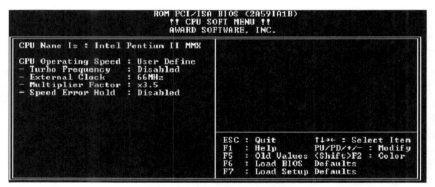

CPU-SOFT-MENU

Keep cool

The heat sink on Pentium II processors is adequate. Only the Socket 7 generation processors need a stronger heat sink beneath the fan. Here you can find a heat sink especially designed for the hotter

5. Power Tuning in the Depths of the PC

running Cyrix processors in your PC store. In any case, there should always be heat-conducting paste between the CPU and the heat sink.

Overclocking

❖ Make certain the external clock is correctly selected
Use CPU Operating Speed to set the external clock to the next-higher processor level. Use the table in the User's Manual.

❖ Don't forget the internal clock
Use Multiplier Factor to set the internal clock correctly to the next-higher processor level.

❖ Activate turbo mode
Turbo mode will only be displayed if it is supported by your CPU's external clock. Use it if available since a 2.5% speed increase isn't bad.

❖ If nothing else works then you've either set the clock rates wrong or your processor can't maintain the pace.

Displaying temperature and voltage in your monitor

More motherboards are being equipped with sensors for displaying temperature and voltage. The concept is called SMB (**S**ystem **M**anagement **B**us) and is done with a small chip called the LM 78. The data is displayed in *Power Management Setup*. Specifically, we're talking about the CPU and motherboard temperature in C (Celsius) and F (Fahrenheit). It may be particularly informative after overclocking to see by how many degrees hotter the processor is running. In addition, it shows all the voltages that are available on the motherboard. These are the two processor voltages (processor and processor core) as well as the + / - voltages of 5 and 12 volts for the drives and the motherboard.

Select the right new motherboard

If you're thinking about replacing the motherboard or getting a new PC in the near future, make sure it supports SMB. This will let you always have your computer under control, especially when it's just done overclocking or is used in a warm environment.

The LM 78 also has a few more internal functions. For example, it has three inputs that can be used to monitor the fan and hard drive. It also has a binary input for monitoring the housing cover (senses open and closed). By coupling the PCI to an ISA bridge in the chipset, you can also use software usually included with the motherboard to display operating system data.

5. Power Tuning in the Depths of the PC

Power Monitor display

As fast as possible - Setting ISA accesses correctly

Remove the weak card

The ISA (Industry Standard Architecture) bus is already outdated. However, you'll still find it on most motherboards for compatibility reasons. Every PC manufacturer still uses old, inexpensive ISA cards for low cost PCs. Like other bus types, the ISA bus is a distribution system for data transmission to the individual system components. It has 62 lines organized in 8 bits, and another 36 in the 16-bit area of the slot. Clocking is a leisurely 8 MHz. Data throughput of 8 MB/sec is theoretically possible, but multi-clocking of the 16-bit area drops this down to around 3 MB/sec.

ISA cards are also found still in new Pentium PCs, usually as a sound card or modem / ISDN card. Old 486s will have many or even all cards in ISA bus format. The ISA bus should run at 8.3 MHz in the system, since old cards especially tend to fail otherwise. The ISA bus clock therefore harks back to the time when 8 MHz processors were state of the art. So manufacturers declared 8.3 MHz as the standard ISA bus clock. The system clock in today's PCs is considerably higher, with the result that a divisor is needed to adapt it.

The divisor factor

Increase the ISA bus clock

Using a divisor of 3 for a 33 MHz system clock gives you an 11 MHz bus clock. In an old 486 system with an ISA video card you will then have 30% more power in the box, since the slow operations of the video card at 8.25 MHz otherwise slows down the whole system.
 However in no case go higher than 11 MHz, even if the ISA cards still run beause they will overheat and fail.

5. Power Tuning in the Depths of the PC

BIOS options
ISA Bus Clock, AT BUS Clock, BUS Clock Selection, ISA Bus Clock Option

The options are *ISA Bus Clock, AT BUS Clock, BUS Clock Selection* or *ISA Bus Clock Option* and you will find them in *Chipset Futures Setup*. The parameters vary widely in their names, but always imply something about the divisor factor. Let's say your system has a 66 MHz processor and runs at an external clock of 33 MHz. Then you have to find a divisor for the 33 MHz such that a maximum of 8.3 MHz remains. In this case that divisor is 4, since 33 / 4 = 8.25 MHz. If you don't have any really old ISA cards in the system, you can adapt the divisor so that the ISA bus clock is increased. If *Auto Configuration* is active, the divisor is automatically set to the correct value.

Too high a bus clock can be lethal

BIOS options
DMA Clock Selection

If the bus clock is permanently set at over 11 MHz, directly coupling the DMA bus clock to the ISA bus clock can destroy the DMA controller on motherboards that are several years old (say, pre-1996). Now you're looking at an expensive motherboard replacement. If your BIOS has *DMA Clock Selection* and you have set the bus clock, for example to 11 MHz, then use *ATCLK/3* instead. The DMA bus clock will then be in the safe range of 3.67 MHz. For safety reasons, it should not exceed the 4 MHz limit.

Wait states for ISA cards

Remove the weak card

Track down a weak card by reducing the 8-bit and 16-bit wait cycles separately from each other. Then when an error occurs, remove one card after the other from its slot until the error goes away. Now you've found the culprit and can replace it with a new card or remove it out even if it's no longer needed.

BIOS options
8 Bit I/O Recovery, 16 Bit I/O Recovery

Some BIOS versions also offer *8 Bit I/O Recovery and 16 Bit I/O Recovery*. This is for using wait states between the CPU and the ISA bus. It's only necessary for outdated cards that can't supply their data to the CPU fast enough. The settings for 8-bit and 16-bit cards can be made independently since 8-bit cards usually require more wait states than the 16-bit cards. Ideal here would be 0 or just 1 wait state. However this often doesn't work. When there is just one weak card, you have to increase the wait states at the expense of the good cards.

5. Power Tuning in the Depths of the PC

Wait states for DMA as well

BIOS options
DMA CAS Timing Delay

In some AMI BIOS versions there is an option called *DMA CAS Timing Delay*, which adds wait states to the DMA access. If possible, this should be *Disabled* so that the DMA can run at full speed. However if you are getting read/write errors on the diskette or hard drive, you'll have to enable it again. The same thing applies to problems with a CD-ROM burner, ZIP drive, scanners or other devices that use DMA.

VLB timing

Timing jumpers
Some plug-in cards also have jumpers for wait state timing. Check the User's Manual for the card and try disabling the performance brake.

BIOS options
Local Bus Ready Delay, Latch Local Bus, Check ELBA#-Pin

If you have a motherboard with VL (VESA Local), you may also find options like *Local Bus Ready Delay* or *Latch Local Bus* in *Chipset Features Setup* or *Check ELBA#-Pin* in *Advanced Features Setup*. These options determine the wait states that the processor initiates when accessing VLB cards. Depending on the BIOS version, there are settings for timing values or just Enabled / Disabled. Smaller values represent faster accesses. Faster access, of course, means more power, especially since it's usually the video card that is on the VESA Bus. However, if the wait states are set too short, the PC will usually go on strike. So just set these values higher by a single increment or switch the option back to *Enabled*.

Optimizing PCI accesses

The PCI bus has significantly more settings than the slow ISA bus. Virtually every expansion card today is available in a fast and easy-to-use PCI version. A high-tech PC today should come with PCI cards exclusively. Otherwise, you have the ISA impediment built-in to slow your work unnecessarily. The PCI accesses are extremely important for good overall performance. It doesn't help to have the memory accesses optimally configured if slow PCI accesses slow the entire system. Depending on which cards are installed in your system, the PCI bus may already be correctly configured by the BIOS manufacturer. However, if you also have MPEG cards or other video accessories in your PC, it can be advantageous to check a few options and change them if necessary.

5. Power Tuning in the Depths of the PC

The PCI bus

The PCI (Peripheral Component Interconnect) bus has a width of 32 bits in its original version and is clocked at 33 MHz for a theoretical throughput of 120 MB/sec. The succeeding PCI variations for Pentiums are configured for 64 bits at 33 MHz for the PCI 2.0 and 66 MHz for the PCI 2.1 version. This brings throughput to 230 MB/sec at 33 MHz and 460 MB/sec at 66 MHz. This is an huge difference compared with the ISA bus. This is because the bus is now separate from the CPU. A host bridge is inserted for controlling data actions. The PCI bus itself can thereby write data to the main memory or read data without processor intervention. This gives the processor time to control other items and improves system performance.

Latency time

BIOS options
PCI Latency Timer, Latency Timer

Since the PCI bus is so much faster than the ISA bus, error-free data exchange dictates that the PCI be delayed. This option is in the *PNP and PCI Setup* or *PCI / Plug and Play* menu. It may be called *PCI Latency Timer* or simply *Latency Timer*. Some BIOS versions let you set the latency time individually. The values contained in the option are the clock cycles of the PCI bus, with settings from 0 - 255, which determine how long the PCI card can use the bus before releasing it for other cards. If, for example, an ISA card requests a data transfer to the bus and the latter is being used too long by a PCI card, the result can be function problems with the cards or even a system hang.

The optimal setting for latency time

1. The ideal case is if you have only PCI cards in your PC. Then you can set the parameter to 255 PCI bus clock cycles so the PCI bus doesn't have to be released briefly for ISA cards and you can get full performance out of your system.

2. If on the other hand ISA cards are installed, the number of clock cycles allotted to the PCI cards for using the bus depends on the cards. The standard value is 32 clock cycles in the Award BIOS and 66 clock cycles in the AMI BIOS. This functions perfectly with most cards. However, audio, video and network cards can come up short here and cause problems. Then you need to reduce the clock cycle. Determining by how much is a matter of experimenting. Lower the setting in increments of 10 until the problem disappears. Of course, this will negatively effect the performance of the PCI bus.

The palette snoop

BIOS options
PCI/VGA Palette Snoop

5. Power Tuning in the Depths of the PC

PCI bus options appear in many areas throughout the menus. You can find the *PCI/VGA Palette Snoop* in *BIOS Features Setup*. When enabled, PCI bus masters can monitor the VGA palette registers for direct writes and translate them into PCI burst protocol for greater speed, to enhance the performance of multimedia video. If not enabled, color errors may be the result and some cards won't work. If you don't have any of the mentioned combinations, definitely disable it.

Among peers - controller and processor

BIOS options
Peer Concurrency

PCI cards work with the system in many ways. Therefore the bus master controller and the processor in a PCI system can be set as peers for data exchange using the *Peer Concurrency* option. This allows both to work simultaneously with the PCI card. This again is important for assuring that smooth data transfer takes place when using audio, video and network cards. Enable the function with *Enabled*.

PCI burst mode

BIOS options
PCI Burst Mode, CPU to PCI Burst Write, PCI Burst to Main Memory

Burst mode is also relevant for PCI cards. The PCI bus uses it for accessing RAM and the CPU. The options are called *PCI Burst Mode, CPU to PCI Burst Write* and *PCI Burst to Main Memory*. They are active by default on today's boards and hard to find. In general, you can enable all options with *Burst Mode*, since they are always faster. If in a rare instance you get errors, simply switch these options off.

BIOS options
PCI Streaming

PCI Streaming has the same effect with data sent in blocks instead of individually. *Enable* it if available.

Passive release

BIOS options
Passive Release

If both ISA and PCI cards are installed in the system, the result can be brief but frequent disturbances in the data flow on the PCI bus. This is because an ISA card is causing the DMA function to hold up bus master operation. Prevent this by enabling the *Passive Release* option.

Delayed transaction

BIOS options
Delayed Transaction

5. Power Tuning in the Depths of the PC

This option has virtually the same effect as passive release. Enable this option as well so the improved compatibility with PCI 2.1 can ensure smooth data flow.

ISA and PCI accesses

❖ Optimal ISA bus clock setting
Change the divisor in the ISA Bus Clock option for more system performance.

❖ Wait states are sometimes necessary
Unfortunately, old cards need wait states. Try to reduce these as much as possible.

❖ Reduce latency time
A very good tuning factor is selecting the perfect latency time so that the PCI bus isn't inhibited too long.

❖ ISA and PCI synchronous in VGA mode
If two cards use a VGA function, the color palette must be synchronized. Otherwise color errors and function disturbances may result.

❖ Permit simultaneous access of controller and processor
The bus master controller and the processor can work simultaneously with the PCI card using the Peer Concurrency function.

❖ Is burst mode for the PCI bus enabled?
If you find the burst mode option in your BIOS, turn it on.

❖ Enable passive release for the PCI bus
By enabling the Passive Release option, data flow is no longer interrupted by an ISA access.

Avoid conflicts with installed plug-in cards

PCI cards are also subject to faults that are not always due to an incorrect configuration in the BIOS Setup. Instead, sometimes they are the result of a wrong physical arrangement on the bus. Most motherboards have four PCI slots. However, only two of them support bus mastering, which enables data exchange with other PCI cards or directly to RAM without processor intervention. Which two of the four are bus master capable and which card requires a bus master slot can be found in the user's manual for the corresponding component. To make sure ISA and PCI cards work properly together, see Chapter 5 and Plug and Play configuration in the next chapter.

5. Power Tuning in the Depths of the PC

Only two of the four PCI slots (white) are bus master compatible

6

Plug and Play Offers No-hassle installation

Plug and Play calls itself "the system of the future." It is intended so that you may plug new computer hardware into place and instantly begin using it. This would be great, if it were only as easy as the manufacturers say. You buy a new card with "PnP" prominently displayed on the package. Excellent, you say, and the salesperson assures you that there's nothing to it. So you get home, plug the card into the slot, turn on the computer, the operating system starts up, and you want to install the necessary drivers. However, already an error message pops up to tell you that the install program can't find the card. Once again, absolutely nothing functions, in spite of the "PnP" on the package. Now the time has come to dial the manufacturer's hotline. Unfortunately, it's busy again, and again, and again. Finally, after the tenth try, you get a technician on the line. At some point during the conversation, he or she explains that you'll need a new motherboard for your one-year old PC in order to use the new card. To relegate such problems to the past, this chapter will explain Plug and Play simply and understandably.

The way it's supposed to be—how PnP functions

In the past, you had to know which I/O address, IRQs and DMAs were still available before you could install a new card. After that you could set the jumpers and insert the card. The selected address was entered in the driver and the card was installed. However, even just learning which system resources (I/O, IRQ, DMA) are free is a science in itself.

It finally occurred to someone that there had to be an easier way. Microsoft and Intel created the Plug-and-Play specification in 1993. Now it's handled completely by the BIOS, which automatically configures expansion boards and other devices during boot-up. Naturally, this only works with cards that don't have fixed settings, since these are supposed to be determined by PnP. Right away, PnP-compatible PCI cards were developed, and the whole system has become an accepted standard. Naturally, there has also been some progress in the meantime, with the rapid pace of PC technology development. PnP is by no means a fully mature entity, because it's still full of inexcusable problems. This is why you often hear the term "Plug and Pray" among those in the know.

6. Plug and Play Offers No-hassle Installation

PCI bus version 2.0 or 2.1

Whether Plug and Play functions as advertised also depends on the PCI bus version used on the motherboard. Motherboards with the FX chipset and PCI version 2.0 shipped until around the middle of 1996. This combination was not fortuitous, and errors in the Plug-and-Play system were numerous. Motherboards with the HX chipset and PCI version 2.1 didn't arrive until the end of 1996. In general, the chipset is the determining factor for the PCI version. The cards themselves aren't visually different. When using PCI cards, it is imperative to note which version you need for your motherboard. This is because the cards are only upwards compatible. This means a card for PCI version 2.1 will run only poorly or not at all on a PCI 2.0 motherboard, but going the other direction works fine. So before using a PCI card, check in the user's manual to verify that the versions are compatible. It's not always the fault of the BIOS configuration if the card doesn't work properly; it could also be the wrong version number. How these errors manifest themselves cannot be precisely defined.

PnP in detail

Plug and Play is somewhat intelligent. It checks all the cards installed in the system and then assigns the IRQs and DMAs for the Plug-and-Play cards.

First, the jumper-set (fixed) interrupts and DMAs for the ISA cards are ascertained. Next come the flexible PCI cards. For this the BIOS has to get information from the Plug-and-Play components. The PnP cards therefore wait for an initialization code from the BIOS. A specified command sequence writes this to a pre-determined I/O address on the card. Now the cards are ready for further instructions from the BIOS, which determines the available resources by communicating with the individual PnP cards. For this purpose the PnP cards have a 256-byte memory with information for the BIOS. This contains a 64-byte header block with the setup information in an IC code, including the type of component (video card, SCSI adapter, ISDN card, etc.) and the manufacturer, as well as the resources that can be allocated.

These variable IRQs and DMAs are now conveyed to the BIOS. The still-available resources are allocated corresponding to the requirements of the Plug-and-Play cards. Once the allocating is done, the result is stored in NVRAM in Upper Memory under the address (E000-EDFF) as ESCD (**E**xtended **S**ystem **C**onfiguration **D**ata). The PnP system uses this data at each boot to compare whether the installed cards or their settings have changed. If nothing has changed, the last combination of system resources from the ESCD is used. The comparison runs faster and the allocation of resources for PnP cards remains the same as long as nothing has changed. However, if the snapshot looks different, first the resources are determined and allocated as described above, then the ESCD is rewritten.

PnP-compatible operating systems, like Windows 95 and 98, also read the ESCD during the system start and then configure their own drivers. Finally, the allocated resources are displayed in a configuration list during the boot process.

6. *Plug and Play Offers No-hassle Installation*

Everything about IRQs, DMAs and port addresses

The main PC resources are IRQs, DMAs and port addresses. They snooze behind the scenes until the user wants to install a new card. Then in the manual, you may read something like "The standard setting is A220, I5, D1 …" What the designations for a non-PnP card mean exactly, and what they do inside the PC, are nowhere to be found. You will be told where the jumpers are on the card, and which values can be set using which jumpers, but how to determine the correct ones remains mostly a secret. A list of the used and available resources never comes with the PC anyway. All the PC manufacturers seem to shy away from providing this additional, but for the non-versed user, quite useful information. To install a new card, you first have to use the MSD diagnostic tool from Microsoft or some other suitable program to determine the resources for non-PnP cards. Then you put the jumpers in place according to the illustrations in the manual. This is probably the hardest part of the whole installation. Now plug the card in place and hope everything works. If it doesn't, you start asking yourself: What is an IRQ, a DMA or a port address, anyway? To make sure you are equipped and can anticipate any future new card installation with a smile instead of a sinking feeling, let's look at the functions in order.

Make a list for IRQ, DMA and I/O addresses

If you have used a diagnostic tool to discover the settings for your ISA cards, make a list of them. Then if you install a new ISA card, you'll have the available resources handy.

In the beginning was the IRQ

An IRQ (Interrupt Request) is an interruption for the processor, which then momentarily interrupts some process for a certain system routine. We know such interruptions in our daily workday. You're in the middle of sorting papers in a file and suddenly the phone rings. The ringing can be pictured as an interrupt request. You put the still unsorted papers aside and answer the phone. Once the conversation is over, you resume sorting. This is exactly how an IRQ works, except with the CPU and cards instead of a telephone and papers.

The IRQ

A chip on the motherboard called the interrupt controller controls the interrupt. It had eight interrupt channels, until the 286 processor came along. Then the interrupt channels were nearly doubled, to 15 channels available. The second controller chip has IRQ 9 coupled to IRQ 2 of the first controller. IRQ 9 on the second controller chip can only be used under certain conditions, and IRQ 2 should not be used at all.

The processor has just one control line through which the interrupt controller sends the interrupt number. Based on the interrupt number, the processor checks an interrupt table in main memory to see which routine it's supposed to carry out. If several interrupts appear at once, they are handled according to pre-determined priorities. The interrupt with the highest priority is processed first, with the rest following in decreasing order (see table on page 109).

6. Plug and Play Offers No-hassle Installation

The keyboard, for example, uses IRQ 1 when a key is pressed, and the interrupt controller forces the processor to pause so the video card can cause the character to appear on the monitor. Once the character has been displayed, the processor goes back to whatever it was doing before. This is how every requested interrupt is handled.

15 interrupt channels isn't much, especially since not all of them can be used for plug-in cards. In fact, channels 0, 1, 3, 4, 6, 8, 13 and 14 are already reserved by the system itself. Interrupts 2 and 9 are especially critical, since they're "tapped" by the interrupt controller. IRQ2 really shouldn't be touched at all. In an emergency and if all else fails, IRQ 9 can be used. If both IRQ 2 and IRQ 9 are used for another purpose, your system will surely come to a stop. This leaves IRQs 10, 11, 12 and maybe 15 for expansions, and these get used up quickly. One each of an ISDN, network, and 3-D video card plus a PS/2 mouse and you've reached the limit. Soon we're looking at possible IRQ duplication on a single channel. The respective devices will then cause problems for each other, and in most cases neither one works.

IRQ 5 is an exception. If there is no LPT 2 resulting from an auxiliary plug-in card in the system, it may be used. If you have a sound card, then it has probably already staked a claim on IRQ 5. Here the engineers need to do some more thinking, though it may not even be necessary, because the USB port and the firewire interface are coming.

The INT for PCI

ISA cards use interrupts directly based on jumper settings on the card. PCI cards, on the other hand, have dedicated interrupt lines from INT A to INT D (INT 1-4), which are not set by jumpers, but are converted (mapped) into normal IRQs by the Plug-and-Play BIOS. INT B then becomes IRQ 12, for example. Operating systems and the BIOS Setup still use the IRQ nomenclature, so INT will only be found in the card or motherboard manual. However the names are managed, it all comes out the same. In addition, PCI cards only use IRQs 8-15. The 8-bit IRQs from 0-7 can only be used by ISA cards.

The BIOS and the operating system can make some software interrupts available. For the most part, these are used by device drivers, and so are not interesting for BIOS tuning.

IRQ	Used by	Status	Priority
0	System timer	Reserved	15
1	Keyboard	Reserved	14
2	Interrupt controller	Use only if necessary	13
3	COM 2	Reserved, can share the IRQ with COM 4	4
4	COM 1	Reserved, can share the IRQ with COM 3	3
5	LPT 2	Available if no LPT 2 is used	2
6	Floppy drive	Reserved	1
7	LPT 1	Reserved	0
8	Realtime clock	Reserved	12
9		Available (don't use if IRQ 2 is already used by a component)	11
10		Available	10
11		Available	9
12	PS/2 Mouse (if present)	Available if no PS/2 mouse is used (can be disabled in BIOS)	8
13	Coprocessor	Reserved	7
14	First (E)IDE controller	Reserved	6
15	Second (E)IDE controller	Available unless otherwise used (can be disabled in BIOS)	5

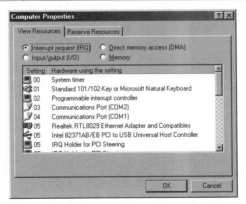

Interrupt list in the Windows 98 Device Manager

The DMA channels

Most of what we have said about interrupts applies equally to DMAs (**D**irect **M**emory **A**ccess). DMA is a technique that allows devices other than the CPU to write to memory (RAM). In most computers this is the preferred technique for quickly transferring lots of data. Basically, the CPU tells the DMA controller which device to access and where in RAM to read or write the data. After these instructions, the DMA controller transfers the requested data and notifies the CPU when it is ready. There are eight DMAs, two of which are reserved for the system itself. In really old motherboards, DMA 0 can also be reserved by the RAM refresh. As you can see in the table, there are 8-bit and 16-bit wide channels. Which type the card uses depends on the card itself. Then either only channels 0-3 (8-bit) or 4-7 (16-bit) are available, of which channels 2, 4 and sometimes 0 are already reserved by the system. If you're using EPP mode for your printer, then DMA 3 is probably already spoken for. If the system has a sound card, it usually reserves DMA 1. Some 16-bit sound cards also reserve a second DMA channel. DMA is often controlled by the card as HDMA (**H**igh **D**irect **M**emory **A**ccess).

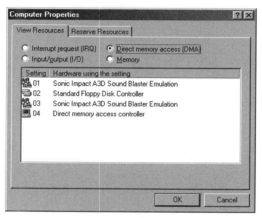

Some sound cards use two DMAs

Like the IRQs, the DMAs are associated with a controller. The DMA controller is responsible for sending data from the device into memory. Normally, the processor sends the data to the port on the card or retrieves data from the memory. Once again the processor is involved in regulating data transport when it could be doing more meaningful tasks. This is why a DMA controller was specially developed. It feeds the data flow directly to memory and controls device access. This removes a lot of the burden from the processor and increases overall system performance.

The DMA

The interplay of DMA controller, card and processor is much more complex than indicated in this brief summary. For a better overview of the functions, we have only summarized the basic sequences:

The card uses the DMA lines to request a data transfer. Now the DMA controller contacts the processor and asks to use the bus system. Once the processor has given permission for this transaction, the controller stores an address in memory and tells it to the card. Now the card can use this specified memory range itself, without the processor influencing the data transfer.

DMA	Reserved by	Use	Bus width
0	*RAM Refresh	Available (*Reserved)	8 bit
1		Available	8 bit
2	Floppy drive	Reserved	8 bit
3		Available	8 bit
4	DMA controller	Reserved	8 bit
5		Available	16 bit
6		Available	16 bit
7		Available	16 bit

Only ISA cards still use the DMA channels. PCI components make use of bus mastering. The available DMAs can all be used for the ISA cards.

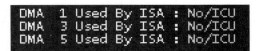

Manual DMA reserving

Port addresses

These are also called "I/O" addresses. To communicate, every card needs an I/O address in memory for buffering data. The address is either fixed by the card or is set using jumpers. Plug and Play does not affect the I/O address. This means you have to make sure that the I/O address is only assigned once, just as with the IRQ and DMA channels. If two devices share the same address, conflict is unavoidable, as both devices will attempt to access the same memory area.

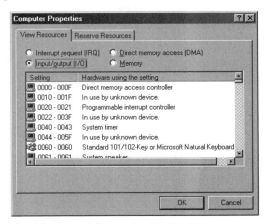

The I/O addresses in Device Manager

6. Plug and Play Offers No-hassle Installation

Determining resources with a system tool

You can use a good tool like *PC Checkup* to exactly determine the IRQs, DMAs and I/O addresses. In the left window tree, click on IRQ, DMA or port information. Now an overview of the IRQ and DMA information as well, as the adapter ROMs and reserved port addresses for the individual components, will appear in the right window.

The DMAs in PC-Checkup

BIOS Option:
Legacy ISA or Used by ISA

This option is useful, especially when installing a new card. You may check which resources the existing cards use before installing and configuring the new card. Now you have a precise summary of which IRQs and DMAs are still available. Set the jumpers accordingly and plug in the card. Then open the PnP/PCI Configuration menu in BIOS Setup and reserve the resources for ISA cards with the *Legacy ISA* or *Used by ISA* option. This eliminates many possible conflicts with other ISA cards or the PnP system.

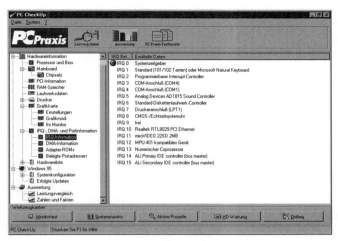

PC-Checkup determines the IRQs very exactly

Windows 95 and "Plug and Play"

Windows 95 was the first Plug and Play-compatible operating system. It works in conjunction with a BIOS which is likewise PnP compatible. During the development and new release stages of 1994/95 however, not all motherboards were shipped with a PnP BIOS. Windows 95 was also intended to be used in older PCs without PnP. Microsoft came up with a very special technique. Every time the computer boots up, the operating system identifies the PnP components again and checks them for changes. As part of this process, the ESCD (**E**xtended **S**ystem **C**onfiguration **D**ata) is read and used. If another component has been added, it tries to recognize this device. Then it looks for suitable drivers in the system. If one is available, it's selected and used. If there are no appropriate drivers for these components, it prompts the user for the correct drivers. These are (we hope) installed and the device is added to the registry database.

How it's done

BIOS Option:
PNP-aware OS, PNP OS Installed

To make sure the BIOS and operating system work together properly, you have the option *PNP-aware OS* or *PNP OS Installed* in *PNP/PCI Configuration*. If a PnP-compatible operating system like Windows 95 is used, *Yes* should be selected. Then the BIOS only configures the components that are necessary for booting, and leaves the rest for the operating system. According to what scheme Windows 95 then distributes the resources is very unclear and apparently known only to the Microsoft developers.

6. Plug and Play Offers No-hassle Installation

Non-PnP components remain undetected and can be called to life only through hardware recognition. This works off a database that assigns drivers to devices based on the addresses. It doesn't always work reliably, since there is an endless number of manufacturers and models. If hardware detection fails, the resources have to be manually entered in the Device Manager. This often works better and may be considerably faster.

ESCD and Windows 95/98

BIOS Option:
Resources controlled by, assigned to: ISA, Reserved, ISA/Legacy

Resource problems with ISA cards

If you have a resource problem with ISA cards, simply reserve the IRQ and DMA for the card using the provided option in the BIOS.

Windows 95 has another feature that it uses with a PnP BIOS: it can update the ESCD when shutting down. Normally, only the BIOS Setup writes to the ESCD. But now, the operating system can enter components that escaped the BIOS directly in the Plug and Play of the BIOS. For example, the IRQs and DMAs for certain components can be reserved in the Device Manager under the *Reserve resources* tab just as in the BIOS Setup under *PNP/PCI Configuration* using the *Resources Controlled by, assigned to: ISA, Reserved* or *ISA/Legacy* option. Resources reserved in this way are then not allocated to non-PnP cards by the operating system or the BIOS. If you want to prevent Windows 95 from changing the ESCD, you can disable this option in Device Manager under *System Components, Plug & Play BIOS*. This is not recommended, however, since the operating system works much better than the BIOS itself. Still, it's amazing that after a system reset the BIOS accepts the changes without complaining, as if it had noticed nothing at all.

6. Plug and Play Offers No-hassle Installation

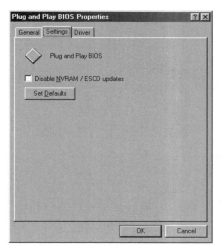

The option that allows the OS to change the ESCD can also be deactivated

You can disable the *Use automatic settings* option and set IRQs, DMAs and I/O addresses manually for particularly unruly devices by going into the Device Manager, selecting the device, and clicking the *Resources* tab. Entering values here will force the device to be used with those values. If you enter a value that is already allocated, an error message will appear in the *Conflicting device list* field.

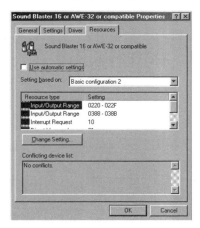

Setting resources manually

IRQ sharing adds more available resources

In contrast to ISA cards, PCI cards support IRQ sharing. This means several PCI components are allowed to share the same IRQ. However, theory is one thing, and practice often another. So Windows 95 first assigns the existing IRQs and only then tries to make multiple cards happy with a common IRQ.

6. Plug and Play Offers No-hassle Installation

Whether that works or not depends primarily on the components themselves. You may well find two components are both capable of sharing according to the technical data in the user's manual, but in reality they can't agree. Older cards are more of a problem in this respect than very new ones.

IRQ sharing problems

If IRQ sharing doesn't work, it's probably the fault of the cards themselves: they don't understand each other. Then you need to intervene manually and, in the Device Manager, allocate the resources for the sharing cards to a different one.

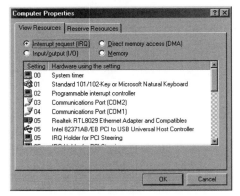

IRQ sharing is covered in Device Manager

Thanks to the constant development of motherboards and devices, Plug and Play has changed very much for the better in Windows 95. A PC running exclusively PnP components under Windows 95 should be problem-free.

Windows 98 and "Plug and Play"

Now Windows 98 can be added to the list of Plug and Play-compatible operating systems. The complete Plug-and-Play architecture has been revised compared with Windows 95. The biggest plus is improved detection of non-PnP cards, which are always the weak spot in such a system. PnP and non-PnP cards also get along much better than before.

Users of a PC without the Plug-and-Play BIOS also get their money's worth. The hardware scan during the installation routine has been made much more thorough.

In addition, the Add New Hardware Wizard is new for Windows 98. First it checks the new Plug-and-Play devices in the system, then summarizes its findings in a list. Then you can simply select which device to install.

The Plug-and-Play devices in the Add New Hardware Wizard

If the device doesn't appear in the list, you can take the next step and have Windows 98 look for non-PnP devices. The automatic hardware detection now tries to find these. If the search comes up empty, you can still run the Hardware Wizard manually, as usual.

Non-PnP hardware is detected

6. Plug and Play Offers No-hassle Installation

"Plug and Play" with DOS, Windows 3.x and Windows NT

DOS, Windows 3.1 and Windows NT are not Plug-and-Play systems. Their components are configured entirely by the BIOS. Go to the BIOS menu *Plug and Play Configuration* or *PNP/PCI Configuration* and set the option *PNP OS Installed* or *Plug and Play O/S* to *No* or *No/ICU*. The rest then happens just as described in the next section.

Allocate IRQs and DMAs

It's best to reserve the IRQs and DMAs for the ISA cards manually, since this will minimize any problems you have with the resources.

Compared with DOS and Windows 3.1, which have nothing to offer in the way of hardware detection, at least NT 4 has a minimum, automatic hardware detection function, which is controlled by simple .INF files. These files contain a list of hardware features that the operating system compares with the hardware in the computer. For precise identification, the BIOS is read from the plug-in card, in which the manufacturers store certain hardware data. If there is agreement with the hardware features in the .INF file, the component is properly detected. As you can see, cards that do not have their own BIOS will always have problems being detected by NT. However, this will change with Windows 2000, which will also provide Plug-and-Play support.

The path to a functioning PnP PC

Configuring a PnP PC is not difficult; it depends more on how the cards behave in the system.

Tell the BIOS which operating system you're using. If it supports PnP, go to the *Plug and Play Configuration* or *PNP/PCI Configuration* menu and set *PNP OS Installed* or *Plug and Play O/S* to *Yes*, or set the *Configuration Mode* to *Use PNP OS*.

PnP and non-PnP operating systems

To start various operating systems (PnP and non-PnP) with a boot manager, you would first have to set the PNP OS Installed option accordingly. You can avoid this by always selecting No. The PC will then take somewhat longer to boot, since the BIOS first has to configure all the cards, and Windows 95/98 also does its configuring. But at least you avoid having to get into the BIOS.

If you don't have an operating system that supports PnP, select *No* or *NO/ICU*.

```
PNP OS Installed     : No
Slot 1 (RIGHT) IRQ : Auto
Slot 2 IRQ           : Auto
```

PnP assignment for the operating system

6. Plug and Play Offers No-hassle Installation

The slow Auto function

This is just like all the other BIOS functions that are set to Auto. Booting takes longer, since Auto first has to process the configuration. If you choose to reduce the bootup time, the resources have to be configured manually.

If you also have a *Resources Controlled by* option, select *Auto*, and the resources will be allocated by the BIOS. If you select *Manual*, you can configure the resources yourself. This lets you reserve IRQs and DMAs for non-PnP compatible components. Be sure to allocate correctly, otherwise the results may be faults in individual cards or the entire system may stop working.

The *Legacy ISA* or *Used by ISA* option reserves an IRQ or DMA for a non-PnP compatible component that is not available to the PnP system. *PCI/ISA PnP* does exactly the reverse. Here IRQs and DMAs are set for PnP-compatible PCI or ISA cards.

```
                      ROM PCI/ISA BIOS
                     PNP AND PCI SETUP
                    AWARD SOFTWARE, INC.

PNP OS Installed    : No          DMA  1 Used By ISA : No/ICU
Slot 1 (RIGHT) IRQ  : Auto        DMA  3 Used By ISA : No/ICU
Slot 2 IRQ          : Auto        DMA  5 Used By ISA : No/ICU
Slot 3 IRQ          : Auto
Slot 4 (LEFT) IRQ   : Auto        ISA MEM Block BASE : No/ICU
PCI Latency Timer   : 0 PCI Clock
                                  SYMBIOS SCSI BIOS  : Auto
                                  USB IRQ            : Disabled
IRQ  3 Used By ISA : No/ICU
IRQ  4 Used By ISA : No/ICU
IRQ  5 Used By ISA : No/ICU
IRQ  7 Used By ISA : No/ICU
IRQ  9 Used By ISA : No/ICU
IRQ 10 Used By ISA : No/ICU
IRQ 11 Used By ISA : No/ICU
IRQ 12 Used By ISA : No/ICU      ESC : Quit          ↑↓→← : Select Item
IRQ 14 Used By ISA : No/ICU      F1  : Help          PU/PD/+/- : Modify
IRQ 15 Used By ISA : No/ICU      F5  : Old Values   (Shift)F2 : Color
                                 F6  : Load BIOS  Defaults
                                 F7  : Load Setup Defaults
```

The IRQ and DMA options

An interrupt for every slot

BIOS Option:

Slot 1 (Right) IRQ to Slot 4 (Left) IRQ

How to find slots 1-4

If you're not quite sure where Slot 1 and Slot 4 are located on the motherboard, either look for a printed number on the motherboard next to the slots or refer to the drawing in your user's manual.

On some motherboards, the interrupts can be allocated individually for each PCI slot. The options are called *Slot 1 (Right) IRQ* to *Slot 4 (Left) IRQ*. The nomenclature "Right" and "Left" is not 100% clearly defined. Slot 1 is supposed to be on the outer edge of the board. If you look at the board from the proper direction, *i.e.*, with the slots towards the front, Slot 1 will be the right outermost one directly adjacent to the ISA slots, and Slot 4 will be the leftmost one. This is what "Slot 1 (Right)" and "Slot 4 (Left)" refer to. If the setting is on *Auto*, an available IRQ is allocated to each occupied slot.

6. Plug and Play Offers No-hassle Installation

The video card and the IRQ

Since it's virtually certain that the video card uses a PCI slot, it also receives an IRQ, although video cards don't even need one. This is a complete waste of scant resources. For the slot where the video card is located, select the setting *NA*. This means the video card is not given an IRQ. Do this with each unoccupied PCI slot. If your video card is coupled to a 3-D accelerator or video converter, then it does require an IRQ. By assigning this manually instead of letting it be allocated by the BIOS, you can speed up the boot time. When the BIOS is being relieved of a chore, it will work faster.

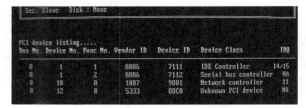

The Slot 1-4 options

Save the new settings and reboot the computer. The configuration list displayed briefly as the system boots shows you which resources are now allocated to the PnP-compatible cards. Sometimes the display is visible too briefly to read. Simply press the (Pause) key when the list appears on the screen, pausing the boot process. Press (Enter) to resume booting.

The configuration list

Half and half

Sometimes PnP cards have jumpers for setting INT A-D. Then it depends on which slot the card will be using. If you have selected Slot 2 for the card, set the jumper to INT B.

Homemade Plug and Play with ICU

New ISA cards are often shipped as PnP versions. These use a serial memory chip in which all the manufacturer's data is stored, as with a Plug-and-Play card. If you want to use these Plug-and-Play cards in your system without PnP BIOS and a PnP-compatible operating system, you can have problems. You have no way of allocating resources to this jumper-less card. The solution is called ICU (**ISA C**onfiguration Utility). This utility determines which hardware is installed and then the individual parameters for the plug-in card. Then the utility, which simulates a PnP BIOS, allocates resources for the card. The configuration is then saved in a file residing on the hard drive. A driver in CONFIG.SYS sees to the card resources when the operating system is started. Normally, the manufacturers ship this or a similar utility with such cards. If this is not the case, you either have to replace the card with a normal ISA version having jumpers or download the utility off the Internet from the motherboard or card manufacturer, or from Intel.

Be sure to set the intended IRQs in the BIOS to *No/ICU* under the *PNP OS* option.

Install the utility and configure the card according to the user's manual.

There's another interesting program at National Semiconductor's Website. It's called *Isolate,* and it reveals detailed information about the ISA Plug-and-Play cards. You can also configure under DOS with it.

You can't get into the BIOS

❖ Is the PNP OS Installed option configured correctly?
  For a non-PnP compatible operating system, never use the Yes setting under PNP OS Installed. Otherwise only those cards that are absolutely needed for booting will be configured and the others won't work at all, since they haven't been allocated resources.

❖ Leave the Resources Controlled by option to the pros
  It's better to use the Auto mode if you're not absolutely certain which IRQs and DMAs your non-PnP compatible cards use.

❖ Slot 1 (Right) IRQ to Slot 4 (Left) IRQ
  Don't assign an IRQ to an empty slot or use Auto if you're unsure which slots (1-4) are occupied. If, by confusing the slots, you inadvertently assigned N/A to the card, the card won't work.

❖ ICU doesn't function correctly
  For the ICU to function correctly, the option PNP OS Installed must be set to No/ICU. Otherwise, the BIOS steals the resources from the utility and the components won't function even if the settings are correct.

Economical and fast SCSI support for SymbiosLogic (NCR)

BIOS Option:
SYMBIOS SCSI BIOS

If you have an Asus or QDI motherboard with SCSI BIOS support, you can use the economical controller from SymbiosLogic. This uses the SYM810 / 810A chip for SCSI-2 or the SYM820 chip for Wide SCSI-2, which is already integrated on the motherboard. Furthermore, it doesn't need its own ROM BIOS. All you have to do is plug in the SCSI adapter card and set *SYMBIOS SCSI BIOS* to *Enabled* in the system BIOS under *PNP and PCI Setup*. If you set the option to *Auto*, the BIOS itself recognizes whether a SymbiosLogic adapter is being used. You have a relatively economical, but full-feature SCSI adapter.

The SYMBIOS SCSI BIOS option

SymbiosLogic adapter
Advantages ❖ Low-cost SCSI adapter ❖ Driver for all operating systems Disadvantages ❖ Used on very few motherboards

7

Using Power Management to Save Energy

Every PC needs a lot of power. To save power during work breaks, BIOS controls the power management. This allows various components to power down after a certain period of inactivity. When you initiate any action (such as pressing a key), the components are activated again. Unfortunately, Windows 95 and NT have problems with this. This is especially true with desktop PCs. In the case of laptops, you generally have to learn how to use the built-in power management, since this will extend precious battery life.

BIOS and power usage

Energy savings will vary according to how the PC is used. This can range from a few cents to a few hundred dollars a year. The main source of power use is your monitor, which uses an average of 70 watts. This means your system is using about 115 watts (including 45 watts for the PC). However, by using power-save mode, you can reduce the power the system requires to about 38 watts (5 watts for the monitor and 33 watts for the PC). This represents a savings of 77 watts, which may not be much for an individual, but can be significant for a business if all PCs used the power-save mode.

Device	Normal mode	Power save mode	Savings
Monitor	70 watts	5 watts	65 watts
PC	45 watts	33 watts	12 watts

Therefore, monitors and motherboards usually include the "Energy Star" label. This is a symbol that the device complies with EPA guidelines.

Energy Star label

7. Using Power Management to Save Energy

Demands on the hardware

Don't expect too much from this rather simple technology. If the hard drive is powered down too often (intervals too short), it uses more energy starting up again than it saved while sleeping. Nor should the mechanical consequences be ignored. The greatest stress for the hard drive(s) comes not from continuously running, but from being turned on and off. The same applies to the monitor. If it is put to sleep too often, the picture tube suffers from the repeated full voltage peaks each time it is turned on. So, if you're looking to save power, you may be saving it on the wrong end, because once the monitor or hard drive has reached the end of its days, the savings are quickly lost in the cost of new hardware. Use the power management functions intelligently.

Power management isn't always ideal

These savings probably aren't worth much for an occasional home user. However, a PC used constantly in an office environment—including a home office—can save a significant amount of money. In our view, a server doesn't need an activated power management setting in the BIOS. This is because the devices that are not used in a 24-hour period can be turned off with a mechanical power manager (switch box) or directly using a network switch. Only the hard drive and the processor cannot be controlled in this way. However, there is hardly time in server mode to turn these components off anyway. Users constantly access the server during the day and it's probably backing up data at night. Risking a system crash in the server caused by a power management utility incorrectly supported by the operating system is not justifiable for the administrator.

Performance suffers as well

The PC must permanently monitor the time intervals for turning components on and off. This costs performance. With maximum power management, the processor may use up to 30% of its computing performance just managing the power. Surely we can find better uses for this performance.

Power management options

The power management system cannot be used by the BIOS alone; the operating system must be capable of APM (Advanced Power Management). This is usually the responsibility of drivers available with MS-DOS 5.0 and Windows. MS-DOS uses the POWER.EXE driver, which is bundled in the CONFIG.SYS with a device command. It's slightly more complicated in Windows 95/98 but can be configured in the Power Management control panel. Windows 98 even supports ACPI (Advanced Configuration and Power Interface), which can be used with several motherboards starting with the TX chipset.

Compared with API, this provides expanded energy management that adapts power management to the energy requirements of an application and to the typical work habits of the user. It can even use the BIOS to put the PC into a deep-sleep mode with extremely low power consumption, and reactivate the devices in response to a keystroke or modem activity, without rebooting. This new technique is called *OnNow*.

7. Using Power Management to Save Energy

Check the Microsoft website for more information. How this function will prove itself in practice remains to be seen.

Power Management
Advantages
❖ Devices can be turned off individually in three stages
❖ Operating systems are providing better and better support
❖ Environmentally responsible
Disadvantages
❖ Operating system problems can result
❖ Time interval for turning off the hard drive is too short
❖ Old BIOS versions do not support power management

Enabling power management

BIOS Option:
Power Management

If you've decided to use power management, you should go to BIOS Setup and the *Power Management* menu. Select the *Power Management* option, and select *Enable* or *Disable* in the AMI BIOS to turn power management on or off.

Power management induced faults
If you are about to install a large program that takes longer to install than your power management settings would allow, temporarily disable the function to avoid problems. The same applies to longer tests (such as benchmarking) and even for backup operations.

Setting options

The Award BIOS provides significantly more versatile settings for power saving mode with its *Disable, Min. Saving, Max. Saving* and *User Define* options. *Min. Saving* represents minimum power management and *Max. Saving* applies maximum power management settings. For example, in *Min. Saving* the system goes into standby mode after one hour, whereas *Max. Saving* causes this to happen after only one minute. The same time spans are used for *Doze Mode* and *Suspend Mode*. The *HDD Power Down* mode is activated in *Min. Saving* after 15 minutes, and after one minute in *Max. Saving* mode. The newer BIOS versions allow the hard drive to be set separately. If you can, your best bet is the *Min. Saving* option or *User Define*. *Max. Saving* makes the intervals too short for controlling a hard drive.

7. Using Power Management to Save Energy

BIOS Option:
PM Control by APM

If the option *PM Control by APM* is set to *Yes*, power management is handled by APM. This allows you, for example, to configure power management from Windows 95/98 as well as changing the setting while running.

When the monitor shuts off

BIOS Option:
Video Off Option

The *Video Off* option causes the video card to switch the monitor to power-saving mode. Your options are *Always on, Suspend Off, Susp, Stby Off and All Modes Off. Always On* prevents the monitor from shutting off in any of the modes. *Suspend Off* switches it off when the system goes into suspend mode, and *Susp, Stby Off* when the system goes into suspend or standby mode. *All Modes Off* turns the monitor off in suspend, standby and doze mode.

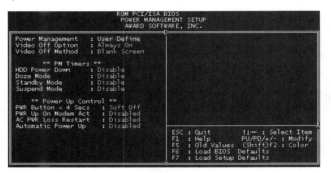

Power Management Setup

How the monitor is turned off

BIOS Option:
Video Method, Video Off Option

The *Video Method* determines which procedure is used to control the monitor when using the *Video Off* option to put the monitor into power-saving mode. The settings are *V/H SYNC+Blank, DMPS* and *Blank Screen*. In *V/H SYNC+Blank* or *Green PC Monitor Power State* the horizontal and vertical line signals from the video card are turned off, so that blanks are written into the video buffer. With *DPMS* (Display Power Management Signaling) or *DPMS Video Power Down Mode*, which only works with a DPMS-capable video card and monitor, the monitor is turned off by a signal from the video card. *Blank Screen* is more like a simple screen saver, just turning the screen black. The line signals are not turned off, so no power is saved in this mode. In fact, it is mainly designed for really old monitors that have no power-

7. Using Power Management to Save Energy

saving mode. *Video Power Saving* in the AMI BIOS also causes the monitor to go into power-saving mode after an inactive interval of *3, 5, 7* or *9* minutes.

"Mechanical" Power Management

BIOS Option:
Suspend Switch

A do-it-yourself Suspend Switch
Many motherboards have the connection for a Suspend switch but sometimes the option is missing in the BIOS. Although the connection still works, it can't be disabled. However, this isn't critical. If you don't have a green Eco button on your PC housing, attach the three-pin Turbo button since only two of the terminals are used in a Pentium PC. The third terminal on one of the two ends remains unused. If necessary, you could also purchase a simple switch from an electronics parts store and install it. Pressing the button will then put the PC into suspend mode.

The *Suspend Switch* is an interesting option, used to enable or disable the suspend connection for a power-saving button on the motherboard. This is a very effective method, since the user can determine exactly when to put the PC to sleep. It also eliminates any problems caused by software control in the APM.

Putting the processor on low simmer

BIOS Option:
Doze Speed, Stby Speed

Doze Speed and *Stby Speed* are used to slow the processor speed by the selected factor. Doze Mode is the first power-saving mode, reducing the processor clock speed by the factor in the *Doze Speed* option. *Stby Speed* works the same way, except that it's responsible for the second stage, the Suspend mode. This lets you reduce the clock even further if desired. This is a good thing for a processor, preventing it from overheating and even allowing time to cool off. *Slow Clock Ratio* in the AMI BIOS works just like *Stby Speed*.

If you have selected *Power Management User Defined*, the following settings can be changed under the *PM Timers* menu option.

Giving the hard drive a rest

BIOS Option:
HDD Power Down, Hard drive Timeout

7. Using Power Management to Save Energy

The Hard drive Sleeper

Another alternative is a "Hard drive Sleeper." This is a small shareware program (either DOS or Windows version) used for setting the power-down times for (E)IDE hard drives.

HDD Power Down or *Hard drive Timeout* determines the length of an inactive phase before the (E)IDE hard drive is powered down. SCSI drives are not compatible with this feature, and anyway they have their own utilities in the software packet included with the SCSI adapter. The problem is, the time span of 1 to 15 minutes is ridiculously short and hardly worth it. The hard drive uses nearly as much energy powering up again as it saved while asleep, not to mention the unnecessary stress on the mechanics from constant starting and stopping. Windows 95/98 solves this problem. The Power Management control panel allows you to set the inactive time for AC operation between 1 and 300 minutes. The 15-minute setting should only be used for notebooks.

Doze Mode

Doze Mode slows the processor clock during an inactive phase starting after anywhere from one minute to one hour. All the other components remain unaffected. We recommend a setting of three minutes here.

Standby Mode

Standby Mode puts the video system and hard drives on standby after an inactive period of one minute to one hour. All other components remain unaffected. Here we recommend a setting of 15 minutes. The AMI BIOS only provides a maximum of 15 minutes in its *Standby Timeout* option anyway.

Suspend Mode

Suspend Mode puts all the components except the processor into suspension after a period of one minute to one hour. Normally select 20 minutes.

Once the inactive periods have been selected, the PC goes into the highest power saving mode in three stages. The recommendations above should be modified according to your own work habits, and may be very different from user to user. If you have a 30-minute break time in your office, for example, it makes little sense to put the PC into Suspend mode after 20 minutes if you're going to wake it up again in 10 minutes. Unfortunately, the AMI BIOS only offers a maximum of 15 minutes for *Suspend Timeout*. That's at least acceptable.

PM Events

The next menu item, *PM Events*, is used to determine what type of event is permitted to bring the PC out of Suspend mode. Any IRQ from 3 to 15 could be used. It's enough if the corresponding COM port (COM1, COM2) or PS/2 mouse port is enabled, so that not only the keyboard—which is always active—but also a movement of the mouse wakes up the PC.

7. Using Power Management to Save Energy

If a modem or ISDN adapter is used, you can also enable the IRQ used by that device so the PC will wake up to answer incoming calls. Depending on your BIOS, this is also what the *Modem Use IRQ* option is designed for. You can select from interrupt 3 or 4, depending on which one the modem uses. Now, for example, the PC can be taken out of Suspend mode to receive a fax while the modem is establishing the connection.

BIOS Option:
COM Ports Accessed, LPT Ports Accessed, Drive Ports Accessed

Some BIOS versions also have a *Power-Down* setting. The options *COM Ports Accessed, LPT Ports Accessed* and *Drive Ports Accessed* allow the use of the devices connected to those ports without waking the PC from Suspend mode. If these options are set to *On*, a printer or modem can be activated without affecting the Suspend mode. Even when the connected devices are in use, the PC can go into Suspend mode.

Power up control for ATX systems

ATX form motherboards have a separately controlled power supply with an electronic switch, providing several additional options in the Award BIOS.

BIOS Option:
PWR Button < 4 Secs

Option *PWR Button < 4 Secs* means the STX switch on the front of the PC case has a dual function, either turning the system off if the *Suspend* setting is active or simply putting the system to sleep. Hold the button down for less than four seconds to enable the Sleep mode or longer than four seconds to completely power down the system. If the *Soft Off* setting is active, the switch has only one function: to power the system down. The *No Function* setting disables the switch completely. Then you have to use the main power switch on the rear of the PC to turn the machine on and off.

BIOS Option:
PWR Up On Modem Act, Power up on Modem

PWR Up On Modem Act or *Power up on Modem* lets you power up the PC in *Soft Off* mode when there is a modem event.

BIOS Option:
AC PWR Loss restart

The *AC PWR Loss restart* option causes the PC to be restarted automatically after a power loss. *Automatic Power up* uses the *Every Day* or *By Date* settings to start the PC at a certain time every day or only on certain days.

7. Using Power Management to Save Energy

Windows 95/98 and power management

In Windows 95, often the PC suddenly quits when going from suspend into normal operating mode. This can manifest itself in various ways, from the blue protection fault screen to the operating system freezing. Somehow the drivers are incompatible with some motherboards, even though the APM standard should ensure compatibility.

Getting around compatibility conflicts

When the PC goes on strike immediately after powering up, it generally indicates a timing problem is causing the hard drive to shut down. Disable powering down of the hard drive in the BIOS and in the operating system.

Setting your own time

Go to Windows' control panels and double-click the Power icon (Power Management in Windows 98), then select the *Advanced* option on the first tab section, and select *Show Suspend command on Start menu*. Clicking this option in the Start menu then immediately puts the PC into Suspend mode. This is a practical solution to putting the PC to sleep when you want.

The option for showing Suspend mode in the Start menu

For problems with power management, go to the *Problems* tab and select the compatibility mode for the APM 1.0 standard. This often works wonders in stabilizing how Windows 95 manages power. For a desktop machine, turn off the automatic power status monitor, since there is no rechargeable battery to monitor.

7. Using Power Management to Save Energy

The setting for suspending hard drives when using AC power under the *Power* icon can be set on the *Drives* sheet for 1 to 300 minutes. This setting can be used just as well for a portable running on battery power.

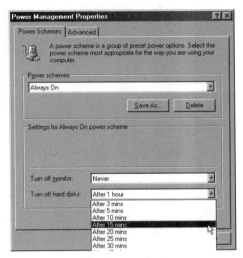

The Power sheet

To access power management for the monitor, open the Display control panel and select the *Screen Saver* tab. The time span for Low-power standby and Shut off monitor can be set from 1-60 minutes if you are using a monitor that meets the Energy Star guidelines.

7. Using Power Management to Save Energy

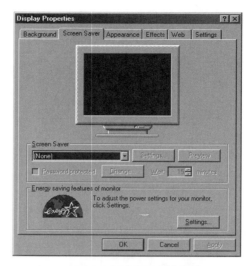

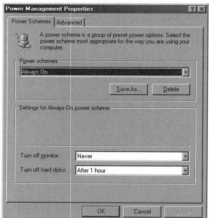

The Screen Saver page of the Display options

Windows 98 even allows you to set *Standby mode, Shut off monitor* and *Shut off hard drives* individually on the *Power settings* tab. You can then save the settings as a power setting and quickly change them when necessary. This is an interesting feature for a portable that alternates between desktop and mobile use. For travel, shorten the shut-off times, and lengthen them for desktop use. A simple mouse click is all it takes to change the settings. In addition, the *Advanced* tab offers a display of the battery monitor in the taskbar for laptops. Even requiring the password when reactivating the PC is possible by checking this option.

7. Using Power Management to Save Energy

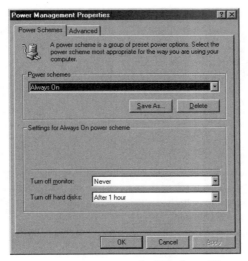

Power management in Windows 98

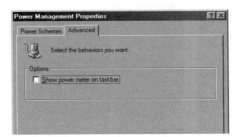

Additional settings offered in Windows 98

Optimal settings for fax servers, servers, workstations and home/office

Finding the optimum settings is not always easy. Now that you have learned all the options and their functions, here are a few guidelines that can be used for particular PC applications. Remember that it's still necessary to use trial and error to determine which values work best for your own working habits.

The fax server

The fax server is used only for sending and receiving faxes. This means you can put it into Suspend mode the soonest, leaving only the modem or ISDN card active with the corresponding setting in *PM*

7. Using Power Management to Save Energy

Events. You can also power down the hard drive if faxes do not arrive frequently. The monitor could also be shut off using the power switch, and only turned back on when needed.

HDD Power Down	Doze Mode	Standby Mode	Suspend Mode
5 minutes	2 minutes	3 minutes	5 minutes

The server

As mentioned earlier, we would not recommend using any power-saving mode for a pure server. Selecting *Power Management disabled* ensures that all the power saving modes remain inactive. The monitor and all other unneeded devices can be turned off directly with the power switch. However, many devices don't have a separate power switch because they are powered by a plug-in power supply. This means that somewhere between three and seven watts are being consumed per device, at an annual cost of $10-$12 per year for each device. Using a switchable power strip or a mechanical power manager can prevent this kind of waste.

The office workstation

An office workstation lends itself well to power management, and you can use the recommendations for the individual options as we described. Set the time values according to your work habits and break times. This will provide optimum energy saving providing you don't get errors from the software or when going from energy saving to normal operation.

HDD Power Down	Doze Mode	Standby Mode	Suspend Mode
Disable	3 minutes	30 minutes	60 minutes

The home/office PC

Energy-saving mode is often less effective for the home or home/office PC, since you are usually on the PC for longer stints and the times when energy saving mode is active are simply too short. This means the devices would be turned on and off at relatively short intervals, which is not conducive to long service life. All in all, the dollar savings are relatively minimal.

HDD Power Down	Doze Mode	Standby Mode	Suspend Mode
Disable	3 minutes	15 minutes	20 minutes

These table values are only recommendations so you can adapt them to your own needs.

Automatically power down all gluttons

Using a master-slave terminal strip from your electronics store, you can make turning off energy consumers even easier. The PC itself is plugged into the master socket and the auxiliary devices into the three slave sockets. Turning your PC on and off switches the other devices.

7. Using Power Management to Save Energy

Define success with the energy-cost monitor

If you want to know exactly how much you're saving in each mode, you can purchase an energy-cost monitor from an electronic supply store and measure it yourself. This is perhaps the most accurate way to determine the best settings for your own circumstances.

The energy-cost monitor, inserted between the wall socket and your PC, measures the PC's power consumption in watts. You can also enter the electricity rate, in two rate groups. The recording mode displays the W/h (watts/hour) and kW/h (Kilowatts/hour) values. The measuring range is from 1.5 W to 3,600 W (depending on model). You can also use the unit to check other power consumers. Hidden energy wasters like printers, modems, active boxes or scanners can be uncovered this way.

Power Management

❖ Is the power manager on?
Power management must be activated via the Enabled or User Defined setting in the power management setup menu.

❖ Is the operating system ready for power management?
For power management to work, the POWER.EXE driver must be enabled for DOS/Windows 3.1. In Windows 95, go to the Control Panel and double-click the Power icon to see the enabling options.

❖ Don't make the settings too short
Leave the settings long enough to avoid needless wear on the components.

❖ Can't receive faxes
If fax reception won't work when in Suspend mode, the problem is the IRQ for the modem/ISDN card isn't activated to resume normal mode or for use when in power-down mode.

❖ Switch manually if necessary
If you keep getting problems in your system when bringing the PC from Suspend into normal mode, disable the power-management system and manually switch off the energy consumers.

Connecting Peripherals to your PC

The ports on the motherboard in your PC are called *integrated peripherals*. Depending on the motherboard, these may include the primary and secondary (E)IDE ports, the FDC port, the serial and parallel ports, and the infrared PS/2 and USB port(s). A FireWire interface will soon join these peripherals. Devices and communications tools connect to the PC in many ways. Depending on what is connected to these ports, various settings are required to ensure that communication takes place at the correct speed without wasting precious resources. The standard BIOS settings make the ports operational, but they are seldom configured correctly. In some cases, as much as 30% more power can be coaxed from the connected components. If you don't have a menu called *Integrated Peripherals / Peripheral Setup* and your BIOS doesn't include *Chipset Features Setup* options, then you have an old motherboard with an external, plug-in combination controller. You must configure this type of motherboard using jumpers instead of using the BIOS.

The best EIDE configuration

In Chapter 2 we examined automatic detection and the various translation modes for the hard drives. There we also delved into the primary and secondary port, PIO mode and connecting a CD-ROM drive.

Individualized port management

BIOS Option:
On-Chip Primary IDE, On-Chip Secondary IDE, Onboard Primary/Secondary IDE

You can enable or disable the onboard ports on the motherboard using the BIOS settings without jumpers. For example, if only the primary port is used, the secondary port can be disabled to free an IRQ. If a SCSI adapter is built in and an (E)IDE hard drive is not used, you can even disable both ports and use one of the newly available IRQs for the SCSI adapter. To accomplish this, the Award BIOS offers the *On-Chip Primary IDE* and *On-Chip Secondary IDE* options, which can be switched using the *Enabled* and *Disabled* selections. You may also see the option *Onboard PCI IDE Enabled* in the newer BIOS versions. The *Primary IDE Channel, Secondary Channel, Both* or *Disable* settings can be used for automatic detection of only the primary, only the secondary or both ports. *Disable* deselects

8. Connecting Peripherals to Your PC

both. In the AMI BIOS, *Option Onboard Primary/Secondary IDE* functions the same way. You can find these options in the Integrated Peripheral Setup or in the Chipset Features Setup.

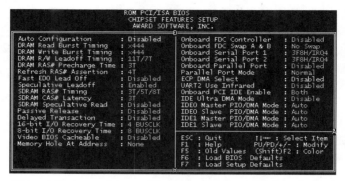

Chipset Features Setup with the port options (right window)

PIO provides more power

BIOS Main Menu
Integrated Peripherals, Peripheral Setup

PIO (Programmed Input/Output) mode determines the data transmission method (including the speed) between the controller and hard drive. Therefore, it is essential to set the correct PIO mode for whichever device is connected to the port, unless the BIOS determines it in Auto mode. If the PIO mode is incorrectly set, you can lose up to 30% of the available performance. Older controllers in combination with a hard drive and a CD-ROM drive on the primary port will cause false interpretations of the mode. For example, the slower PIO for the CD-ROM will also be used for the hard drive, which actually supports PIO 3. The CD-ROM simply slows down the hard drive. Disable Auto mode and manually make the proper setting, which can be found in the BIOS setup under *Integrated Peripherals* or *Peripheral Setup*. Choose from options *Auto, 0, 1, 2, 3* and *4*. Check the user's manual for which mode the device supports.

Be sure to check the PIO mode that your devices use when Auto is selected. Do this by watching the values displayed in the boot table while the PC starts. If the Auto modes do not conform to the devices' user's manuals, enter the correct settings manually in BIOS setup.

Mode	Speed
PIO 0	3.33 MB/s
PIO 1	5.22 MB/s
PIO 2	8.33 MB/s
PIO 3	11.11 MB/s
PIO 4	16.66 MB/s

8. Connecting Peripherals to Your PC

Speeding up the streamer tape drive

As mentioned in Chapter 2, the FDC floppy drive controller can be set in some BIOS versions to 1.44 MB or 2.88 MB. If you are running a streamer tape drive on the floppy controller, you can use this trick to reduce the tedious wait for backup to be completed.

QIC 80 and Travan streamer tapes

Simply selecting the 2.88 MB setting in the Standard CMOS Setup will make your streamer tape about 15% faster. To format diskettes in the 1.44-MB floppy drive, you then must use a DOS command to force the drive to a 1.44-MB format. If you format more diskettes than you backup data, constantly entering the DOS commands can become a bother. In that case, reset the option in the BIOS.

Correctly configuring the serial ports

Serial interfaces, also called V.24 or RS232, are still used in today's PC for the mouse or modem. They are referred to as COM1 and COM2, and use a 9- or 25-pin connector on the rear of the PC for attaching various devices. If the manufacturer has not identified the ports, you can assume that the 9-pin connection is COM1 and the 25-pin is COM2. COM1 is usually dedicated to the mouse if no PS/2 mouse port is available. COM2 is often used for an external modem or for serial communication with a null modem cable.

Switch connectors in the BIOS

You've probably experienced the irritation of 9- and 25-pin COM terminals that should be the other way around. If the ports are configurable in the BIOS, you won't even have to open the PC to reverse the connections. Simply reverse the addresses of COM1 and COM2 in the BIOS to accomplish the same thing

A radio clock receiver, graphics digitizer, selector, switching board, data acquisition device, etc., can be connected to this port. Using an auxiliary card, you can gain an additional two serial ports, COM3 and COM4, which need to be configured with jumpers.

The serial port

Two types of serial interfaces are available, depending on which UART (Universal Asynchronous Receiver Transmitter) is used. The UART is responsible for sending data to and from the port. Some inexpensive motherboards continued to use the old UART 8250 until 1996. This version is only capable of data transfer rates of 9,600 bits/s, which is sufficient for most devices. However, if you want to operate a higher speed modem on your COM port, you need the new UART 16550 chip. This not only provides a significantly higher data-transfer rate, but also has a 16-byte cache that uses FIFO (First In First Out) for buffering data. Then using a 56K modem won't be a problem.

8. Connecting Peripherals to Your PC

How do you find which UART is in your PC? First, check the user's manual included with your motherboard. Second, you may use the Windows 95/98 Device Manager or the MSD (Microsoft Diagnostics) tool that was included with the operating system. Find this tool either in the DOS directory of the hard drive or in a subdirectory of the installation CD.

Here's how:

Windows 95/98

In the Start menu, click **Settings | Control Panel**, double-click Modems, and then select the *Diagnostics* tab.

Double-click the corresponding port (for example, COM2).

To display the UART type, click on *More info...*

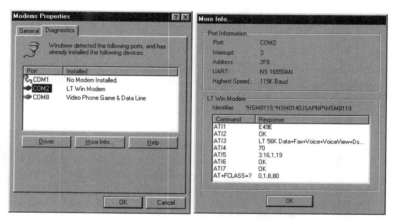

The UART type is displayed in modem properties

MSD

Start the tool by running msd.exe from your DOS directory or from the installation CD.

It will take a moment for MSD to check your system; the status message "MSD is examining your system..." will be displayed.

When the main menu appears, select *COM-Ports...*

All available COM ports and their values are displayed.

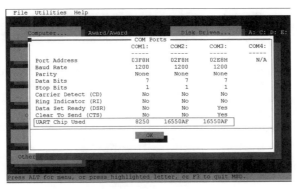

COM port UARTs as shown by MSD

UART	Data transfer
8250	9,600 bits/s
8250 A	9,600 bits/s
16450	9,600 bits/s
16550 A, AF, AFN	115,200 bits/s

BIOS settings

BIOS Option:
Onboard Serial Port 1, Onboard Serial Port 2

Enough theory, now we come to the settings in the Award BIOS Setup. To make sure the ports are active from the start, *COM1* and *COM2* are set in the standard configuration under *Onboard Serial Port 1* and *Onboard Serial Port 2*. The ports can also be set as *COM3* and *COM4* if desired. The I/O addresses and IRQs are shown in the following table:

COM Port	Address	IRQ
None	Not active	Not active
COM1	3F8h	4
COM2	2F8h	3
COM3	2E8h	4
COM4	3E8h	3

In more recent BIOS versions, the COM ports (1-4) are no longer indicated, but rather the I/O addresses and IRQs for the ports.

BIOS Option:
Serial Port IRQ, Serial Port Address

8. Connecting Peripherals to Your PC

The AMI BIOS provides the options Serial Port IRQ and Serial Port Address, which are also labeled with the port number. Here again the addresses and IRQs are set directly. Another option provided is Serial Port FIFO, used for enabling or disabling the cache.

Select *Enabled* so that the highest data-transfer rate can be used. Disable this only if you have problems with an old modem or other device.

If you want to operate a modem faster than 9,600 baud on your COM port, you must have a port with the new UART chip. Should your motherboard only have a UART 8250, get a serial interface card with the 16550 chip and disable your old ports via the BIOS or jumpers.

The PS/2 mouse has its own port

BIOS Option:
PS/2 Mouse Function Control, Mouse Support Option

Many new motherboards provide a PS/2 interface for the mouse. Thanks to the higher data-flow rate, it runs much smoother and more evenly than the mouse on the COM port. However, there's no such thing as a free lunch—this requires its own IRQ. To use the port, you have to enable it in the BIOS under *PS/2 Mouse Function Control* or *Mouse Support Option*.

There is a PS/2 mouse in the BIOS and no female?
Manufacturers often save money by using only a male PS/2 terminal on the motherboard, requiring you to order the female connector from the manufacturer. Also, computer cases are sometimes used without a cutout for the female plug. Although present on the motherboard, it's covered by the case panel. Often, you can attach a PS/2 port that fits in a slot on the back of the case.

PS/2 mouse
Advantages
❖ Mouse pointer runs smoother
❖ Can also be used if COM2 and COM3 are already used
Disadvantages
❖ Uses a high interrupt
❖ Not present on every motherboard

Disable the COM1 port if it's not needed. This frees IRQ 4. Some components can't use it, however, since it's such a low interrupt. Its use is limited mainly to old ISA cards. If you are lacking an interrupt for a PCI card, then none of this will help. You'll have to attach a normal mouse to the COM port and make interrupt 12 of the PS/2 connection available.

If there is no PS/2 mouse port on your motherboard, you can get one on an auxiliary plug-in card, assuming an interrupt is available.

An on-board infrared port

BIOS Option:
IR Function

Many new motherboards support an infrared port, the IrDa port. Developed for wireless data transmission, this has not yet established itself. Cableless data transmission between a laptop and printer is very practical, though very few people use it. Still, it's offered on the new motherboards as a terminal strip.

Infrared port
Advantages
❖ Data transmission without cables
Disadvantages
❖ Not present on every motherboard
❖ Infrared port emitter and receiver diodes are not included with the motherboard
❖ COM2 goes out of commission
❖ Needs a DMA

Retrofitting is simple

You have to order the infrared emitter and receiver from the motherboard manufacturer. Contact the company or your computer dealer and have the exact part number/serial number for the motherboard ready.

To install, open the case and plug the cable for the emitter/receiver unit into the male IrDa connector provided on the motherboard. Consult the user's manual to see where the connector is located on the board and which direction the plug should face when inserted.

Now you can use *BIOS Features Setup* to enable the *IR Function* option, which enables the IrDa port. Unfortunately, this automatically reserves COM2, making it unavailable for any other device. You also need another DMA channel.

The parallel ports—accessing printers and scanners

BIOS Option:
Onboard Parallel Port

SPP	
Advantages	
❖ Supported by any printer	
❖ On many motherboards	
❖ Up to three LPT ports possible	
Disadvantages	
❖ Data transfer only 300 KB/s	

The motherboard usually provides just one printer port, LPT1. More than one port is not required. However, the BIOS administers two ports through the various I/O addresses and IRQs. You can see how these are configured in the table below. The standard port is always LPT1, but this can be changed using the *Onboard Parallel Port* option. The board itself naturally only has one parallel port, which can be used as LPT1 or LPT2.

Two printers, one port
If you want to use two printers and you don't have enough interrupts for an additional port, simply use an A-B switcher. These switch boxes work like a Y-divider for switching between printer A and printer B that are connected together on a single port. Depending on which printer you wish to use, simply set the switch accordingly.

If you need a second printer port, you will need to purchase an additional parallel port in the form of a plug-in card. These cards are always jumpered to LPT1. You need to either configure the on-board port as LPT2 or jumper the plug-in card for LPT2. If you have a sound card installed, there will definitely be problems, since it is set for either IRQ7 or IRQ5. Then you need to consult the user's manual to see which IRQs can be used with the sound card, and find which ones are available in your PC. The parallel ports can be expanded to a total of three (LPT1 - LPT3).

LPT Port	Address	IRQ
LPT1	378H	7
LPT1	3BCH	7
LPT2	278H	5

The standard setting correctly configures the parallel port by your address and the IRQ, and does not need to be changed. You do need to check for the correct mode (SPP, EPP, ECP) and correct if necessary as described below.

8. Connecting Peripherals to Your PC

The parallel port

Several modes are available for the parallel port. SPP (Standard Parallel Port) was originally intended only for connecting printers and is only found on older motherboards. Hewlett Packard, Intel, Microsoft and Zenith revised SPP in 1990. This resulted in the enhanced modes, EPP (Enhanced Parallel Port) and ECP (Extended Capabilities Port). Now they are used also for connecting scanners, ZIP drives, networks, streamers, CD-ROMs, etc. They have also acquired more horsepower compared with the original type. SPP mode was designed for a data-transfer rate of only 300 KB/s and 8-bit data width. The eight data lines allow eight data bits to be sent in parallel at the same time. The serial port uses just one data line. Therefore, the parallel port is eight times faster than the serial port. Data transport may be unidirectional or bi-directional. In unidirectional mode, the computer is the sender and the printer the receiver. In bi-directional mode, both act as sender and receiver.

SPP mode for printers

The SPP is designed for connecting printers and is therefore included on every motherboard. Older motherboards without selection capability in the BIOS only offer SPP mode.

EPP mode for other devices

EPP

Advantages
❖ Data transfer rate: 2 MB/s

Disadvantages
❖ Needs an IRQ and DMA
❖ Only for non-printer devices

EPP mode is an enhancement of SPP, using hardware handshaking for even higher performance than a simple bi-directional port. Naturally, the device itself must also be EPP capable. This means that in EPP mode you should only run devices that are designed for it. The maximum data transfer rate is 2 MB/s.

ECP mode is often supported

ECP

Advantages
❖ Data transmission rate: 2 Mbits/s
❖ Up to 128 devices are supported
❖ Supported by many devices

Disadvantage
❖ An IRQ and DMA are required

8. Connecting Peripherals to Your PC

ECP is an interesting mode that can be used like EPP. In addition, it provides a 16K FIFO buffer similar to the serial interface. Data compression is used as well. Here the data-transfer rate is a maximum 2 MB/s, and up to 128 devices can be operated. Unfortunately, EPP or ECP mode also requires an IRQ and DMA. The DMA is not a problem, but there is often a shortage of IRQs. On the other hand, ECP mode also supports printers.

Having the right support

For a normal printer, simply select SPP mode in the Parallel Port Mode option.

If you're using a printer and a scanner on the same port, select ECP mode if the scanner supports it.

For all other devices, consult the user's manual to see which mode is required. The connected device must always support the selected mode, otherwise you will either have problems or you will waste an IRQ and DMA channel by enabling the enhanced mode.

USB is no problem for Windows 98

USB
Advantages
❖ Latest technology
❖ Supports up to 128 devices
❖ Data-transfer rate: 12 Mbits/s
❖ Don't need an IRQ or DMA for each device
Disadvantages
❖ Still not many devices on the market
❖ Not supported by every operating system

BIOS Option:
USB Function, On-Chip USB Controller, USB IRQ

If your motherboard is new enough to support USB (Universal Serial Bus), you must first enable it in the BIOS. You will find the options in *Chipset Setup* or *Integrated Peripherals* under the names *USB Function, On-Chip USE Controller* and *USB IRQ*. Select *Enabled* to activate USB support. An additional feature, not yet offered by all BIOS versions, is *USB Keyboard/Mouse Legacy Support* or *USB Keyboard Support*, which fully supports a USB keyboard as well as a traditional keyboard. In this configuration, the hardware on the motherboard simulates a standard keyboard. A USB keyboard will work without this special support under Windows 98, but not if you want to use it to get into the BIOS or just to use DOS; then you have no choice but to connect a standard keyboard. This is rather inconvenient if this option in the BIOS is missing. The same problem occurs with a USB mouse or a USB joystick when you want to run games under DOS.

8. Connecting Peripherals to Your PC

USB

The idea behind USB is to create a single interface for every device. Compaq, Intel, IBM, Microsoft, NEC and many others have cooperated on this. Up to 128 devices can be simultaneously connected. In this arrangement, hubs are connected to the port as distributors for 16 devices each. The USB port has a maximum transfer rate of 12 Mbits/s in 32-bit mode. The real highlight is hot plugging of devices, which allows you to plug and unplug them while the PC is running. The operating system immediately controls the device(s) with the drivers. You no longer have to power down the PC and restart to connect a peripheral device. Supply voltage is also provided through the USB port. There is naturally a limit to be observed. Current consumption of the devices is given in loads. A load corresponds to 100 milliamps. Devices in the Low Power category use a maximum of one load, and devices categorized as High Load consume a maximum of five loads. Only one High Power device may be connected to a port. Monitors and other big power consumers have their own, dedicated power supply.

USB devices such as the mouse, keyboards, joysticks, modems, loudspeakers, printers, CD-ROMs, MO drives, microphones, ISDN, scanners, streamers, etc., are gradually appearing on the market. Although they are still more expensive than the traditional devices, this is compensated by the fact that installation is simpler and no external IRQs and DMAs are required. USB is also a solution for easily connecting the individual devices to multiple PCs. Simply unplug a joystick, for example, from one USB PC and attach it to another.

The USB terminal is always there

Many motherboards in the AT form factor do have a USB port, but there's no terminal on the rear of the case. First, you have to obtain a terminal from the motherboard manufacturer. Don't buy just any terminal from another OEM—it probably won't fit, since the wiring assignments on the plug are not standard and may be configured differently.

Contact your motherboard OEM or dealer and have the exact part number and product information for the motherboard ready.

Open the case and plug the USB terminal connector cable into the appropriate pin connector on the motherboard. Consult the user's manual to find the exact location of the pin connector and determine the proper plug orientation.

ATX motherboards already have the terminals integrated on the board.

If a USB port is absent from your motherboard, you can add one by purchasing an additional plug-in card.

Windows 98 makes it easy

If the USB port is enabled, Windows 98 will recognize it at startup. Enabling it after the fact in the BIOS will also work, since Windows will find the port anyway and install the appropriate drivers. If USB doesn't work properly with Windows 98, a BIOS update will help. The cause is usually that support of the USB port is not properly interpreted in the BIOS itself. This is often why hot swapping doesn't work. If a device is unplugged and then plugged in again, either nothing will work in the device or the computer will simply crash.

Also possible in Windows 95

In Windows 95b, also called OSR2, this works by getting a driver update from the Windows 95 CD with version number 2.1. Find it in the \OTHER\USB folder.

Run supp.exe and note the instructions. When you restart Windows 95, USB support will be available.

Naturally, the BIOS options first have to be enabled. Note that the support isn't as stable as in Windows 98. Users of Windows 95a will, for better or worse, have to update to Windows 98 or do without USB.

FireWire—the interface of the future

FireWire
Advantages
❖ Latest technology
❖ Up to 63 devices can be connected
❖ Data-transmission rate: 400 Mbits/s
❖ Ideal for video and editing
Disadvantages
❖ Still not a lot of devices on the market
❖ Currently only available as external host adapter

FireWire promises almost limitless performance and connection possibilities. What's behind it, and when will FireWire be available on the market? IEEE-1394 (Institute of Electrical and Electronics Engineers) was the original designation for FireWire, but this was changed again in 1995 into "IEEE 1394-1995 Standard for a High Performance Serial Bus." Apple Computer invented the bus as early as 1986. The most commonly used designation, however, remains "FireWire." The 8940 host adapter is already on the market as a plug-in card for the PCI bus. Consumer devices, primarily in the video sector including cameras and video editing systems, are leading the way. FireWire provides a digital connection for 63 devices without hubs (distributors) at a data transfer rate of 400 Mbits/s. Adapters with a rate of 1.2 Gbits/s are in development. Data transmission uses a six-conductor cable. The simultaneous data transport of the 1394 bus provides the guaranteed bandwidth and latency required for high-speed data transfer over multiple channels.

Ports

❖   Are the EIDE ports turned on?
Only enable the corresponding port, so that no IRQ is wasted. If a device doesn't work on the primary or secondary port, check whether that port is turned on.

❖   PIO is important for performance
If performance of the device on the primary or secondary port is unsatisfactory, check the PIO setting.

❖   Are the COM ports configured correctly?
If the devices don't work on COM1 or COM2, check whether the ports are enabled and configured to the right address.

❖   Do you have a PS/2 mouse port?
If the PS/2 mouse causes problems, the reason may be a non-enabled port or an IRQ conflict with another component.

❖   The infrared port doesn't work together with COM2
If you want to use the onboard infrared port, COM2 is automatically disabled.

❖   Is the parallel port turned on?
If your printer doesn't work on LPT1, either the parallel port is not enabled or it is configured to LPT2, which is not supported by the program from which you wish to print.

❖   Is the parallel port in the correct mode?
The connected device must be configured for the selected mode, or it will not function properly.

❖   Do you have a USB port?
If the BIOS provides for USB but you have no terminal, you can retrofit the motherboard with the appropriate connection.

9 Burning Your Own BIOS

It's sometimes necessary to replace the old basic software in the BIOS with new software. To do this quickly, and without changing the BIOS chip, use an *update*. Such an update can really be useful, for example, if the 528 Meg limit is thereby removed or new hardware refuses to run with the old BIOS version. That is very often the case with 1996 motherboards, when an Intel processor is swapped for an AMD K6 or Cyrix 6x86. The BIOS does not yet support these, and either doesn't recognize them or recognizes them incorrectly.

Even if the processor does then run under a false interpretation with this BIOS version, it will not achieve its full performance because certain functions are not supported. The Plug & Play versions are also changed specifically regarding various devices that have recently appeared. These devices include an EIDE CD burner, a 2.88 Meg floppy, an EIDE-ZIP, an LS-120 drive or the ISA-PnP support, which is still not yet available.

You can get very frustrated when you add a part and then learn from the user manual for the motherboard that the part is not to be found at all in the technical data. In this case, you can return the new item or install a new motherboard with the corresponding support. Fortunately, you can also use a better and simpler method of using a BIOS update. You'll find the necessary software for most brand-name boards on the Internet or possibly from your favorite computer dealer.

Upgrades, tools and manuals - The BIOS sources in review

Before starting, first determine whether a BIOS update is available for your motherboard. Updates unfortunately are not always the main concern for some manufacturers. Therefore, the latest version isn't always available. This is especially true for very low cost "no name" products. To get any upgrade at all, you must know the BIOS-ident line, the version number and the manufacturer of the motherboard. You'll learn how to find and understand the BIOS-ident line later in this chapter.

9. Burning Your Own BIOS

Check the following manufacturers and websites for possible updates on your BIOS	
Abit	http://www.abit.com.tw/
Aopen	http://www.aopen.com.tw/
Asus	http://www.asus.com/
American Megatrends (AMI)	http://www.megatrends.com/
Atrend	http://www.atrend.com/
Award	http://www.award.com/
Chaintech	http://www.chaintech.com.tw/
Compaq	http://www.compaq.com/
Dell	http://www.dell.com/filelib
DFI	http://www.dfiusa.com/
Ellitegroup (ECS)	http://www.ecs.com.tw/
Elito	http://www.elito.com/
Epox	http://www.epox.com/
FIC	http://www.fica.com/
Freetech	http://www.freetechcom/
Gigabyte	http://www.giga-byte.com/
Iwill	http://www.iwill.com.tw/
Intel	http://www.intel.com/
MSI	http://www.msi.com.tw/
MR-BIOS	http://www.mrbios.com/
Phoenix	http://www.ptltd.com/
QDI	http://www.qdigrp.com/
Shuttle	http://www.shuttle.com/
Siemens	http://www.mch.sni.de/
Soyo Computer	http://www.soyo.com.tw/
Tyan	http://www.tyan.com/
Vobis	http://www.vobis.de/
Wim's BIOS Page	http://www.ping.be/bios/
These websites and addresses are current as of presstime but can change without notice.	

Determining the motherboard manufacturer

Once you have noted the BIOS-ident line, you also need to know who manufactured your motherboard. This is because you can only get a BIOS update from the manufacturer and not the BIOS producer. The motherboard manufacturer changes the BIOS version as needed and, therefore, is responsible for the update. The exact type designation will lead more quickly to an update during your search. You'll have a big advantage if you can get on the Internet and go to the website of the motherboard manufacturer and download the upgrade. The upgrade will always consist of a flash program and an update file. Many producers offer the flash program and the update file separately for downloading. The flash program is the same for many BIOS versions from the same manufacturer but the update file is different for each motherboard. Also, read the text file (called README.DOC or something similar) if one is included. It usually describes the new features added to the BIOS.

The fastest way to go

If you cannot find the name of your motherboard manufacturer in the user manual or printed somewhere on the board, go to Wim's BIOS Page on the Internet. You can find the manufacturer there using the ident line. You can then download the update either directly using Wim's BIOS page or from the manufacturer's website. If no update is listed for your motherboard, there either isn't an update available or you still have an older motherboard without flash-ROM.

If you do not have access to the Internet, either have the manufacturer mail the BIOS update to you on a diskette or determine whether the motherboard manufacturer has a bulletin board. (However, remember that you'll need at least a modem to retrieve the file from the bulletin board.)

The version is crucial

However you manage to obtain the update of your motherboard, it's important the version of the update matches your BIOS. Otherwise, your PC may not boot or work correctly. Therefore, always compare very carefully and, in case of doubt, preferably skip the BIOS update, or first prepare a substitute BIOS in case of trouble. Remember, an update is also not always better than the version you're currently using. If your PC runs well and an update is not absolutely necessary because of a new device or other problems, it might be better not to install an update. The primary purpose of an update is to remove problems-not just to have the latest software version.

BIOS-ident line deciphered - Understanding BIOS-ID codes

Each BIOS displays a BIOS-ident line on the screen after you turn on the PC. It combines letters and numbers that can be considered a string of identification characters. It's usually located at the lower left corner of the screen and contains the BIOS release date and the code to the identify the motherboard and the chipset manufacturer. The version number is also indicated at the upper left-edge of the screen near the BIOS manufacturer. If you want to write down the code, the best method is to pause the boot process by pressing the [Pause] key after the content with the code appears. Then press any key to continue the boot process when you've written down the code. Only the code is definitive for the BIOS version, not the sticker on the BIOS chip. That usually contains only an unimportant series number.

How it's determined

This is an example of the BIOS-ident line of a motherboard with an Award BIOS. Displayed to the lower left is the combination 2A59IA2AC-00. The first five characters 2A59I identify the chipset (it's the Intel Triton TX chipset in this combination). The next combination A2 indicates the manufacturer of the motherboard (Atrend in this example). The numbers that follow determine the model from the manufacturer. The model identified here with AC-00 is the ATC-5000.

9. Burning Your Own BIOS

Example for the Award-BIOS		
Chipset	Producer	Model
2A59I	A2	AC-00

The procedure is similar for the BIOS from AMI. Although the combination 51-0618-001223-00111111-071595-82430VX-F is longer, you'll find the manufacturer in the third number group. The combination 1223 indicates Biostar. Only with these combinations of Award and AMI will you find all manufacturers and models on Wim's BIOS Page under *http://www.ping.be/bios*. Furthermore, you can download your update immediately by linking to the manufacturer's website.

Example for the AMI-BIOS		
See Table	Producer	See Table
51-0618-00	1223-	00111111-071595-82430VX-F

The complete BIOS-ident line

Anyone still interested in the rest of the official BIOS-ID code can check the number combination from the displayed code in the following table. Note the dashes in the combination are part of the number combination.

Number from left	Designation	Value	Function
1	Processor type	X 4 5	80386 SX 80486 Pentium
2	Size of the BIOS	0 1	64 K 128 K
4 - 5	Major version number		
6 - 7	Minor version number		
9 -14	Reference number (Motherboard manufacturer)		
16	Stops in the event of a POST-error	0 1	Off On
17	Initializes the CMOS for each booting operation	0 1	Off On
18	Pins 22 and 23 are blocked by the keyboard controller	0 1	Off On
19	Mouse support in the BIOS/keyboard controller	0 1	Off On
20	Wait for <F1> when an error is found	0 1	Off On
21	Displays floppy error during the POST	0 1	Off On
22	Displays video error during the POST	0 1	Off On

23	Displays keyboard error during the POST	0	Off
		1	On
25 - 26	BIOS date (month)		
27 - 28	BIOS date (day)		
29 - 30	BIOS date (year)		
32 - 39	Chipset identification		
41	Keyboard controller version number		

Flash-BIOS or not?

If your PC is by chance already open and the power supply disconnected, slide your finger over the protective sticker on the BIOS chip. If you feel a depression about the size of a dime in the center, forget about a simple update per flash. Your BIOS is still housed in an EPROM and not in an EEPROM. Therefore, you'll have to buy a new BIOS chip with the current basic software from the motherboard manufacturer and use it to replace the one you have. That is normally not worth the trouble because the chips are hard to find and quite expensive. In this situation, you can buy a new inexpensive motherboard for a few dollars more.

BIOS up(to)date - A new BIOS per flash

You still need to look for a few basic items yet when updating your PC's BIOS. In many cases, you'll have to open your computer to set the jumpers for the programming voltage. Pay close attention to the warranty provisions of your dealer so you don't void the warranty. Some manufacturers use a protective seal that you must break to open the case. The manufacturer now has proof that you opened the case and can therefore contest the warranty. Therefore, set the matter straight with the manufacturer before opening a case with a protective seal.

Data backup is important

Always back up your data before working inside your computer. Also, print the current settings of all BIOS menus so you can reset all options after the update. All current settings will be lost during the update, and only the defaults will be available.

Tools and user manual

You may also need tools to open the computer to set the jumper for the program voltage. A few motherboards no longer have such jumpers. In that case you activate the program voltage either in the BIOS itself or with the flash program. Check in the user manual whether such jumpers are present and where they are located on the motherboard.

Also read the "Readme file" supplied with the programming utility. You can find even more information there often along with an update description from the manufacturer.

9. Burning Your Own BIOS

The new flasher from Award

The Award flash program comes in various versions. Version 5.33 has an advantage over the older ones. It recognizes when the update file does not match the one in the system. After the prompt of *Do you want to update? Y/N,* the message *The program files part numbers do not match with your system* appears. You now know that something is wrong with the update. If you still want to use the file despite the warning message, merely start the program at the DOS prompt with *AWDFLASH 2Axxxxxx.bin/PY.* The parameter /PY causes even a non-matching update file to run.

Displaying the parameters

If you would like to know what functions the Award flasher still has that you can execute via the input query, then enter awdflash /? at the DOS prompt. All options and examples will then be displayed.

Flashers are touchy

Each BIOS or motherboard producer has a proprietary flash program that runs either only with his board or with his BIOS. Asus and Intel have such special flash programs whose operation is board related. The Award flasher runs on nearly any board with an Award-BIOS, just as the AMI flasher runs with an AMI-BIOS. MR-BIOS is an exception and even has a flasher that runs with nearly any BIOS and board. If you want an entirely normal update without experimenting, it is also a good idea to use the flash program provided for this purpose.

Enough theory, now let's quickly get the BIOS update and the rest. Then we can get on with it.

The preparation

- ❖ Phillips screwdriver
- ❖ Tweezers
- ❖ Flash program
- ❖ Update file
- ❖ Boot diskette

Step by step on the way to success with the Award flasher

Updating without a boot diskette

You can also start an update directly from the C:\ drive. However make sure that the autoexec.bat or config.sys files do not load any memory manager or TSR programs. Then call the flasher from its directory and proceed just as you would with a boot diskette.

Create a boot diskette for your system.

1. Enter *format a: /s* at the DOS prompt to format the disk and transfer the system files.

2. Copy the flash program onto the same diskette as the update file.

    The BIOS files from the Internet or bulletin board are often packed as ZIP files. In such cases, first unpack them using a corresponding tool and then copy them onto the diskette.

3. Note or write down the filename of the update file, for you'll later have to enter it in the input screen.

It is important that you start the PC with the boot diskette containing only the system files. That prevents the autoexec.bat or config.sys files from accidentally starting a memory manager (Himem.sys, EMM386.exe) or TSR program lurking in memory.

Moving the flash jumper at a later time

If you have already updated the BIOS and suddenly notice while the computer is still running that you have forgotten to move the flash jumper, do not switch off the computer. Move the jumper into the correct position carefully and without using metallic tools. Now repeat the update once more and the damage is removed.

4. Check in the user manual for your mother board whether or not your board has a flash jumper and where it is located on the board. If you have to move a flash jumper, open the case with the Phillips screwdriver and move the jumper, preferably with tweezers, to the prescribed position.

    If the flash jumper is overlooked, it can happen that only parts of the BIOS update are written. That shouldn't happen, for the jumper is after all designed essentially as write protection. If writing does take place with "write protection", there will be confusion in the EEPROM, and the computer will no longer start.

5. Insert the boot diskette, and start the PC. It should now boot from the diskette.

    If that is not the case, check the *Boot Sequence* setting in *BIOS Features Setup* in the BIOS Setup to see whether it is set to *A, C*. If the setting is to *C, A* or something different which is not *A*, the PC boots from a different medium.

6. If booting takes place from a diskette, call the flash program at the DOS prompt with *AWDFLASH.EXE* and the (Enter) key. The program will appear with the input screen for the update file.

7. Now, enter the filename of the update file in the *Filename to program* (for example, *BIOSTAR.BIN*) field and confirm with the (Enter) key.

The Award flasher with the screen for entry of the update file

Updating without a boot diskette

If you want to make a backup of only the old BIOS file, you can skip entering the update file. Simply leave the field empty and confirm by pressing the `Enter` key. The field for entry of the filename of the backup file will appear. Now enter the filename and confirm with the `Enter` key. The file is written to the data carrier. However you should see the "Source file not found!" error message. You can ignore this error message and exit the program by pressing `Enter`.

The Award flasher will then display first of all, in the *Error Message* field, the prompt about backing up the old BIOS file: *Do you want to save BIOS Y/N?*

8. Confirm with the `Y` key. The *Filename to Save* field will now appear, so you can enter the name of the backup file.

9. Enter here *XYZ.BIN* or a different filename which is valid for you. The filename can have a maximum of 8 characters and the extension has to be *.BIN*. Confirm again with the `Enter` key.

    The file will be written into the directory that also contains the program file. With that you'll have the old BIOS file (backup) on the update diskette automatically and immediately available in case of need.

The command for backing up the BIOS

The input field for the filename of the backup file

10. Only select the menu item for writing the update once that is completed. After the update file has been written, the Award flasher automatically prompts you to update. *Do you want to update? Y/N* appears in the *Error Message* box.

11. Confirm with the Ⓨ key. Do not interrupt the burning process for any reason, and wait until the flash program reports that the update has been successful. The Award flasher will then display a message, for example: *Please power off or reset system.*

9. Burning Your Own BIOS

If something goes wrong, do not switch off the computer under any circumstances! Otherwise it will be no longer able to boot, and there will be no chance to copy back the old BIOS file. In a manner of speaking, the computer will then be clinically dead. You won't be able to bring it back to life without digging into your box of tricks or, in the worst case, without a new BIOS chip from the motherboard manufacturer. Therefore always try first to write the backup file back again into the BIOS from the beginning. Only once that is working should you restart the computer. If you have chosen the flash program and the update file carefully and have followed these instructions, normally nothing will go wrong.

12. Put the jumper back into the starting position and look in your user manual to see whether your BIOS has a jumper for CMOS restart.

13. Then insert the jumper for the restart, wait a bit, and then put the jumper back into the original position.

   If your motherboard has no such jumper, or you can't find it, it's not a problem. The first time you boot up you'll then get the error message *CMOS-Checksum Errors*.

14. Call the BIOS setup and select *Load setup defaults*.

   You have now taken care of the error message for the next time you boot, and your computer should start from the inserted boot diskette. Now close the case once again for safety.

Boot-block causes problems

The BIOS consists of several blocks in the EEPROM. One of these is also a boot block. Many BIOS versions also need an update of the boot block, because problems will otherwise occur when you do a warm boot of the computer. If your computer no longer starts in such a case, run the Advanced Features in the flash program and rewrite the boot block.

15. Following a successful BIOS update, you'll in any case have to reenter all the settings of the old BIOS according to your printouts.

Configure any new options that may be available according to the suggestions described in the book..

Other flashers and their use

Depending upon which flasher program you are using, a few menu items in text mode will appear for backing up the current version and one for writing the update. Many will also have additional features for the writing of the boot block in the BIOS or for comparing the update file to the BIOS content. The comparison is also extremely practical, for you can thus determine whether your update has been copied into the BIOS free of errors.

However, absolutely the first thing you should do in this case is to start the menu for backing up the old BIOS file onto the diskette. Always think of it as "life insurance" for your BIOS. The plan for the update as a whole is the same as for the Award flasher, only the menus being somewhat different.

Intel motherboard and MR-BIOS

If you used a MR-BIOS update for the BIOS on an Intel motherboard, you'll have problems if you want to write back the original BIOS file with the Intel flasher, say because you perhaps don't like the MR-BIOS quite as well as you thought you would. Therefore back up the Intel BIOS using the MR-BIOS flasher and not the one from Intel. Writing back with the MR flasher will then work without a hitch.

Emergency fixes should things go wrong

As already mentioned, do not switch off the computer during the update phase, and do not reboot it using a reset. If you do, the basic software will not be completely installed in the BIOS, meaning it won't work either. The computer can no longer boot after a restart. It is thus not possible to write either the old version of the BIOS present on the diskette as a backup file, or the new version into the BIOS. An unfortunate accident, such as a power outage at just this moment, can also cause your BIOS to give up the ghost.

CPR for the motherboard

Many motherboard producers have had the foresight to integrate a recovery jumper into the motherboard. That is usually the case with Intel motherboards.

Motherboard with recovery-jumper

1. The jumper is put into the recovery position and the previously used bootable update diskette is inserted.

    After being switched on, the computer will attempt to write a recovery file from the BIOS block into the flash ROM. There is no monitor display in that case. You recognize the process only from a beep tone of the computer and the flashing of the floppy LED indicator. The file transfer is finished when the floppy LED goes out.

2. Switch off the computer and return the recovery jumper to its original position.

3. Now boot the computer again from the update diskette and copy the backup file which you have hopefully prepared beforehand with the flash program into the BIOS.

If it works, you are in luck and can attempt a new update. However, check again carefully to find out why the previous version didn't work!

Motherboard without recovery-jumper

A similar procedure will also work with many motherboards that have an Award BIOS but no recovery jumper.

1. If you are able to work with a monitor which is only black, first take out the PCI video card and install an ISA video card.

9. Burning Your Own BIOS

2. Insert the bootable update diskette and start the computer. Your computer will boot if the BIOS contains a functional boot block.

3. Now use the flash program to write the backup file into the BIOS.

4. The computer should be in its old state again after rebooting.

This tip is extremely hot; we haven't even tried it yet ourselves. Therefore don't rely upon it absolutely. You are better off preparing a replacement BIOS.

Other motherboards

If your motherboard has no recovery function and also no Award BIOS, the only way out is a reprogrammed BIOS chip that you can order according to the ident-line data. It isn't always easy however to contact the manufacturer, particularly when it is in Taiwan or elsewhere in the East and can be reached, if at all, per E-mail over the Internet. In many cases the BIOS producer will then help you to contact the motherboard manufacturer. If your motherboard no longer happens to be the most current, you can then forget about a new BIOS chip. For the cost compared with that for a new board will then be too high.

SCSI integrated - "Sticking on" NCR-functionality

If you want to use MR-BIOS on your motherboard with NCR-support, the NCR-functionality will fall flat. MR-BIOS simply doesn't support it. If you have a SymbiosLogic adapter and want to install a MR-BIOS, or you already have a MR-BIOS on a motherboard with NCR-functionality and want to install a SymbiosLogic-adapter, there is then the possibility of "sticking it on".

The BIOS is expanded

"Pasting on" with the HEX-Editor

The same result can also be achieved with a HEX editor. Use it to open the mrbios.bio file and remove the empty lines at the beginning. Then open the ncrbios.bin file and copy the contents of the file. Now reopen the mrbios.bio file and insert the copy of ncrbios.bin. Then save mrbios.bio. The patch is ready. However, again you need to watch the total file size here.

You have to patch the BIOS file of the MR-BIOS. For that you'll need a file from the SymbiosLogic FTP-server. The filename is *flash307.exe* and we call it after downloading it. It is a self-extracting zip file containing several files, among others the 16K file important to us, *P8XX_16.rom*.

1. For the sake of simplicity, change the name of the P8XX_16.rom file to ncrbios.bin.

2. Next change the name of the 92K file mrbios.bio or the like to a different filename, for example, mrbios.bin.

3. We then link the *ncrbios.bin* file with the *mrbios.bin* file using a DOS-command. The command is entered as follows: *copy /b ncrbios.bin + mrbios.bin mrbios.bio*. The /b in the command designates a binary file (not ascii text) and the plus (+) makes the two files into one with the content of both files. Be sure in that case that the *ncrbios.bin* file is entered first. It will then also be at the beginning of the file in the combination.

4. You'll see the result in the size of the new file, *mrbios.bio*. The 16K ncrbios and the 92K mrbios yield the 108K (110,592 bytes) *mrbios.bio*.

5. If you did not get the same result, something is wrong. In this case, do not use the file at all. It would make the BIOS incapable of functioning.

6. On the other hand, if you did obtain the proper size, then nothing more stands in the way of an update. The flash program will write it into the EEPROM, just like an entirely normal BIOS update.

However, keep in mind that you are patching the original MR-BIOS file at your own risk.

Working with logos (for example, EnergyStar/Vobis)

If you're tired of seeing the EPA logo on the opening screen you can change it. To do this you'll need two utility programs and a drawing program similar to MS-Paint. You create the logo in .bmp format at a size of 136 x 126 pixels.

First, draw it only in black/white. It's best to select a black background and draw the logo in white. You can also use already finished logos that are to be found on the Kaotica Internet page. Using the BMP2EXE program, you can then insert up to 16 colors into the logo and convert the whole thing into the EPA format. You can now insert the EPA file into the BIOS file using the CBROM program. The *CBROM.EXE* file contains an aid with examples. You simply start the file without entering any parameters.

9. Burning Your Own BIOS

The CBROM.EXE parameters

Then the BIOS has to get an update using the new BIOS file, and you'll already have the new logo on the screen the next time you boot up. The utility programs, BMP2EXE and CBROM, were still to be found on the Kaotica Internet website pages up until a few weeks ago. However they have now unfortunately been forced to remove them again from their pages for reasons having to do with licensing. Finished logos and tips as well as a list of those motherboards that the CBROM program works with are still available. The CBROM program and converter are still available from the Pionix website. You can also change the logo in the Award BIOS with the converter as a replacement for BMP2EXE. You may still be able to find the BMP2EXE program on some other FTP-server and download it. You can find other methods for producing your own logo on the Award website.

The "convertor" program for EPA-logos in the Award-BIOS

9. Burning Your Own BIOS

Creating a replacement BIOS for testing purposes

Do you like to experiment with your BIOS? The best approach is then to make a "duplicate" of it. For that you'll first of all need the designation of your BIOS chip, that is to say, the EEPROM type. On the BIOS you'll find a sticker from the manufacturer. Pull off the sticker carefully and note the designation. Current types are 28F010, 28F001 or 29EE010. You'll now need an EPROM burner and an EEPROM of the same type as that present on the motherboard.

You can get the EEPROM from an electronics store. It is not particularly expensive, but it is not worth spending the money for an EPROM-burner just to burn a few chips. For that reason ask in the store whether the sales person can copy the EEPROM for you on his burner. The whole process takes just a few minutes and is surely worth a small "tip".

Building your own EPROM burner

If you do not have the possibility of copying your EEPROM in an EPROM burner, you can still copy the EEPROM directly on your motherboard using a trick that is not entirely without risk.

1. To do this, loosen the BIOS in the socket on the motherboard in such a way that it still makes contact, but can be easily pulled out. Only the tips should still be inserted in the socket.

Professional EPROM burners

If you want to change a BIOS rather frequently, you can buy a zero insertion force socket in an electronics store. You'll then no longer need to be so careful with the pins on the chip. The zero insertion force socket is installed in the motherboard socket in the open condition. The BIOS chip is then positioned loosely in the zero insertion force socket. and then tightened by closing the lever. If the chip is changed during operation, the risk of causing a short will then be much less than when the chip is inserted in the narrow socket on the motherboard.

2. It is also advantageous if you first remove the chip entirely and reinsert it.

    It can happen, for reasons having to do with the production technology, that the pins are spread rather widely apart and can be inserted in the socket only by applying force. If this is the case, position the chip sideways on a flat surface and gently press the pins inward until they point straight down.

3. Test to see whether the chip can be inserted easily and without touching the pins. If it can, reinsert the old chip very lightly.

4. By all means pay attention to the little notch on the edge of the chip. It must always be on the same side of the socket as before, so the chip is not inserted backwards with polarity being reversed.

9. Burning Your Own BIOS

If you are no longer quite sure on what side the notch of the old EEPROM was located, take a close look at the socket. It will also have a notch (mark). The notch on the EEPROM must always match the one on the socket.

5.   Switch on your computer and call the BIOS setup program.

If the screen remains black, the BIOS is not correctly inserted in the socket. Switch the computer off again and eliminate the contact problem by inserting the chip somewhat more firmly and uniformly. Switch the computer on again. It should now function normally.

6.   Make sure that the shadow RAM function option for the system BIOS is active.

The computer will then continue to run quite normally with the copy in memory, when the chip is later removed.

7.   Close the BIOS setup and boot the computer with the update diskette which you previously prepared for a BIOS update.

8.   Then call the flash program and back up the BIOS version onto the diskette.

9.   This is the crucial part. Pull the EEPROM out of the socket without touching the pins and insert the new one without causing a short in the socket..

Be careful not to touch the pins when you insert the chip and make sure the polarity is correct. If the chip is inserted incorrectly, it is surely "shot". If you do have bad luck, the motherboard will also be scrap, because the chipset or the voltage regulator will also make the trip to the happy hunting grounds.

10.   Once the chip is sitting in the socket, you can then simply write the backup file of the old BIOS onto the new one. However be sure to do that with a MR-BIOS flasher.

It communicates directly with the flash -ROM like a burner and will not return any error message due to the "empty" chip. You now have two identical BIOSes. Keep one as a backup, so you can experiment with the other one without danger.

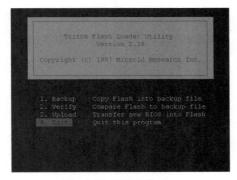

The MR-BIOS flasher

The EEPROM with the burner

If you have an EPROM burner available, then it is quite simple. Insert the original and the new EEPROM in the sockets provided for the purpose, select the correct type and copy the chip. Should you want to know what chip was used for your EEPROM, carefully pull up the sticker on your 28 or 32-pin DIP IC-chip. Certain chips are also not always easy to find in electronics stores; perhaps you can have the manufacturer order one.

You do not absolutely have to buy an EEPROM, you can also use an EPROM of type 27C010. It works on most motherboards and is much, much cheaper than an EEPROM. However, there is no flash ROM for it, and you can no longer update it in the computer. On the other hand, it does have the advantage that it cannot be overwritten by accident.

Each EPROM burner has different keys and functions for burning EPROMs. Thus make it a point to read through the operating instructions carefully, if you do not know your way around. Otherwise you could accidentally erase the original ROM chip, and you really don't want to do that.

Type	Manufacturer	Voltage
Am29F010	AMD	5
Am28F010, Am28F010A	AMD	12
AT28C010, AT28MC010, AT29C010, AT29LC010, AT29MC010	Atmel	5
CAT28F010V5, CAT28F010V5I	Catalyst	5
CAT28F010, CAT28F010I	Catalyst	12
28F010	Fujitsu / ISSI	12
HN58C1000	Hitachi	5
HN28F101, HN29C010, HN29C010B, HN58C1001, HN58V1001	Hitachi	12
A28F010, 28F001BX-B, 28F001BX-T, 28F010	Intel	12
M5M28F101FP, M5M28F101P, M5M28F101RV, M5M28F101VP	Mitsubishi	12
MX28F1000	MXIC	12
MSM28F101	OKI	12
KM29C010	Samsung	5
DQ28C010, DYM28C010, DQM28C010A,	SEEQ	5
DQ47F010, DQ48F010	SEEQ	12
M28F010, M28F1001	SGS-Thomson	12
28EE011, 29EE010	STS	5
TMS29F010	Texas-Instruments	5
TMS28F010	Texas-Instruments	12
W29EE011	Winbond	5
W27F010	Winbond	12
X28C010, X28C010I, XM28C010, XM28C010I	XICOR	5

BIOS update

❖ No update is found
  If you haven't found any update for your BIOS-ID on the Internet, then your motherboard manufacturer is not making one available, or your motherboard doesn't have a flash BIOS.

❖ The flasher doesn't start
  Either the flasher is not suitable for the motherboard / BIOS, or you have loaded a memory manager from your autoexec.bat or config.sys.

❖ The computer no longer boots
  Does the screen simply stay black following the update? That is a bad sign. Either the update file was not the right one for the motherboard, or something went wrong when the EEPROM was being burned. Try to reburn the BIOS by carrying out emergency measures.

❖ The CMOS-Checksum Errors message is displayed
  That is normal, if you have not deleted the data in the CMOS using the corresponding jumper. Go into the BIOS setup and execute the menu item Load Setup defaults.

❖ The hard drive isn't found
  The update has worked, only now "Disk Boot Failure Insert System Disk And Press Enter" is displayed after the POST. The update caused all the settings to be deleted. You first have to reenter all settings in the BIOS setup.

❖ The home-brew EPROM-burner crashes
  The flash program freezes when the empty BIOS is to be burned. That is a sign that the Shadow-Ram option for the system BIOS in the BIOS Setup is not switched on. The system no longer has a BIOS program, because the copy in RAM is missing.

Nearly inseparable - On motherboards, chipsets and the BIOS

You have prepared a replacement BIOS and are experimenting with either the burning of a different BIOS version or the running of a BIOS from a different producer, such as MR-BIOS. A test version of the MR-BIOS for the Triton chipset is also available free of charge on the Internet website. If you want to modify an existing BIOS version according to your own ideas, you are then included among the BIOS programmers who create their own setup using Assembler, Pascal or C. For that you'll first need the precise designation of your chipset and the corresponding documentation from the manufacturer that will require hours of study on your part.

An intimate relationship

The BIOS has to fit the chipset on the motherboard with great precision. A different BIOS version with program data for a different chipset won't work reliably, because the internal register is wrong or not even under control. The controllers, among other things, are also integrated into the chipset that contains the programmable registers. They are of interest to the programmer, because they can be changed. The registers can be set in part using the options in the BIOS setup. However, many registers in the chipset contain either no option, or the option is masked by the manufacturer, and invisible to the user. Sometimes you can make such options visible and then modify using a tool (see page XXX).

Programming a BIOS yourself

It is an advantage for the programmer to create his own setup, allowing him to set all those options of importance to him. The programmer can address the chipset via two I/O ports. An index register is programmed using in and out-commands which then control a specific function. Just how such a BIOS program, that is to say, the basic software, arises, which is then burned into the EPROM, goes way beyond the confines of this book and would easily fill a separate volume. The higher programming languages alone demand years of study from the programmer, to be able to understand and also to convert the commands. However one thing basically holds true: the chipset and the BIOS must fit together, otherwise no communication between the two will be possible. The computer won't even start or will remain hung up somewhere. Even if it runs with a similar BIOS version for a different motherboard type, such as the ATX version instead of the AT version, a loss of data due to some defective function cannot be ruled out.

Changing the menus and options in the finished BIOS

Creating a completely new BIOS or changing the BIOS menus and options using a high-level programming language is not everyone's bag. However, using the Modbin tool available on various Internet websites, among others the Pionex site, you can make any number of changes in the Award BIOS. First, load the BIOS file generated beforehand with the flasher as a backup file into the program. Then you can change everything to *Enabled* or *Disabled*, from the menu items to individual functions. Hidden menu items can also be made visible and will also be made completely functional. From the BIOS message via the CPU registers to the PCI-slots, you can change everything and save it in the BIOS file. All the new functions will be available following an update with the modified file. You have now become a BIOS programmer in spite of it all.

An example:

You want to find out with the program which functions are hidden in your BIOS that you might be able to use.

1. Once you start Modbin, the cursor will automatically point to *Load File* in the menu. The first thing you have to do is to load the BIOS file. If the BIOS file is present in the same directory, which will be indicated in the window to the right, you'll need only to press the [Enter] key to load it.

2. You'll now be able to move with the cursor through the menu items to get an overview.

3. One interesting menu is the Chip-set Setup Default. Select it by pressing the [Enter] key. The main menu will appear.

The main menu of the BIOS in Modbin

4.   You'll now see which main menus are hidden in your BIOS version. The item status *NORMAL* displays the menu, and *DISABLED* will hide it.

5.   To get from the main menus to the submenus, press the `Pg Up` and `Pg Dn` keys. You'll surely run into hidden options there.

The hidden options are "flushed out"

In fact, and in our BIOS, there is also one more very important option in the *Integrated Peripherals* menu. The *DISABLED* setting disables the USB controller. However it is present and completely functional on the motherboard, as determined by the chipset, controller chips and expansion slot. The only thing is, you cannot switch it on in the BIOS, because the option is hidden.

9. Burning Your Own BIOS

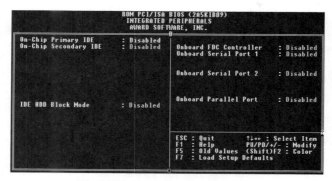

The USB controller is not present

6. Move the cursor to the *On-Chip USB Controller* option and change it with the ➔ key to *DISABLED*. Using the ➕ key in the numeric keypad block on the keyboard, you are now able to select *NORMAL*. The same is true for the *USB Keyboard Support* option.

The hidden options are made visible

7. Pressing the [Enter] key saves the changed settings.

8. With the [F2] key, you can have the "original" BIOS setup displayed at any time. Leave it after looking it over, just as you would exit the BIOS setup of your computer.

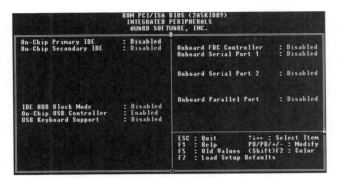

The missing setting options are now present

9. Select *Update File* from the Modbin menu to save the changes in the BIOS file.

10. Now all you need to do is copy the new BIOS file into the EEPROM, like a normal BIOS update, and you'll have a free USB controller available.

There is more than enough of such or similar cases in the "BIOS jungle", because the manufacturer alone determines which functions in the BIOS are "open".

Security Techniques Against Hackers

Are you concerned about other users gaining access to the important data on hard drive on your offic PC? Perhaps no one is interested in the data but simply wants to insert a virus onto your PC. This can happen several times if you do not effectively protect your PC from unauthorized access.

However, the more protective options enabled, the longer it takes for your PC to start. Therefore, enable only what you need. Although protective options are helpful, it can be a serious problem when you forget your password. No one can give you any further help there, if you were the only one in possession of the password.

Back up the BIOS

One day you turn on your PC but it fails to detect either the disk drive or the hard drive. In that case, a likely reason is the CMOS battery is dead. Other possibilities include someone deleting the settings with the *Load Setup Defaults* option, a virus or a defective operating system changing the data in the CMOS so nothing will work. To make sure that no hours of tuning are lost, you need to back up the BIOS settings. You can do this in three ways: by printing a hard copy, by making notes or by backing up your CMOS onto a diskette. Then you can be certain that you can restore the original settings.

The hardcopy method

This method is relatively simple and practical. If the character set of the BIOS program matches that of the printer, all characters and frames would appear on the paper as they appear on the screen. Unfortunately, that is not always the case. Because the BIOS uses the US character set, many characters are also displayed incorrectly. This is true in particular for special characters that are used for the frames and dividing lines. However the menu items and options are usually always printed legibly. Use the `Print Screen` key. If your printer is turned on and still not printing, the sheet feed is not being correctly controlled. If so, you must start it manually on the printer. The displayed page will now also be printed. Follow the same procedure for all the pages in the BIOS containing options that you can set. Then staple the pages together so you'll have your own BIOS manual.

10. Security Techniques Against Hackers

```
                    ROM PCI/ISA BIOS (2A5KIB09)
                         BIOS FEATURES SETUP
                         AWARD SOFTWARE, INC.

Virus Warning              : Disabled   Video  BIOS Shadow  : Enabled
CPU Internal Cache         : Enabled    C8000-CBFFF Shadow  : Disabled
External Cache             : Enabled    CC000-CFFFF Shadow  : Disabled
Quick Power On Self Test   : Enabled    D0000-D3FFF Shadow  : Disabled
Boot Sequence              : C only     D4000-D7FFF Shadow  : Disabled
Swap Floppy Drive          : Disabled   D8000-DBFFF Shadow  : Disabled
Boot Up Floppy Seek        : Disabled   DC000-DFFFF Shadow  : Disabled
Boot Up NumLock Status     : Off
Gate A20 Option            : Fast
Typematic Rate Setting     : Disabled
Typematic Rate (Chars/Sec) : 6
Typematic Delay (Msec)     : 250
Security Option            : Setup
PS/2 mouse function control: Disabled
PCI/VGA Palette Snoop      : Disabled
OS Select For DRAM > 64MB  : Non-OS2   ESC : Quit           ↑↓→ : Select Item
Report No FDD For WIN 95   : No        F1  : Help           PU/PD/+/- : Modify
                                       F5  : Old Values     (Shift)F2 : Color
                                       F7  : Load Setup Defaults
```

Example of a hardcopy of BIOS settings.

Printer driver problems

Many printers require their own driver before they can print. This is not only true under Windows, but also under DOS. If the hardcopy method doesn't work, refer to your printer manual and install any drivers that may be needed.

The handwritten method

Another method, although slightly less practical, is simply to write down all the settings in the BIOS menus. This method is perhaps most suitable for very advanced users who do not want to write down all the settings, but only the ones they changed. All automatic or default settings are ignored. However, for those with less experience, we recommend writing down all the options.

Backup method

The quickest, but not necessarily safest, method is to back up the BIOS using a program that reads the data from the CMOS and stores it in a file. You can keep the file either on a diskette or on the hard drive. If you lose your settings, you will then need only to copy them back using the program.

The disadvantage of this approach is that if you've forgotten your password and have therefore intentionally deleted your BIOS settings , you'll be back where you were before copying back the BIOS settings. So, remove the password from the BIOS for the backup. Depending upon which program you're using to back up your CMOS, it is not guaranteed that 100% of your data will be restored.

Shareware programs are available for this purpose. The commercial programs often consist of an entire program package that can backup not only the CMOS, but also the other system files. It is best to test the program for reliability before you devote yourself to time-consuming tuning. See Chapter 13 for more information on software for backing up and restoring the CMOS.

10. Security Techniques Against Hackers

Write protecting diskettes

It's possible in some BIOS versions to block the disk drive for write accesses. This option is particularly important in offices where users have PCs featuring disk drives. Otherwise, unauthorized individuals can steal your data without your noticing it. All that it takes is for you to leave the room briefly while the PC is running.

> ### Perfect CMOS-backup
> Prepare a boot diskette and copy the program for CMOS backup onto it. Have the program write a backup onto the diskette. If necessary, you will be able to boot with the diskette and write back the CMOS. Once you restart the computer, all your settings will be back.

Your PC is protected only by a *User Password,* and the *Security Option* in the *BIOS Features Setup* is moved to *Setup* that merely prevents access to the BIOS Setup. It will then also be possible for someone to start your PC after working hours and copy the data onto a diskette. However, you can prevent this if you set the *Floppy Disc Access Control* option in the *BIOS Futures Setup* to *Read Only*. This measure prevents thieves from stealing your data using a diskette.

The Floppy Disk Access Control option

Programs copied unnoticed onto the hard drive

Many employees install or copy programs onto "their" office PC. A frequent example is games. However this can also quickly spread a virus by means of infected files. This is especially critical if your PC also happens to be connected to a network. Therefore, it is best to switch off the onboard controller for the floppy in the BIOS Setup. Then protect BIOS Setup itself from changes with a supervisor password.

Switching off the floppy and the QIC in the BIOS

10. Security Techniques Against Hackers

Switching off the boot option for disk drives

The *Boot Sequence* option in the *BIOS Features Setup* is very useful if the disk drive is to do all of its work operating your PC, but without the possibility of booting the computer from it. Select the drives here in the same way they are queried in sequence by the BIOS from a bootable data carrier. If the setting *C; A* or *SCSI, C; A* is selected, booting occurs from the hard drive and not from the disk drive. This prevents unauthorized people from gaining access to your computer using a boot diskette. That could easily happen if your PC is protected by software that prompts for a password before starting the operating system and not by the password in the BIOS. However, that software is not enabled by a boot diskette so anyone will have free access to your hard drive from the DOS prompt *A:\>*. The same is true under 95/98/NT with the password query enabled and the break keys shut off, otherwise you wouldn't even need a boot diskette. Using an active disk drive can also defeat any other operating system with password protection. Therefore, turn on the *A; C;* option only when it is necessary to boot from a diskette for some special reason, or when a new operating system is to be installed.

Switching off other drives

If you have other bootable drives installed in your PC and the boot sequence option has the setting LS/ZIP, C or CD-ROM; C; A in the BIOS Setup, it means you can also boot with a ZIP-, LS-120- or CD-ROM-drive. This is true even if you've switched off the floppy drive. Therefore, switch this option to C; A or SCSI, C; A.

Passwords are almost perfect protection

Any BIOS can protect the PC from unauthorized entry by using a password. Many BIOS versions even offer two protective options called the *USER PASSWORD* and the *SUPERVISOR PASSWORD*. Both options are found in the main menu of the BIOS Setup and can also be used with different passwords. However, it's also possible to assign a password to only one of the two options. In this case, use the *USER PASSWORD* so any user must know the password to boot the PC or call the BIOS Setup. You'll then have common password for access to the PC and for the BIOS Setup.

The supervisor password offers still further protection on a workstation, so that the user cannot call the BIOS Setup with his password and make changes. Once a *SUPERVISOR PASSWORD* is entered, it will be the only means by which the BIOS Setup menus can be opened. If the *USER PASSWORD* is used to open the BIOS Setup, it's also possible for only the *USER PASSWORD* to be changed. All the other menu items cannot be opened for security reasons. With the supplementary *Security Option* in the Award *BIOS Features Setup*, you can further specify with *System* or *Setup* whether the password is requested each time the system boots or only for the BIOS Setup. If you don't need a burdensome password query for the system on your home PC, but would like for example to prevent family members from experimenting with your BIOS Setup, then select a *USER PASSWORD* and set the *Security Option* to *Setup*. Should you then for some reason want to block access to the PC entirely, then merely reset the *Security Option* to *System*.

10. Security Techniques Against Hackers

Examples

The PC is used as a workstation computer

Enter a *Supervisor Password* for yourself and a *User Password* for the user. Set the *Security Option* to *System*. Tell the user what User Password you selected, so that (s)he can gain access to the system for the first time and then enter her/his password. If he calls the BIOS Setup and enters his password, he will then be able to open only the *User Password* menu. The other menus will be blocked. They can be accessed only with the Supervisor Password.

The PC is to be used as a workstation computer in an office and you're the only user. To prevent unauthorized persons (cleaning personnel, for example) from gaining accesss to the PC, specify a User Password and set the *Security Option* to *System*. You'll then have protected the PC and the BIOS Setup with a password.

The PC is used only at home. Since all family members are to have unlimited access to the PC, only the BIOS Setup is to be protected from changes. Then specify a User Password and set the *Security Option* to *Setup*. You're now only prompted for a password for the BIOS Setup and you have eliminated the entry when you switch on the PC.

Setting the password in the Award BIOS

1. When you want to specify a password, simply select the *USER PASSWORD* or *SUPERVISOR PASSWORD* option in the BIOS Setup main menu.

2. An input box (*Enter Password*) will appear, in which you can enter a password up to eight characters in length. If possible, use all the available spaces to achieve maximal security.

3. Once you have decided on your password, enter it and then press the [Enter] key. Notice that it is replaced by several asterisks (********). This is done for security reasons. Otherwise, someone could get your password simply by looking over your shoulder.

The screen for password confirmation

4. The input box (*Confirm Password*) will appear again to confirm the password. Enter the password again and confirm it by pressing the [Enter] key. The password is now valid and you will be prompted for it the next time you start your PC.

10. Security Techniques Against Hackers

The correct way to select the password

A hacker can try several passwords because even entering multiple incorrect passwords doesn't crash the PC. Although passwords can be case sensitive (a distinction is made between uppercase and lowercase letters), do not simply enter your name with uppercase and lowercase letters in alternating sequence. That is too simple and is probably the first thing any hacker tries to use.

Deleting the password

If the *USER PASSWORD* or *SUPERVISOR PASSWORD* is to be deleted again, the procedure is like that for installing a new password.

1. The input box for the password is not filled but confirmed immediately with the [Enter] key.

2. Then the message *Password Disabled, Press any Key to Continue* appears. The password is deleted.

3. It is logical that only people who know the *USER PASSWORD* or *SUPERVISOR PASSWORD* can delete because the computer prompts you for these first.

Creating the password in the AMI-BIOS

The specification of the password is similar in the AMI WINBIOS. Select the option *Supervisor* or *User* in the main menu under *Security*. An input box with a keyboard will appear. This lets you to enter the password using the mouse. However, only passwords with a maximum of six characters are possible here.

The input screen in the AMI-WINBIOS

Forgetting the password

Passwords work fine, but you can be in serious trouble if you forget the user password. Therefore, write down the password and store it in a secret, safe place. Otherwise, if you have lost the password, refer to Chapter 11 for tricks that might help you.

10. Security Techniques Against Hackers

Everything for security

❖ **Print Screen key doesn't work**
If you press the Print Screen key and nothing happens, even if your printer is turned on, it means that the BIOS does not correctly support sheet feed. Trigger it on your printer manually. If the sheet is not then ejected entirely, try the same thing again.

❖ **Only the menu for the User Password can still be opened in the BIOS Setup**
If you are only able to open the User Password menu in the BIOS Setup, it means you have also specified a Supervisor Password. The only way to enter the other menu options is by entering the supervisor password.

❖ **The password in the BIOS Setup can no longer be deleted**
There is no separate menu option for deletion. Go to the menu for the user or supervisor password and leave the input box blank. Confirm with the Enter key and it is already deleted.

11

BIOS Troubleshooting

You've probably already discovered how frequently BIOS problems occur. Your PC often operates with incorrect settings, and even though it runs, it won't run at its full performance.

The same result can occur when installing more hardware components. Everything is suddenly garbled and the PC no longer works. The year 2000 can also become a problem for older PCs. This chapter provides some solutions for this potential problem.

Restoring old BIOS

We mentioned in Chapter 9 that it is very important to generate a backup copy using the flash program. Every flash program we are aware of supports this option. Do not simply rely upon those recovery methods still available in case of problems. They do not always operate in a satisfactory manner. Should this case then actually occur, you have to buy a newly programmed BIOS chip from the motherboard manufacturer. Not only is this a difficult procedure, it's usually also expensive and takes time.

Backing up the old BIOS first

Every flasher has a menu option that lets you back up the old BIOS to a file, either after the start or before the final writing of the BIOS file. Always back up the BIOS onto a diskette, for it does little good to have the file on a hard drive you can no longer access. If the PC fails to operate properly after the update you can restore the old BIOS. To do this, simply use the backup file instead of the update file. Then your original will be back in the BIOS ROM. This is easy to do. Therefore, if you fail to get an OK message from the flasher at the end of the update, do not turn off or reboot the PC. Instead, try again to get the update file into the BIOS. If you do not succeed after several attempts, try to restore the backup file.

Emergency start using jumpers

You have a serious problem if the computer refuses to boot after the update. The reason is that an incorrect update file not matching the present motherboard was written into the BIOS. The backup file can be recovered only with a BIOS that is at least partly functional; the computer has to at least still be able to boot from the *A:* drive.

However, you may be in luck if you use an Intel motherboard equipped with a recovery jumper. The computer can use it to execute an emergency start and restore the backup file. All the other motherboards can be restored either only by experimenting or by buying a new BIOS. Carefully compare all data once more before the update. The correct update is indicated often by an additional number or letter.

Resetting the CMOS with [Ins] or jumpers

If the computer absolutely refuses to start after a tuning of the BIOS, some of the settings for system components must be wrong. Although this doesn't damage the hardware, the components are mutually blocking one another. Except for a possible beep tone, the screen remains black.

Don't rule out the possibility that incorrect data was written into the CMOS. The checksums will then no longer match and the error message *CMOS Checksum error* of the BIOS appears. That can also be the case following a BIOS update. A new BIOS is in the system, but the data in the CMOS remains from the earlier version. You can normally eliminate this by calling the BIOS Setup.

However, the latter may also not work in individual cases and the error message reappears on the monitor. In this case you have to delete the CMOS and reset all the settings to the default values. To do this, press and hold the [Ins] key at the same time you turn on the computer. Many motherboards also have a reset jumper for this purpose. It's usually located near the BIOS and the CMOS battery. It often has two settings made possible by three pins. One configuration connects the battery voltage to the CMOS and the other erases the CMOS. When you remove the jumper, it also interrupts the battery voltage. The CMOS requires about 30 minutes until it has finally lost its data. With the other jumper position, the CMOS is erased immediately.

Removing or Shorting the Battery

If the master passwords provide no help, you'll need to delete the contents of the CMOS. This also means the settings in the BIOS are also lost. Therefore, make certain to have a backup of the options. The job of reentering the settings later will then be quickly finished. Although many options are possible for deleting CMOS contents, you must open the computer as the first step.

Using reset jumpers

1. Check in the user manual for your motherboard to see whether there is perhaps a jumper or DIP-switch for resetting the CMOS.

2. If one is present, move it into the reset position.

3. Then leave the jumper or DIP switch in this position for about 30 minutes until the CMOS is finally erased.

The time needed for deletion will vary greatly according to how the motherboard manufacturer has designed the jumpers. Some merely disconnect the battery voltage, while others trigger a reset immediately, in which case the data in the CMOS will also then be immediately deleted.

Coin cell but no jumper

If there are no jumpers present, and your motherboard has either a coin cell or an external lithium battery connected to the motherboard with a two-pole red/black cable, it is still relatively simple.

Fooling the battery
If you do not want to remove the coin cell for fear of bending or breaking the clip, simply insert a strip of paper beneath it.

1. Remove the coin cell from the retaining clip. Be careful not to pull up the contact arm; it's easy to bend or break it. Instead, grip it at the sides, raise it gently and pull it out over the plastic rim.

2. Now wait for about 30 minutes before reinstalling the coin cell, until the voltage present in the capacitors has dissipated entirely.

Only then is the CMOS erased, and you can reinstall the coin cell.

The coin cell in its clip on the motherboard

With a lithium battery but no reset-jumper

You have installed an external lithium battery in your computer.

1. Disconnect the cable connecting the battery to the motherboard.

2. Wait before reconnecting the cable also in this case until you are sure the CMOS is receiving no further voltage from charged capacitors and erased.

3. Watch the polarity when reconnecting the cable.

11. BIOS Troubleshooting

"Dallas" module but no reset jumper

Did you fail to find either a coin cell or an external lithium battery? That can only mean that your motherboard already has a few years on it and still has a battery in the clock chip. That is a little black box bearing the Inscription "Dallas". This makes life really difficult. You cannot remove the battery from the chip. The only way to save your motherboard is to desolder the chip completely. This also has risks because of "electrical voltage fields" from the soldering iron. This can destroy the other chips. If you want to do this, make certain to wait at least 30 minutes before resoldering the chip. This will provide enough time for the CMOS to be entirely erased.

1. Desolder the chip carefully using an electronic soldering iron and a desoldering suction pump or desoldering braid.

2. Wait at least 30 minutes before resoldering.

3. Now resolder the chip back onto the motherboard.

The clock chip (timer) with integrated battery on the motherboard

Battery but no reset jumper

It's possible that you will not find either a coin cell or an external lithium battery and no little black box. Then your motherboard is truly old and still has a battery soldered to it. It's easy to distinguish the battery from the other components due to its size. It is a rounded, blue part with the label Ni/Cd, soldered between two relatively thick contacts near the BIOS. Either desolder the battery (electrical voltage fields) or buy a 39ohm/1W resistor that is then clamped parallel to the battery. In this case, too, wait about 30 minutes before you turn on your PC again and test the result.

1. Methods for desoldering the battery:

1. Carefully desolder the battery from the motherboard with an electronic soldering iron and a desoldering suction pump or desoldering braid.

2. Wait at least 30 minutes before resoldering.

3. Now resolder the battery to the motherboard.

2. Methods for attaching the resistor:

1. Clamp a 30 ohm resistor parallel to the battery using alligator clips, or wrap the wire ends of the resistor around the poles of the battery.

2. Wait at least 30 minutes.

3. Remove the resistor.

Access denied - Password cracking made easy

Password cracking - the Master Password

Master passwords are circulated illegally for each BIOS and can be entered to replace the forgotten password. Manufacturers constantly change the master password. Therefore, we don't claim that the passwords in the following table will always work or that this is even a complete list

AWARD	AMI
AWARD_SW	AMI
AWARD?SW	AMI?SW
Awkward	AMI_SW
ALLy	A.M.I
ALFAROME	BIOS
BIOSTAR	HEWITT RAND
HLT	LKWPETER
j262	PASSWORD
j256	
lkwpeter	
LKWPETER	
SER	
SKY_FOX	
Syxz	
589589	
589721	

II. BIOS Troubleshooting

Older motherboards still have a jumper for manually switching the video mode to monochrome or color graphics. You can use this to switch the password function on or off in the MR-BIOS. The function is on in the "mono" setting and off in the "color" setting.

Some shareware programs can read the password from the BIOS. However, this is of use only when the password is not enabled as the system password, and it is thus still possible to boot the computer to run the program. It is then possible to read the user password and the supervisor password. This chapter shows that even the protection of the system with a password is not 100% reliable.

If you have forgotten only the Setup password

Many users soon forget the Setup password because it's only required for the BIOS Setup. Just so that you won't have to open the computer again, you can also delete the CMOS with the "DEBUG" command and a few parameters. You must enter the *DEBUG* command in the real mode, in other words, not in the MS-DOS prompt of Windows. Otherwise, it will not work. Therefore, enter the command at the DOS prompt. Also, be very careful about the characters you enter.

1. The *C:\DEBUG* command calls the program itself.

2. Then enter the parameter *O* for Output, which sends the byte-word to an output port. The address of the output port will appear after that as a numerical value.

3. End the program with *Q* for Quit.

For the AMI and Award BIOS:

```
C:\DEBUG
-O 70 17
-O 71 17
Q
```

For the Phoenix BIOS:

```
C:\DEBUG
-O 70 FF
-O 71 17
Q
```

The CMOS is deleted immediately after execution. As you can see from this example, there are always a few gaps in security. A password is not 100% protection for your PC. Hackers are always ready to dig up and exploit such weaknesses. Access can in this way be made more difficult, but not prevented. If you have to be absolutely sure that your data won't fall into the wrong hands, use a ZIP disk or other removable storage and keep it in a safe.

11. BIOS Troubleshooting

System errors - The BIOS error messages

It's possible for BIOS to generate error messages. You'll either see the error as messages on the monitor or hear them as beep codes. The beeps are used whenever the screen can no longer be controlled as the result of a serious hardware error. The selection of the error messages on the screen as well as the beep codes is again unfortunately different for each BIOS manufacturer. They consist of long and (or) short tones, in different numbers and of different pitch, separated by a pause. Please see the Appendices for more information on the individual error messages.

Diagnosis with the POST codes

Besides BIOS codes, POST codes are also available. These POST codes are hexadecimal codes that are sent straight to I/O-port 80h during the POST routine of the BIOS. To use them, you will need a special POST diagnostic card for the ISA- or PCI-bus. It's inserted in an unused slot and displays the POST-code using a 2-digit LED-display. You can then compare the values displayed with those in a table supplied with the unit. Your favorite computer store should have a diagnostic card.

Exact diagnosis
Remove all expansion cards except for the video card and controller card. Otherwise, the result of the diagnosis may not be correct.

The following are examples of POST codes to detect errors with hardware components.

11. BIOS Troubleshooting

POST code	Description
01	Processor test 1 (flags, Iflags)
02	Processor test 2 (register)
03	Initialize chips (FPU,DMA-page,timer,DMA,interrupt controller,EISA registers)
04	Test memory refresh toggle
05	Blank video, initialize keyboard
06	Eprom checksum (=0)
07	Test CMOS interface and battery status
08	Setup low memory (first 256 KB, OEM chip set)
09	Early cache initialization
0A	Setup interrupt table
0B	Test CMOS RAM check sum
0C	Initialize keyboard
0D	Initialize video interface
0E	Test video memory
0F	Test DMA controller 1
0G	Test DMA controller 2
0H	Test DMA page registers

You can quickly identify the POST diagnostic test generating the error. Anyone who experiments with hardware or repairing PCs will quickly recover their investment using such a card. There are also other diagnostic ports that are distinguished by a different I/O address:

Diagnostic port	Address
XT	60h
Compaq	84h
PS/2 models	90h
Award	300h
MCA	680h

You can select the port to be used for diagnosis on many cards using jumpers. Still others, however, are permanently configured for their purpose and have to be purchased correspondingly.

12

Other BIOS Chips in your PC

Several additional BIOS chips that you'll find on the expansion cards and elsewhere in the PC have the same job: control the corresponding device. These BIOS chips also contain software similar to that in the system BIOS. These, too, can be produced on devices, for example, the CD-burner by using a firmware update per flash.

Video cards

The BIOS-ROM of the video card contains the basic data, such as initialization routines, BIOS functions and the character sets. Just after a reset or after turning on the PC, the CPU jumps to the selected initialization string in the program code. That initializes the registers of the VGA chip and sets the interrupt vectors for the interrupts.

You can replace the BIOS chip on many video cards and exchange it for a new version. Still other manufacturers even install a proper flash-BIOS into which it is possible to write an update using software, just as with the system BIOS. The BIOS version in the video card, together with the driver for the operating system, is crucial to the performance of the card.

The BIOS-ROM on the video card

12. Other BIOS Chips in your PC

There is a software interrupt that permits the software to communicate with the video card. In most cases this is INT 10h. You can access the registers through it and graphics mode, character input and output as well as read and write the screen pixels thus controlled.

CD-ROM burners

Most CD-ROM burners, whether SCSI or EIDE, also have a BIOS that you can update if necessary. Manufacturers are always releasing new controller variants and chipsets to which the device has to interface. Therefore, CD-ROM burner manufacturers also offer firmware updates for their devices. You can get these updates off the Internet or from the manufacturer or dealer. Such an update works similar to the system BIOS. Software writes the update file into the BIOS chip of the device. You have to move jumpers or install shorting bridges for that purpose, particularly in the case of SCSI-burners. Make certain to read all "Read-me" files included with the software. If the update for some reason goes wrong, for example, because you have used the wrong update file and can no longer access the original, you may have to send the burner back to the manufacturer for repair.

SCSI host adapters

Bootable SCSI host adapters also use BIOS to control the attached devices. They are identified in sequence by the SCSI-BIOS. The BIOS queries an ID number for that purpose, one after the other, and the connected device responds with its manufacturer and device identifier. This process is indicated by a status report listing all the devices found. It appears after the system start, between the memory test and the boot table.

Here, too, as with the system BIOS, a key combination specified by the manufacturer calls a SCSI host adapter. Many also make use of a separate program for the configuration of the adapter. The setting options range from the booting sequence to synchronous data transfer, transfer rates, separation or termination. Each manufacturer and each model has its own menus and options, just as in the case of the system BIOS.

Network cards

A network card also has its own BIOS. It transfers control of the system to the network server. For that purpose, the network card BIOS queries Interrupt 18h of the system BIOS. It would also bring the system to a halt by the generation of an error message, if no bootable medium can be found in the PC. Following that, Interrupt 18h is diverted by a "no boot routine" to the network, from which booting then takes place. You can only use network cards that don't contain a separate BIOS to link PCs that have their own bootable drive for data exchange.

13

Useful Tuning and Analysis Software

BIOS Setup does not always offer the settings provided with BIOS and the chip. Depending on the BIOS version, motherboard manufacturers mask various settings so they are not used. These are usually sensitive settings that could cause more damage than advantage if an incorrect parameter were used. Therefore, creative programmers have developed tuning software with which those who are to tune their BIOS can increase the speed of their PC by using the masked settings.

A benchmark test is an important part of BIOS tuning because after every change in the settings you must determine whether the change has enhanced performance. If the change reduces rather than enhances performance, the change in the setting can be reversed immediately. Without a benchmark test, for example, if you are left to guessing, you may not be able to tell whether performance has improved. However, there are considerable differences in benchmark programs. Not all are appropriate for our purposes.

Use TweakBIOS to Change Hidden Settings

The motherboard manufacturers determine which options are available for the BIOS settings. Because critical settings are often hidden from the user, any enhanced performance that such settings would provide is not available. However, TweakBIOS (available on the Internet as freeware) will let you change some BIOS settings, depending on the chipset you are using. You can find TweakBIOS on the Internet (http://miro.pair.com/tweakbios/index2.html).

At startup TweakBIOS looks for hardware components in the CMOS memory and displays what it finds. It also indicates whether the component is supported. Such components include the CPU to PCI Bridge, the PCI to PCI Bridge, the PCI to ISA Bridge, the IDE or USB Controller and the VGA Display Adapter. If a component is selected in the main menu, the available options and their settings are displayed. The visual presentation and the use of the options correspond almost entirely to the normal BIOS Setup.

13. Useful Tuning and Analysis Software

The Main Menu in TweakBIOS

When you select an option, a Tip appears that informs you how the settings can be improved. A colored star (*) appears in front of the settings for every option. The star appears in three colors that indicate the status of the value. Green indicates the value is unchanged, red indicates it is changed but not saved and white indicates the change has already been saved to the CMOS.

This provides a continuous overview of the many settings available in the various parts of the menu. Since the settings become active as soon as they are saved to the CMOS, you do not have to reboot.

The concealed options of the chipset

13. Useful Tuning and Analysis Software

The motherboard manufacturer determines which options are indicated in your TweakBIOS. Make certain to follow the suggestions offered by the program author when you make changes. However, keep in mind that these changes, not normally offered in the BIOS, can be very sensitive.

The motherboard manufacturers hide them to prevent a "total optimizing" of the system. Although you may not damage the hardware, any software on the hard drive may not run after a few crashes. However, if you tune carefully, you can attain the full performance that otherwise remains hidden and, therefore, unused.

A good example of this is the missing settings for SDRAM Modules. They run on a good motherboard at idle speed rather than full speed. Despite modern storage techniques, the PC does not come to its full capacity. The same principle holds for SDRAM Modules as for DRAM Modules (see Chapter 5). Lower values are usually faster. The options are listed in the following table:

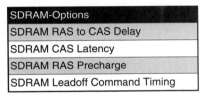

SDRAM-Options
SDRAM RAS to CAS Delay
SDRAM CAS Latency
SDRAM RAS Precharge
SDRAM Leadoff Command Timing

The motherboard manufacturers often also conceal the options for the EDO Module in the BIOS Setup. They need to be included in a successful tune up.

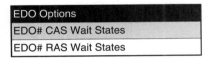

EDO Options
EDO# CAS Wait States
EDO# RAS Wait States

As you can see, the tuning possibilities are virtually limitless with the lost options. Exercise extreme caution when setting the options in the submenu of the IDE controller (for example, the Intel PIIX4 IDE controller).Fine-tuning in this case can lead to total data loss from the hard drive. Therefore, first back up the hard drive and then proceed by incremental tests.

The freeware version of TweakBIOS cannot back up the original settings before tuning. However, the professional version offers a security feature that lets you save the CMOS to a file and then return the original settings of the CMOS if the changed setting proves to be a disadvantage. By using TweakBIOS, you not only get a good tuning tool, but also a good program for backing up and restoring the CMOS. If you're using the freeware version, press F4 to produce a screen shot and save it in a text file. This lets you compare the settings and reverse them if you prefer. In the 1.52b version the program supports the following motherboard and graphic adapter chipsets. An update file that is available on the same Internet site makes the program applicable for additional, current chipsets.

13. Useful Tuning and Analysis Software

Motherboard Chipsets
Intel LX/NX
Intel ZX
Intel 430FX
Intel 430HX
Intel 430 VX
Intel 430 TX
Intel 440LX
Intel BX/EX (Update)
Natoma (440FX)
Orion (450KX/GX)
AMD-640
VIA VP
VIA VP-2
VIA VP-3 (Update)
ALI Aladdin 2
OPT1 Viper and Vendetta
UMC 881
SIS (Update)

Graphic Adapter Chips
Matrox Mystique
ET 6000

AMI Setup

AMI Setup was mainly intended for AMI BIOS versions released before 1995. Because it's no longer current for today's versions, it doesn't always work well with them. Although development has stopped, you may still find it available on many shareware servers on the Internet. In part, AMI Setup replaces BIOS Setup with the added feature that it reveals hidden settings and can change them. It also has tools for AMI BIOS. In a configuration menu that is program-specific, you can determine options for Reboot, Warning Beep, Language or the display of Setup entries.

13. Useful Tuning and Analysis Software

Choose the type of Setup you wish in the main menu:

Standard Setup

Enhanced Setup

Change the Register

Password

Load Standard Settings

Load Saved Settings

Print the Present Setup

Analyze BIOS ID

Reference Manual for Selection

There are also useful tools such as Measure the DMA Speed, Display Battery Status, Change the Register, Back up the CMOS and EISA memory to a file. The Save and Restore the CMOS option is always useful. It will run from a batch command so you won't need to start the entire program and click around in the menu. By using the batch command, you can simply save or restore the CMOS at the DOS level.

Enter the name of the backup file for the *FILENAME* (for example, cmosbkup.sav). In this example, make certain to follow DOS naming conventions so the filename must have eight or fewer letters and the extension must have three or fewer letters.

Function	Batch Command
Save	AMISETUP - SAVE:CMOS:FILENAME
Restore	AMISETUP - RESTORE:CMOS:FILENAME

13. Useful Tuning and Analysis Software

CMOS Backup & Restore

As mentioned in Chapter 10, many programs are available that let you write the content of the CMOS into a file and then save it to the hard drive or a diskette. Many programs are small enough to permit them to be saved to a boot diskette. They can then be used to restore all the settings of the CMOS, in case those settings are lost. The "CMOS SAVE and RESTORE" software, available on the Internet pages of PC Praxis, serves this purpose very well. You can find this type of software with TweakBIOS (full version), AMI Setup, BIOS 310 from Eleventh Alliance, Parastat from Paraland, and TechFacts from Dean Software Design. You can also probably find others by using your favorite web search engine (for example, by typing "cmos backup").

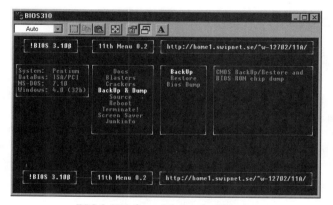

BIOS 310 from Eleventh Alliance

The program BIOS 310 from Eleventh Alliance uses graphic menus and is small enough to fit on a diskette. Here is an example of how to back up the CMOS.

Backup:

1. Place the cursor on the menu *Backup and Dump.*

2. Using the ➔ key, place the cursor on *Backup* and press (Enter).

3. The following message appears in the lower window:
   Enter file/device where to back up CMOS settings: A:\CMOS065C.BIO.

4. You can use either the path/filename suggested by the program or one of your own choices.

5. Press (Enter) to copy the file to the disk.

13. Useful Tuning and Analysis Software

Avoid problems with the password

Before the final backup, delete the password from the BIOS. If you forget your password and have no other recourse than to delete the CMOS, you will have the same problem again after Restore.

Changing settings rapidly

If you use various settings in your BIOS and therefore have to change settings frequently, store the various combinations of settings in several files under different filenames. Using Restore you can then load the configuration you wish.

Restore:

1. To restore a file to the CMOS proceed as you did to back up a file, but choose *Restore* rather than *Backup* from the menu.

2. Use the automatically selected file or enter the path/filename of the backup file in the lower window.

3. Press (Enter) to write the backup file into the CMOS.

4. Restart the PC to make operative the newly entered settings in CMOS.

CMOS Save and Restore

The program CMOS Save and Restore is also small enough to fit on a diskette. Although it does not have a graphic interface, it's easy to use.

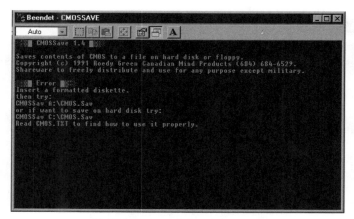

CMOS Save and CMOS Restore

Save

1. If you start the program without parameters, it presents a simple example (see above) for use.

2. The program asks for a program command and the path/filename of the Save or Restore file (CMOSSAV A:\CMOS.SAV). Normal DOS naming conventions are used. Therefore, you cannot use more than eight letters for the filename and three for the extension.

3. Press the Enter key to save the CMOS to the disk. CMOS successfully saved is given as the status report.

Restore

1. Restoring the file to the CMOS proceeds like the saving of the file, only you use the program command CMOSREST instead of CMOSSAV.

2. Press Enter to write the file from the disk to the CMOS.

TechFacts 95

In addition to some functions that are less interesting, this system utility also offers a Backup and Restore program for the CMOS file.

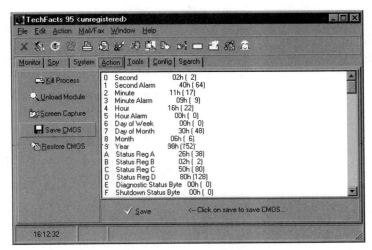

The System Utility "TechFacts" includes a Backup and a Restore feature.

The Save CMOS and Restore CMOS buttons are included on the Action tab. If either of the two is selected, an additional button appears under the window; you must click on this button to perform the final Backup or Restore.

Test the Functionality

When you've selected a program, first print the BIOS settings so that in case of function failure, you can re-enter the BIOS settings manually. Then test the Backup and Restore features. Once you have determined that your program reliably backs up and restores the CMOS files, you can discard the hard copy.

Low-level Benchmarks and Determining Your Success

The Benchmark

This is a procedure that tests the performance of the PC using the values of the individual components: processor, memory, video card, hard drive, and CD-ROM drive. The test results can be given using various indicators. Some procedures, such as WinTune or PC Checkup, report all the values for the individual components; other procedures, such as Winbench 97, Winstone 97, or Sysmark 32, produce an accumulative value for the components using simulated standard applications such as word processors, spreadsheets, databases, and image processors. These test results can then be compared with previously attained results or with those from another PC.

13. Useful Tuning and Analysis Software

Wintune

The Wintune benchmark program is fast, precise and user-friendly. Also, the detailed display for the values of CPU, Video, Disk, and Memory, contributes to BIOS tuning, since it shows specifically which values have changed.

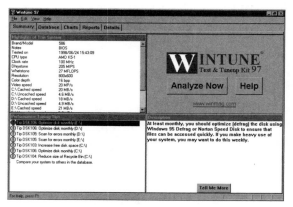

The detailed display of Wintune

It also analyzes the hardware and software in the system. It displays the operating system with its version number, information on the PC model, System Bus, BIOS Type, APM Version and other details. Comparison with other systems from a database is also possible. The values are then given as a report in adjacent lists or in charts (either 2-D or 3-D). The graphic representation avoids a reciprocal confusion of the values by showing only one value from each selected list. The values can be stored in a file for future reference, if you wish.

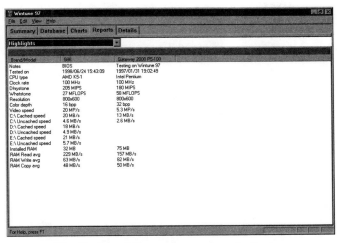

The display of the memory values in the tree

If you change the settings for memory in the BIOS, use "Memory" to compare them immediately with the previous settings. For memory alone, 22 values that were produced by an extensive test are displayed in a convenient overview. If you click on the icon in front of a value, you will get an explanation for the value; the same procedure is available for the values of CPU, Video, and Disk. In this way, you can monitor the effect of even the slightest change in the BIOS Setup on the performance of the system.

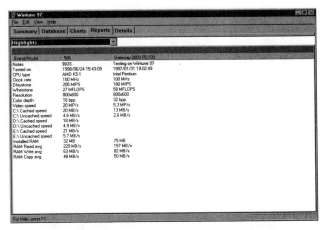

Comparison of the performance with that of another computer

The program is available from Windows Magazine as freeware on the Internet or as a shareware CD. As the menu entry *About Wintune 97 . . .* indicates, it was produced by CMP Media; it is presently

13. Useful Tuning and Analysis Software

available as Wintune 2.0 for Windows 3.x, as Wintune 97 for Windows 95 and NT, and most recently also as Wintune 98. In addition, you can now download "Wintune 95 Results." This is an update for the two Tune-Up-Kits, Wintune 2.0 and Wintune 97, and enhances them by adding some comparative values for the newest MMX processors.

Here's what it looks like in practice:

The following settings, determined by *Auto Configuration,* were on the test processor:

Option	Previous Value
DRAM Read Burst Timing	X333
DRAM Write Burst Timing	X333

1. Start the program and execute the test routine by clicking on the *Analyze Now* button.

2. Save the displayed values in the program with *File, Save Current Results* or print the test report with *File, Print.*

3. Call up the BIOS Setup and change the settings.

On the test computer the settings were changed as follows:

Option	Subsequent Value
DRAM Read Burst Timing	X222
DRAM Write Burst Timing	X222

4. Restart the program and compare the results with each other by saving them under different names or printing them.

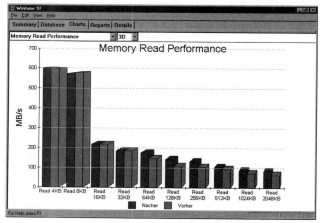

Before and After in graphic 3-D Representation

13. Useful Tuning and Analysis Software

5. If you have obtained favorable results, you can retain the altered settings; if the test yields negative results, you can restore the original settings.

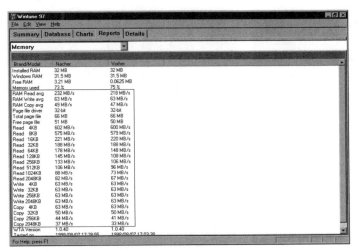

Comparison with Wintune

We retained the changes shown above on our test computer. In the right column of the graphic, the original settings are stored as "Before"; in the left column the values of the optimized settings are stored as "After." This presentation is available under the tab as *Reports* and through the option *Memory*. The data to be compared is marked beforehand in the *Database* tab.

In this instance you can observe exactly how the memory management and thus the performance are considerably improved by a change involving only two settings.

After that, proceed to the setting *DRAM RAS to CAS;* on our test processor, *Auto Configuration* has set them at the value "3."

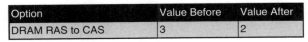

Option	Value Before	Value After
DRAM RAS to CAS	3	2

Change the setting to the value "2" by repeating steps 1-5.

Option	Value Before	Value After
DRAM RAS Precharge Time	4	3

Now proceed in the same manner with the options *DRAM RAS Precharge Time* or *DRAM R/W Leadoff Timing*

Another example illustrates the performance data of the PC when the external or internal cache memory is disabled in the BIOS.

Option	Extcache	Intcache	Optimal
CPU Internal Cache		Disabled	Enabled
External Cache	Disabled		Enabled

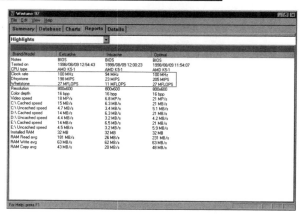

The Performance Comparison

The individual values in the three columns can easily be compared to determine how much performance is lost by disabling the internal or external cache. Not only does the processor performance decrease, measured in MIPS (millions of instructions per second) or MFLOPS (millions of floating point operations per second); but also the entire performance of the PC decreases.

One more example illustrates the decrease in performance of the hard drive when Block mode is disabled in the BIOS. The data transfer and thus once again the entire performance of the PC is impaired.

Option	Normal	Block Mode Off
HDD Block Mode	Enabled	Disabled

13. Useful Tuning and Analysis Software

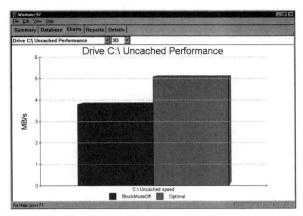

Graphic illustration of hard drive performance with and without Block mode

Regardless of which settings you change in the BIOS, you should always test the results immediately after the change. One change can often affect the values of all components, either positively or negatively. An increase in the speed of one component can decrease the speed of another component, so strive for a configuration that reconciles the various components.

InfoPro

InfoPro, made by Eastern Digital, is a diagnostic tool for Windows 95 and contains some benchmark tests in addition to denoting system settings; it tests the CPU, motherboard, memory, hard drive, CD-ROM and video card. The individual test routines have a maximum of seven minutes runtime; therefore, this benchmark is also convenient for tuning the BIOS settings.

Because the tests can be used individually, they offer an opportunity to test the altered settings at each stage of the BIOS tune. The program is shareware with a 14-day trial time.

13. Useful Tuning and Analysis Software

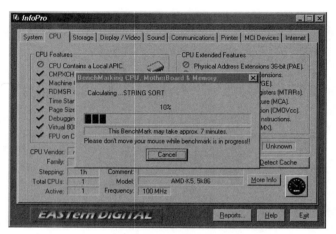

InfoPro with tests for CPU, motherboard, and memory

Winbench

The programs PC-Bench 8.0 for DOS and Winbench 4.0 for Windows 3.x, NT 3.1 and OS/22.1, produced by ZIFF-Davis, are products for the final testing of all tuning actions performed on the BIOS.

Since the tests are performed with great precision, they require more time than the tests performed by programs mentioned above. When you're testing settings in the BIOS, we recommend first applying a faster "pre-test" to find the best setting and then to perform a final test with Winbench. Before you begin tuning, run a benchmark test with the present parameters and save the results of the test; you will then be able to compare these results with the results obtained after tuning is complete.

Winbench 97

Winbench 97 is a synthetic subsystem-level benchmark that determines the performance of the PC through tests of the graphics, video, processor, disk, and CD-ROM. Since it is a 32-bit program it runs under Windows 95 and NT.

13. Useful Tuning and Analysis Software

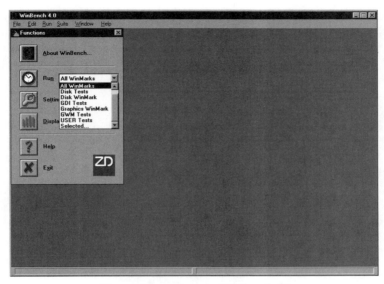

The setting options in Winbench 97

It consists of several smaller programs. For example, CPU-Mark performs both a 16-bit and a 32-bit processor test, Graphic-Winmark thoroughly tests the video card, Disk-Winmark for disk performance and CD-ROM Winmark. The tests are performed by 32-bit programs, produced by acclaimed manufacturers, programs that are copied into a work list using scripts and are then called up as needed. As the program runs, the values are exhibited; when the program is finished it is deleted from the work list. The test routines determine which programs are employed in the test process; if all the test routines are employed, the process requires about 50 mnutes on a Pentium 133 with 32 Meg of RAM.

Winstone 97

Winstone 97 is a benchmark program from the same manufacturer. It runs under Windows 95, NT3.51 and 4.0. The business tests usually require about 16 Meg of RAM and the high end tests usually require about 32 Meg of RAM. Either test requires an additional 150 Meg free on the hard drive. It performs similarly to Winbench 97 except it uses other scripts and methods of measurement. This brings us to the "Business" or "High-End" groups. Programs are assigned according to the group. The test routine for the High-End test requires about 32 minutes on a Pentium 133 with 32 Meg of RAM; for the Business test it requires about 19 minutes. Higher Winstone values mean greater performance throughout the entire system. Other processor manufacturers also use this program for the P-Rating (Pentium Rating). This P-Rating is determined based on a performance comparison of other processors with the original Intel processor.

13. Useful Tuning and Analysis Software

Thus the benchmark is conducted in a defined Hardware Environment. A P-Rating of 200 equals the performance of a Pentium processor with 200 MHz. The CPU clones usually run at considerably less MHz: The Cyrix P200+ runs at 75 MHz x 2 = 150 MHz and performs the equivalent of an Intel Pentium 200 that runs at 66 MHz x 3 = 200 MHz. The following programs are used to test the performance of the corresponding categories:

The Business Group		
Program	Category	
Adobe Page Maker 6.0	Graphic/DTP	
Corel Draw 6.0	Graphic/DTP	
Microsoft Power Point 7.0	Presentation	
Borland Paradox 7.0	Database	
Microsoft Access 7.0	Database	
Lotus Word Pro 96	Word Processor	
Microsoft Word 7.0	Word Processor	
Microsoft Excel 7.0	Spreadsheet	

The High-End Group	
Program	Category
Microsoft Visual C++	Application Programming
Adobe Photoshop 3.0.5	Image Processing
Micrografx Picture Publisher 6.0	Image Processing
Bently Systems Micro Station 95	CAD/3-D
Visual Numerics PV-WAVE 6.0	CAD/3-D
Advanced Visual Systems Application Visualization System (AVS) 3.0	CAD/3-D

In the meantime the newer versions of Winstone 98, 3-D Winbench 98, and Winbench 98 have arrived on the market.

SysMark 32

Sysmark 32 is another benchmark test that, like Winstone 97, is oriented to the practical needs of the PC user. To determine performance levels with precision it incorporates programs from acclaimed software manufactures that have united themselves as BAPCo (Business Applications Performance Corporation). A few hardware manufacturers have also joined this corporation. Together they seek to develop benchmark tests for specific applications. Sysmark 32 is one such test. BAPCo introduces eight other Sysmark tests at its website.

Again in this case the application programs are copied to the hard drive and run in a subsystem through script management. The Pentium 100 is set as the standard of comparison. The number of points your system attains determines how much faster it is than the Pentium 100; e.g., if your system attains 150 points in the test, it operates 1.5 times as fast as the Pentium 100. Since this test executes the application programs, it takes rather long to run, and thus is best used as a final test. It produces very exact results.

Benchmark Programs like Sand in the Sea

Many more benchmark programs that provide good results are available on the market, especially on the Internet and on shareware CDs. Many of these limit themselves to the measurement of hard drives, RAM and cache, graphics or 3-D graphics. Others are integrated into diagnostic tools. Such programs are also useable but the accuracy of their measurements can only be determineed by one's own tests. If the measurements are not sufficiently sensitive, they will not register a gain in performance if the gain is only slight. For that reason, use the programs recommended here, so that you don't spend time futilely attempting to coax higher performance from your PC.

Determining Tolerances

If you are not certain how high the tolerance values are in an unfamiliar benchmark program, run the test several times in succession and compare the values. If the values differ considerably, the test is not useable.

Appendix A:
BIOS Information

The BIOS Manufacturers

Not only are the addresses of the BIOS manufacturers important for getting an update or reaching the support service, also important are the listing and explanation of the error codes and beeps of the BIOS that are output on an error. Many users are also interested in the operational routine of the POST. Therefore, in this chapter we have summarized the data that can be very useful in case of errors. This will tremendously speed up and simplify users' search for the cause of the error.

American Megatrends, Inc.
6145-F North Belt Parkway
Norcross, GA 30071
http://www.ami.com

MR-BIOS
Microid Research, Inc.
1538 Turnpike Street
North Andover, MA 01845
http://www.mrbios.com

Intel Corp.
5200 North East Elam Young Parkway
Hillsboro, OR 97124
http://www.intel.com

Award Software International, Inc.
777 East Middlefield Road
Mountain View, CA 94043
http://www.award.com

Phoenix Technologies, Ltd.
411 East Plumeria Drive
San Jose, CA 95134
http://www.ptltd.com

BIOS Error codes

The error codes of the BIOS are very helpful in troubleshooting on the PC. If something doesn't work the way it is supposed to, the POST of the BIOS establishes this and can inform the user in three different ways. One way is the display of defined error messages on the screen. If the monitor can no longer be controlled due to a serious hardware error, beeps are output via the system speakers. They are not always as precisely defined as the error messages on the screen, however, they do offer a good clue. The third

Appendix A: BIOS Information

and also most precise variant for tracking errors is the POST code. However, you can only display this through additional hardware. For this purpose you have to purchase an expansion card (POST card). The two-figure LED display then displays the ID which you can compare with the POST code in the tables.

Award BIOS error codes

BIOS ROM checksum error - System halted

The checksum of the BIOS code in the BIOS chip is wrong. The BIOS has to be replaced or rewritten by flash.

CMOS battery failed

The CMOS battery is discharged and has to be replaced.

CMOS checksum error - Defaults loaded

The checksum of the CMOS is wrong. The BIOS default values are being loaded. This can happen as a result of an almost discharged battery or through the updating of the BIOS. If no BIOS update is occurring, replace the battery and reconfigure the system with your saved settings.

CPU at nnnn

Displays the speed of the CPU.

Display switch is set incorrectly.

The setting for monochrome or color graphics is wrong. Either the jumper for the video setting has to be changed or the Video Selection has to be corrected in Setup. The message merely compares the setting of the jumper on the motherboard with the setting of BIOS Setup.

Press ESC to skip memory test

The user can press the (Esc) key to skip the memory test.

Floppy disk(s) fail

The floppy disk controller or the drive cannot be found or initialized. Either the controller is not correctly installed or the onboard controller is disabled in the BIOS Setup.

HARD DISK initializing Please wait a moment...

Some hard drives take longer to be intialized.

HARD DISK INSTALL FAILURE

Cannot find or initialize the hard drive controller or the drive. Make sure the controller is installed correctly. If no hard drives are installed, be sure the Hard Drive selection in Setup is set to NONE.

Appendix A: BIOS Information

Hard disk(s) diagnosis fail

An error occurred in the diagnostic routine of a hard drive. The cause could be a defective hard drive.

Keyboard error or no keyboard present

The keyboard cannot be intialized. Check whether the keyboard is properly connected and do not press any keys during the POST. If you wish to use the system without a keyboard, you have to set the *Halt On All, But Keyboard* option in the *Standard CMOS Setup*. The BIOS will then ignore the keyboard.

Keyboard is locked out - Unlock the key

One or more keys are being continuously pressed during the keyboard test. Either the keys are stuck or something is on the keyboard.

Memory Test :

This message shows the complete memory test. The checked memory is decremented.

Memory test fail

When the POST detects an error in the memory, it outputs the information with the type and address.

Override enabled - Defaults loaded

The system cannot boot with the existing CMOS configuration and therfore overwrites the existing configuration with the BIOS default values. Now the minimum configuration is loaded again, and you will have to reset the BIOS settings.

Primary master hard disk fail

The POST has detected an error in the primary master IDE hard drive.

Primary slave hard disk fail

The POST has detected an error in the primary slave IDE hard drive.

Secondary master hard disk fail

The POST has detected an error in the secondary master IDE hard drive.

Secondary slave hard disk fail

The POST has detected an error in the secondary slave IDE hard drive.

AMI BIOS error codes

8042 Gate-A20 Error!

Gate A20 in the keyboard controller is defective. The keyboard controller needs to be replaced.

Appendix A: BIOS Information

C: Drive Error

Drive C: is not responding. With a non-IDE hard drive, run the Harddisk utility to solve the problem. Caution, you will lose all data.

D: Drive Error

Drive D: is not responding. With a non-IDE hard drive, run the Harddisk utility to solve the problem. Caution, you will lose all data.

C: Drive Failure

Drive C: is not responding. Either the cable connection or the hard drive is defective.

D: Drive Failure

Drive D: is not responding. Either the cable connection or the hard drive is defective.

Address Line Short

The address logic for the memory is producing errors.

BUS Timeout NMI at Slot X

(EISA) slot x was disabled due to a timeout.

Cache Memory Bad, do Not Enable Cache!

The cache memory has an error. Do not enable the cache in the BIOS Setup or replace the chip.

CH-2 Timer Error Non fatal

The system timer on the motherboard is producing errors.

CMOS Battery State Low

The battery is almost discharged and has to be replaced.

CMOS Checksum Failure

After saving the Setup data in the CMOS, a checksum is calculated. If there is a difference in the checksum after the most recent boot, this error message appears and you will have to call BIOS Setup to make corrections.

CMOS Memory Size Mismatch

The memory size saved in the CMOS does not match the one detected by the POST. You will have to call BIOS Setup to make corrections.

Appendix A: BIOS Information

CMOS System Options Not Set

There are errors in the settings saved in the CMOS or the settings are no longer present. You will have to call BIOS Setup to make corrections.

CMOS Time and Date Not Set

The time and date are not set in the CMOS. You will have to call BIOS Setup to make corrections.

Display Switch Not Proper

The setting for monochrome or color graphics is wrong. You will either have to change the jumper for the video setting or correct the Video Selection in Setup. The message simply compares the setting of the jumper on the motherboard with the setting of BIOS Setup.

Diskette Boot Failure

The diskette in the boot drive is defective. You cannot start the system with this diskette. Use a new diskette with the system files.

DMA #1 Error

DMA #2 Error

An error has occurred in the first/second DMA channel on the motherboard.

DMA Error

An error has occurred in the DMA controller on the motherboard.

DMA Bus Time-out

The DMA bus signal was triggered by an ISA component for longer than 7.8 microseconds. This results in a time-out.

EISA CMOS Checksum Failure

After saving the Setup data in the CMOS, a checksum is calculated. If there is a difference in the checksum after the most recent boot, this error message appears and you will have to call BIOS Setup to make corrections.

EISA CMOS Inoperational

A read/write error has occurred in the expanded CMOS-RAM. You will have to call BIOS Setup to make corrections. The battery may be weak and in need of replacement.

(E)nable (D)isable Expansion Board?

An NMI (**N**on **M**askable **I**nterrupt) has occurred in the EISA bus. Press [E] or [D] to enable or disable the expansion board.

Appendix A: BIOS Information

Expansion Board not ready at Slot X

The AMI BIOS cannot find an expansion board at EISA-Slot X. Check the card and the installation.

Expansion Board disabled at Slot X

The expansion board at Slot X is disabled.

Fail-Safe Timer NMI Inoperational

Components that use the fail-safe NMI timer will not function properly.

Fail-Safe Timer NMI

The fail-safe NMI timer is generated.

FDD Controller Failure

The BIOS cannot communicate with the floppy controller. The cause can be in the cable connection or in the controller.

HDD Controller Failure

The BIOS cannot communicate with the hard drive controller. The cause can be in the cable connection or in the controller.

INTR #1 Error

POST detected an error in the first channel of the interrupt control.

INTR #2 Error

POST detected an error in the second channel of the interrupt control.

Invalid Boot Diskette

The system is able to read the diskette, but the operating system cannot start.

Create a new boot disk (*Format A:\ /S*).

I/O Card Parity Error at xxxxxx

 A parity error has occurred on an ISA expansion card. If the address is known, it will be included in the display.

ID information mismatch for Slot X

The ID of the EISA expansion board at Slot X does not match the ID in the CMOS-RAM. You will have to fix the problem using the EISA configuration program.

Appendix A: BIOS Information

Invalid Configuration Information for Slot X

The configuration data of the EISA expansion board at Slot X are wrong. Therefore the card cannot be configured.

K/B Interface Error

The keyboard interface on the motherboard is defective.

Keyboard Error

The keyboard has a problem with the system. If this occurs frequently, replace the keyboard.

Keyboard is locked ... Unlock it

The keyboard is locked. You need to unlock the keyboard lock at the computer case.

Memory mismatch, run Setup

The memory has been changed. Start BIOS Setup and save the settings.

Memory Parity Error at XXXX

A parity error in the main memory has occurred. If the address can be localized it will be included in the display. Otherwise the message appears with ????.

No ROM Basic

The BIOS cannot find an operating system.

On Board Parity Error

A parity error in the onboard main memory has occurred. The address will be localized and displayed with xxxx (hex).

Off Board Parity Error

A parity error in the main memory in the expansion slot has occurred. The address will be localized and displayed with xxxx (hex).

Parity Error ????

A parity error has been detected in the main memory. The address could not be localized.

Software Port NMI Inoperational

The software port NMI (**N**on **M**askable **I**nterrupt) is not working. While the system is able to function, it hangs when an NMI occurs.

Appendix A: BIOS Information

Software Port NMI

A software port NMI (**N**on **M**askable **I**nterrupt) has been generated.

BIOS Beeps

Award BIOS

The Award BIOS generates short and long beeps in varying number and is incredibly brief in the breakdown of errors. These are only divided into three groups. The fourth message is the signal for everything is all right.

Beeps	Description	Problem solution
1x short	Everything is ok	
2x short	Small error, also usually displayed on the monitor.	Fix error or press F1 to continue boot procedure.
1x long 2x short	Error in video card	The video card or the memory on the video card is defective and needs to be replaced.
1x long 3x short	Error in the keyboard controller	Probably the keyboard controller is defective. Replace the chip on the motherboard.

AMI BIOS

The AMI BIOS generates short beeps in varying number or also short and long beeps in combination. The breakdown of the errors is somewhat more exact than with the Award BIOS.

Appendix A: BIOS Information

Beeps	Description	Problem solution
1	DRAM-Refresh Error	Check the RAM modules to make sure they are correctly seated in the socket. If all the modules are correctly seated, but the error persists, have your dealer check the modules for errors.
2	Parity error	See above
3	Memory error in the first 64K	See above
4	System timer error	The motherboard is defective and needs to be replaced.
5	Processor error	Have the dealer check the processor.
6	Keyboard controller/Gate A20 error	The keyboard or the keyboard controller on the motherboard is defective. Replace it!!
7	Interrupt error from the processor	Have the dealer check the processor.
8	Read/write error in the video card memory	The video card or the memory on the video card is defective and needs to be replaced.
9	ROM-BIOS Checksum is incorrect	The BIOS needs to be replaced or updated.
10	Read/write error in the shutdown register of the CMOS	The motherboard is defective and needs to be replaced.
11	Error in the cache memory	The module of the external cache memory is defective and needs to be replaced. The cache is integrated on newer motherboards and the motherboard needs to be replaced.
1x short 3x long	Error in the main memory	Check the RAM modules to make sure they are seated correctly in the socket. If all the modules are seated correctly, but the error persists, have your dealer check the modules for errors.
1x long 2x short	No video card found	No video card is installed.
1x long 3x short	No monitor found	The monitor is not connected or the cable is defective.
1x long 8x short	Error in video memory	The video card or the memory on the video card is defective and needs to be replaced.

MR-BIOS

MR-BIOS emits a sound sequence of high and low beeps. The first two sound signals are followed by a pause, and then the actual beep code.

Appendix A: BIOS Information

Beeps	Description	Problem solution
LH-LLL	Checksum error in the BIOS	The BIOS needs to be replaced or updated
LH-HLL	Error in DMA page register	The motherboard is defective and needs to be replaced
LH-LHL	Error in the keyboard controller	Probably the keyboard controller is defective. The chip on the motherboard can be replaced.
LH-HHL	Error in the memory refresh	See LH-LLLL to LH-LHHL
LH-LLH	Error in the DMA controller	The motherboard is defective and needs to be replaced
LH-HLH		
LH-LLLL	Error in memory bank 0	Check the RAM modules to make sure they are seated correctly in the socket. If all the modules are seated correctly, but the error persists, have your dealer check the modules for errors.
LH-HHHL	Error in the interrupt controller	The motherboard is defective and needs to be replaced
LH-LHHH	Error in the system timer	The motherboard is defective and needs to be replaced
LH-LHLLH	Read/write error in the CMOS	BIOS Setup must be executed to correct the error.
LH-HHLLH	Error in the real-time clock	The motherboard is defective and needs to be replaced
LH-LLHLH	Error on the video card	The video card or the memory on the video card is defective and needs to be replaced.
LH-HLHLH	Error in the keyboard controller	Probably the keyboard controller is defective. The chip on the motherboard can be replaced.
LH-LHHLH	Parity error in memory	See LH-LLLL to LH-LHHL
LH-HHHLH	Error in the I/O channel	The motherboard is defective and needs to be replaced
LH-LLLHH	Gate A20 error	The motherboard is defective and needs to be replaced
LH-HLLHH		
LH-LHLHH	Error in the real-time clock	The motherboard is defective and needs to be replaced

Phoenix BIOS plus und Version 1.x

The Phoenix BIOS emits three beeps in variable number, separted by a pause.

Appendix A: BIOS Information

Beeps	Description	Problem solution
1-1-3	Read/write error in the CMOS	BIOS Setup must be executed to correct the error.
1-1-4	Checksum error in the BIOS	The BIOS needs to be replaced or updated
1-2-1	Error in the timer	The motherboard is defective and needs to be replaced
1-2-2	Initialization error of the DMA	The motherboard is defective and needs to be replaced
1-2-3	Read/write error of the DMA page register	The motherboard is defective and needs to be replaced
1-3-1	Refresh error in RAM	Check the RAM modules to make sure they are seated correctly in the socket. If all the modules are seated correctly, but the error persists, have your dealer check the modules for errors.
1-3-1	Error in the first 64K of memory	See above
1-3-4		
1-4-1		
1-4-2	Parity error in the first 64K of memory	See above
3-1-1	Error in the DMA controller	The motherboard is defective and needs to be replaced
3-1-2		
3-1-3	Error in the interrupt controller	The motherboard is defective and needs to be replaced
3-1-4		
3-2-4	Error in the keyboard controller	Probably the keyboard controller is defective. The chip on the motherboard can be replaced.
3-3-4	Error in video memory	The video card or the memory on the video card is defective and needs to be replaced.
3-4-1	Initialization error of the video card	See above
3-4-2	Error checking the screen activation	The monitor is not connected or the cable is defective.
4-2-1	Error in the timer chip	The motherboard is defective and needs to be replaced
4-2-2	Error of the shutdown register	The motherboard is defective and needs to be replaced
4-2-3	Error in Gate A20	The motherboard is defective and needs to be replaced
4-2-4	Interrupt error in Protect mode	The motherboard or the processor is defective and needs to be replaced
4-3-1	Error in memory above 64K	See 1-3-1 to 1-4-2
4-3-2	Error in the timer chip	The motherboard is defective and needs to be replaced
4-3-4	Error testing the real-time clock	See above
4-4-1	Error testing the serial ports	See above
4-4-2	Error testing the parallel ports	See above
4-4-3	Error testing the coprocessor	The coprocessor is defective and needs to be replaced. Processors that include the coprocessor need to be completely replaced.

Appendix A: BIOS Information

Phoenix BIOS Version 4.x

The latest version of the Phoenix BIOS emits four beeps in variable number, separated by a pause. However, the error communication is no longer as precise as it was in Version 1.x.

Beeps	Description	Problem solution
1-2-2-3	Checksum error in the BIOS	The BIOS needs to be replaced or updated
1-2-3-1	Error in the timer chip	The motherboard is defective and needs to be replaced
1-2-3-3	Error in the DMA controller	The motherboard is defective and needs to be replaced
1-3-1-1	Refresh error in RAM	Check the RAM modules to make sure they are seated correctly in the socket. If all the modules are seated correctly, but the error persists, have your dealer check the modules for errors.
1-3-3-1	Error im RAM	See above
1-4-2-1	CMOS-Error	BIOS Setup must be executed to correct the error.

POST Codes - The Power On Self Test

The PC executes a self test right after it is powered up. This is called the POST (**P**ower **O**n **S**elf Test). These POST codes are hexadecimal codes that are sent directly to the I/O port 80h during the POST routine of the BIOS. A special POST diagnostics card for the ISA or PCI bus is necessary to make them visible. You plug this card into a free slot; it displays the POST code through a 2-figure LED display. You can then compare the code with the displayed values through a supplied diagnostic card or the following table. You can get a diagnostics card in any electronics specialty shop.

Code (hex)	Name	Description
C0	Turn off Chipset Cache	OEM Specific-Cache control
1	Processor Test 1	Processor Status (1FLAGS) Verification. Tests the following processor status flags: carry, zero, sign, overflow, The BIOS sets each flag, verifies they are set, then turns each flag off and verifies it is off.
2	Processor Test 2	Read/Write/Verify all CPU registers except SS, SP, and BP with data pattern FF and 00.
3	Initialize Chips	Disable NMI, PIE, AIE, UEI, SQWV Disable video, parity checking, DMA Reset math coprocessor Clear all page registers, CMOS shutdown byte Initialize timer 0, 1, and 2, including set EISA timer to a known state Initialize DMA controllers 0 and 1 Initialize interrupt controllers 0 and 1 Initialize EISA extended registers.

Award BIOS 4.51 PG		
Code (hex)	Name	Description
4	Refresh Toggle	RAM must be periodically refreshed to keep the memory from decaying. This function ensures that the memory refresh function is working properly.
5	Blank video, Initialize keyboard	Keyboard controller initialization.
6	Reserved	
7	Test CMOS Interface and Battery Status	Verifies CMOS is working correctly, detects bad battery.
BE	Chipset default Initialization	Program chipset registers with power on BIOS defaults.
C1	Memory presence Test	OEM Specific-Test to size on-board memory
C5	Early Shadow	OEM Specific-Early Shadow enable for fast boot.
C6	Cache presence Test	External cache size detection
8	Setup low Memory	Early chip set initialization Memory presence test OEM chip set routines Clear low 64K of memory Test first 64K memory.
9	Early Cache Initialization	Cyrix CPU initialization Cache initialization
A	Setup Interrupt Vector Table	Initialize first 120 interrupt vectors with SPURIOUS_INT_HDLR and initialize INT 00h-1Fh according to INT_TBL
B	Test CMOS RAM Checksum	Test CMOS RAM Checksum, if bad, or insert key pressed, load defaults.
C	Initialize Keyboard	Detect type of keyboard controller (optional) Set NUM_LOCK status.
D	Initialize Video Interface	Detect CPU clock. Read CMOS location 14h to find out type of video in use. Detect and Initialize Video Adapter.
E	Test video Memory	Test video memory, write sign-on message to screen. Setup shadow RAM - Enable shadow according to Setup.
F	Test DMA Controller 0	BIOS checksum test. Keyboard detect and initialization
10	Test DMA Controller 1	
11	Test DMA Page Registers	Test DMA Page Registers.
12-13	Reserved	
14	Test Timer Counter 2	Test 8254 Timer 0 Counter 2.
15	Test 8259-1 Mask Bits	Verify 8259 Channel 1 masked interrupts by alternately turning off and on the interrupt lines.
16	Test 8259-2 Mask Bits	Verify 8259 Channel 2 masked interrupts by alternately turning off and on the interrupt lines.
17	Test Stuck 8259's Interrupt Bits	Turn off interrupts then verify no interrupt mask register is on.
18	Test 8259 Interrupt Functionality	Force an interrupt and verify the interrupt occurred.

Appendix A: BIOS Information

Award BIOS 4.51 PG		
Code (hex)	Name	Description
19	Test Stuck NMI Bits (Parity I/O Check)	Verify NMI can be cleared.
1A		Display CPU clock.
1B-1E	Reserved	
1F	Set EISA Mode	If EISA non-volatile memory checksum is good, execute EISA initialization. If not, execute ISA tests an clear EISA mode flag. Test EISA Configuration Memory Integrity (checksum & communication interface).
20	Enable Slot 0	Initialize slot 0 (System Board).
21-2F	Enable Slots 1-15	Initialize slots 1 through 15.
30	Size Base and Extended Memory	Size base memory from 256K to 640K and extended memory above 1MB.
31	Test Base and Extended Memory	Test base memory from 256K to 640K and extended memory above 1MB using various patterns. NOTE: This test is skipped in EISA mode and can be skipped with ESC key in ISA mode.
32	Test EISA Etended Memory	If EISA Mode flag is set then test EISA memory found in slots initialization. NOTE: This test is skipped in ISA mode and can be skipped with ESC key in EISA mode.
33-3B	Reserved	
3C	Setup Enabled	
3D	Initialize & Install Mouse	Detect if mouse is present, initialize mouse, install interrupt vectors.
3E	Setup cache Controller	Initialize cache controller.
3F	Reserved	
BF	Chipset Initialization	Program chipset registers with Setup values
40		Display virus protect disable or enable
41	Initialize Floppy Drive & Controller	Initialize floppy disk drive controller and any drives.
42	Initialize Hard Drive & Controller	Initialize hard drive controller and any drives.
43	Detect & Initialize Serial/Parallel Ports	Initialize any serial and parallel ports (also game port).
44	Reserved	
45	Detect & Initialize Math Coprocessor	Initialize math coprocessor.
46	Reserved	
47	Reserved	
48-4D	Reserved	

Appendix A: BIOS Information

Award BIOS 4.51 PG		
Code (hex)	Name	Description
4E	Manufacturing POST Loop or Display Message	Reboot if Manufacturing POST Loop pin or display message is set. Otherwise display any messages (i.e., any non-fatal errors that were detected during POST) and enter Setup.
4F	Security Check	Ask password security (optional).
50	Write CMOS	Write all CMOS values back to RAM and clear screen.
51	Pre-boot Enable	Enable parity checker Enable NMI, Enable cache before boot.
52	Initialize Option ROMs	Initialize any option ROMs present from C8000h to EFFFFh. NOTE: When FSCAN option is enabled, ROMs initialize from C8000h to F7FFFh.
53	Initialize Time Value	Initialize time value in 40h: BIOS area.
60	Setup Virus Protect	Setup virus protect according to Setup
61	Set Boot Speed	Set system speed for boot
62	Setup Numlock	Setup NumLock status according to Setup
63	Boot Attemp	Set low stack Boot via INT 19h.
B0	Spurious	If interrupt occurs in protected mode.
B1	Unclaimed NMI	If unmasked NMI occurs, display Press F1 to disable NMI, F2 reboot.
E1-EF	Setup Pages	E1- Page 1, E2 - Page 2, etc.
FF	Boot	

AMI BIOS

Checkpoint	Description
01	Processor register test about to start,and NMI to be disabled.
02	NMI is Disabled. Power on delay starting.
03	Power on delay complete. Any initialization before keyboard BAT is in progress.
04	Any initialization before keyboard BAT is complete. Reading keyboard SYS bit, to check soft reset/ power-on.
05	Soft reset/ power-on determined. Going to enable ROM. i.e. disable shadow RAM/Cache if any.
06	ROM is enabled. Calculating ROM BIOS checksum, and waiting for KB controller input buffer to be free.
07	ROM BIOS checksum passed, KB controller I/B free. Going to issue the BAT command to keyboard controller.
08	BAT command to keyboard controller is issued. Going to verify the BAT command.

227

Appendix A: BIOS Information

Checkpoint	Description
09	Keyboard controller BAT result verified. Keyboard command byte to be written next.
0A	Keyboard command byte code is issued. Going to write command byte data.
0B	Keyboard controller command byte is written. Going to issue Pin-23, 24 blocking/unblocking command.
0C	Pin-23, 24 of keyboard controller is blocked/ unblocked. NOP command of keyboard controller to be issued next.
0D	NOP command processing is done. CMOS shutdown register test to be done next.
0E	CMOS shutdown register R/W test passed. Going to calculate CMOS checksum, and update DIAG byte.
0F	CMOS checksum calculation is done, DIAG byte written. CMOS init. to begin (If "INIT CMOS IN EVERY BOOT IS SET").
10	CMOS initialization done (if any). CMOS status register about to init for Date and Time.
11	CMOS Status register initialized. Going to disable DMA and Interrupt controllers.
12	DMA controller #1,#2, interrupt controller #1,#2 disabled. About to disable Video display and init port-B.
13	Video display is disabled and port-B is initialized. Chipset init/ auto memory detection about to begin.
14	Chipset initialization/ auto memory detection over. 8254 timer test about to start.
15	CH-2 timer test halfway. 8254 CH-2 timer test to be complete.
16	Ch-2 timer test over. 8254 CH-1 timer test to be complete.
17	CH-1 timer test over. 8254 CH-0 timer test to be complete.
18	CH-0 timer test over. About to start memory refresh.
19	Memory Refresh started. Memory Refresh test to be done next.
1A	Memory Refresh line is toggling. Going to check 15 micro second ON/OFF time.
1B	Memory Refresh period 30 micro second test complete. Base 64K memory test about to start.
20	Base 64k memory test started. Address line test to be done next.
21	Address line test passed. Going to do toggle parity.
22	Toggle parity over. Going for sequential data R/W test.
23	Base 64k sequential data R/W test passed. Any setup before Interrupt vector init about to start.
24	Setup required before vector initialzation complete. Interrupt vector initialization about to begin.
25	Interrupt vector initialization done. Going to read I/O port of 8042 for turbo switch (if any).
26	I/O port of 8042 is read. Going to initialize global data for turbo switch.
27	Global data initialization is over. Any initialization after interrupt vector to be done next.

Appendix A: BIOS Information

Checkpoint	Description
28	Initialization after interrupt vector is complete. Going for monochrome mode setting.
29	Initialization after interrupt vector is complete. Going for monochrome mode setting.
2A	Color mode setting is done. About to go for toggle parity before optional ROM test.
2B	Toggle parity over. About to give control for any setup required before optional video ROM check.
2C	Processing before video ROM control is done. About to look for optional video ROM and give control.
2D	Optional video ROM control is done. About to give control to do any procesing after video ROM returns control.
2E	Return from processing after the video ROM control. If EGA/VGA not found then do display memory R/W test.
2F	EGA/VGA not found. Display memory R/W test about to begin.
30	Display memory R/W test passed. About to look for the retrace checking.
31	Display memory R/W test or retrace checking failed. About to do alternate Display memory R/W test.
32	Alternate Display memory R/W test passed. About to look for the alternate display retrace checking.
33	Video display checking over. Verification of display type with switch setting and actual card to begin.
34	Verification of display adapter done. Display mode to be set next.
35	Display mode set complete. BIOS ROM data area about to be checked.
36	BIOS ROM data area check over. Going to set cursor for power on message.
37	Cursor setting for power on message ID complete. Going to display the power on message.
38	Power on message display complete. Going to read new cursor position.
39	New cursor position read and saved. Going to display the reference string.
3A	Reference string display is over. Going to display the Hit <ESC> message.
3B	Hit <ESC> message displayed. Virtual mode memory test about to start.
40	Preparation for virtual mode test started. Going to verify from video memory.
41	Returned after verifying from display memory. Going to prepare the descriptor tables.
42	Descriptor tables prepared. Going to enter in virtual mode for memory test.
43	Entered in the virtual mode. Going to enable interrupts for diagnostics mode.
44	Interrupts enabled (if diagnostics switch is on). Going to initialize data to check memory wrap around at 0:0.
45	Data initialized. Going to check for memory wrap around at 0:0 and finding the total system memory size.
46	Memory wrap around test done. Memory size calculation over. About to go for writing patterns to test memory.

Appendix A: BIOS Information

Checkpoint	Description
47	Pattern to be tested written in extended memory. Going to write patterns in base 640k memory.
48	Patterns written in base memory. Going to findout amount of memory below 1M memory.
49	Amount of memory below 1M found and verified. Going to findout amount of memory above 1M memory.
4A	Amount of memory above 1M found and verified. Going for BIOS ROM data area check.
4B	BIOS ROM data area check over. Going to check <ESC> and to clear memory below 1M for soft reset.
4C	Memory below 1M cleared. (SOFT RESET) Going to clear memory above 1M.
4D	Memory above 1M cleared. (SOFT RESET) Going to save the memory size.
4E	Memory test started. (NO SOFT RESET) About to display the first 64k memory test.
4F	Memory size display started. This will be updated during memory test. Going for sequential and random memory test.
50	Memory test below 1M complete. Going to adjust memory size for relocation/ shadow.
51	Memory size adjusted due to relocation/ shadow. Memory test above 1M to follow.
52	Memory test above 1M complete. Going to prepare to go back to real mode.
53	CPU registers are saved including memory size. Going to enter in real mode.
54	Shutdown successfull, CPU in real mode. Going to restore registers saved during preparation for shutdown.
55	Registers restored. Going to disable gate A20 address line.
56	A20 address line disable successful. BIOS ROM data area about to be checked.
57	BIOS ROM data area check halfway. BIOS ROM data area check to be complete.
58	BIOS ROM data area check over. Going to clear Hit <ESC> message.
59	Hit <ESC> message cleared. <WAIT...> message displayed. About to start DMA and interrupt controller test.
60	DMA page register test passed. About to verify from display memory.
61	Display memory verification over. About to go for DMA #1 base register test.
62	DMA #1 base register test passed. About to go for DMA #2 base register test.
63	DMA #2 base register test passed. About to go for BIOS ROM data area check.
64	BIOS ROM data area check halfway. BIOS ROM data area check to be complete.
65	BIOS ROM data area check over. About to program DMA unit 1 and 2.
66	DMA unit 1 and 2 programming over. About to initialize 8259 interrupt controller.
67	8259 initialization over. About to start keyboard test.
80	Keyboard test started. clearing output buffer, checking for stuck key, About to issue keyboard reset command.
81	Keyboard reset error/stuck key found. About to issue keyboard controller interface test command.

Appendix A: BIOS Information

Checkpoint	Description
82	Keyboard controller interface test over. About to write command byte and init circular buffer.
83	Command byte written, Global data init done. About to check for lock-key.
84	Lock-key checking over. About to check for memory size mismatch with CMOS.
85	Memory size check done. About to display soft error and check for password or bypass setup.
86	Password checked. About to do pogramming before setup.
87	Programming before setup complete. Going to CMOS setup program.
88	Returned from CMOS setup program and screen is cleared. About to do programming after setup.
89	Programming after setup complete. Going to display power on screen message.
8A	First screen message displayed. About to display <WAIT...> message
8B	<WAIT...> message displayed. About to do Main and Video BIOS shadow.
8C	Main and Video BIOS shadow successful. Setup options programming after CMOS setup about to start.
8D	Main and Video BIOS shadow successful. Setup options programming after CMOS setup about to start.
8E	Mouse check and initialization complete. Going for hard disk, floppy reset.
8F	Floppy check returns that floppy is to be initialized. Floppy setup to follow.
90	Floppy setup is over. Test for hard disk presence to be done.
91	Hard disk presence test over. Hard disk setup to follow.
92	Hard disk setup complete. About to go for BIOS ROM data area check.
93	BIOS ROM data area check halfway. BIOS ROM data area check to be complete.
94	BIOS ROM data area check over. Going to set base and extended memory size.
95	Memory size adjusted due to mouse support, hdisk type-47. Going to verify from display memory.
96	Returned after verifying from display memory. Going to do any init before C800 optional ROM control
97	Any init before C800 optional ROM control is over. Optional ROM check and control will be done next.
98	Optional ROM control is done. About to give control to do any required procesing after optional ROM returns control.
99	Any initialization required after optional ROM test over. Going to setup timer data area and printer base address.
9A	Return after setting timer and printer base address. Going to set the RS-232 base address.
9B	Returned after RS-232 base address. Going to do any initialization before Co-processor test
9C	Required initialization before co-processor is over. Going to initialize the coprocessor next.

Appendix A: BIOS Information

Checkpoint	Description
9D	Coprocesor initialized. Going to do any initialization after coprocessor test.
9E	Initialization after coprocessor test is complete. Going to check extended keyboard, keyboard ID and num-lock.
9F	Extd keyboard check is done, ID flag set. num-lock on/off. Keyboard ID command to be issued.
A0	Keyboard ID command issued. Keyboard ID flag to be reset.
A1	Keyboard ID flag reset. Cache memory test to follow.
A2	Cache memory test over. Going to display any soft errors.
A3	Soft error display complete. Going to set the keyboard typematic rate.
A4	Keyboard typematic rate set. Going to program memory wait states.
A5	Memory wait states programming over. Screen to be cleared next.
A6	Screen cleared. Going to enable parity and NMI.
A7	NMI and parity enabled. Going to do any initialization required before giving control to optional ROM at E000.
A8	Initialization before E000 ROM control over. E000 ROM to get control next.
A9	Returned from E000 ROM control. Going to do any initialization required after E000 optional ROM control.
AA	Initialization after E000 optional ROM control is over. Going to display the system configuration.
00	System configuration is displayed. Going to give control to INT 19h boot loader.

MR-BIOS

Code (hex)	Description
00	Cold Start, output EDX register to I/O ports 85h, 86h, 8Dh, 8Eh for later use
01	Initialize any Custom KBD controller, disable CPU cache, cold initialize onboard I/O chipset, size & test RAM, size cache
02	Disable critical IO (monitor, DMA, FDC, I/O ports, Speaker, NMI)
03	Checksum the BIOS ROM
04	Test page registers
05	Enable A20 Gate, issue 8042 SelfTest
06	Initialize ISA I/O
07	Warm initialize custom KBD controller, warm initialize onboard I/O chipset
08	Refresh toggle test
09	Test DMA Master registers, test DMA Slave registers
0A	Test 1st 64K of base memory
0B	Test Master 8259 mask, test Slave 8259 mask

Appendix A: BIOS Information

Code (hex)	Description
0C	Test 8259 Slave, test 8259 slave's interrupt range, initialize interrupt vectors 00 - 77h, init KBD buffer variables.
0D	Test Timer0, 8254 channel0
0E	Test 8254 Ch2, speaker channel
0F	Test RTC, CMOS RAM read/write test
10	Turn on Monitor, Show any possible error messages
11	Read and checksum the CMOS
12	Call Video ROM initialization routines, Show Display sign on message, Show ESC Delay message
13	Set 8MHz AT-Bus
14	Size and test the base memory, Stuck NMI check
15	No KB and PowerOn: Retry KB init
16	Size and test CPU Cache
17	Test A20 OFF and ON states
18	Size and test External memory, Stuck NMI check
19	Size and test System memory, Stuck NMI check
1A	Test RTC Time
1B	Determine Serial Ports
1C	Determine Parallel Ports
1D	Initialize Numeric Coprocessor
1E	Determine Floppy Diskette Controllers
1F	Determine IDE Controllers
20	Display CMOS configuration changes
21	Clear screens
22	Set/reset Numlock LED, perform Security functions
23	Final determination of onboard Serial/Parallel ports
24	Set KB Typematic Rate
25	Initialize Floppy Controller
26	Initialize ATA discs
27	Set the video mode for primary adaptor
28	Cyrix WB-CPU support, Green PC: purge 8259 slave, relieve any trapped IRRs before enabling PwrMgmt, set 8042 pins, Ctrl-Alt-Del possible now, Enable CPU Features
29	Reset A20 to OFF, install Adapter ROMs
2A	Clear Primary Screen, Convert RTC to system ticks, Set final DOS timer variables
2B	Enable NMI and latch.
2C	Reserved
2D	Reserved

Appendix A: BIOS Information

Code (hex)	Description
2E	Fast A20: Fix A20
2F	Purge 8259 slave; relieve any trapped IRRs before enabling Green-PC. Pass control to INT 19 boot
32	Test CPU Burst
33	Reserved
34	Determine 8042, Set 8042 Warm-Boot flag STS.2
35	Test HMA Wrap, Verify A20 enabled via F000:10 HMA
36	Reserved
37	Validate CPU: CPU Step NZ, CPUID Check. Disable CPU features
38	Set 8042 pins (Hi-Speed, Cache-off)
39	PCI Bus: Load PCI; Processor Vector init'd, BIOS Vector init'd, OEM Vector init'd
3A	Scan PCI Bus
3B	Initialize PCI Bus with intermediate defaults
3C	Initialize PCI OEM with intermediate defaults, OEM bridge
3D	PCI Bus or PLUGnPLAY: Initialize AT Slotmap from AT-Bus CDE usage
3E	Find phantom CDE ROM PCI-cards
3F	PCI Bus: final Fast-Back-to-Back state
40	OEM POST Initialization, Hook Audio
41	Allocate I/O on PCI-Bus, logs-in PCI-IDE
42	Hook PCI-ATA chips
43	Allocate IRQs on the PCI Bus
44	Allocate/enable PCI Memory/ROM space
45	Determine PS/2 Mouse
46	Map IRQs to PCI Bus per user CMOS, Enable ATA IRQs.
47	PCI-ROM install, note user CMOS
48	If Setup conditions: execute setup utility
49	Test F000 Shadow integrity, Transfer EPROM to Shadow-RAM
4A	Hook VL ATA Chip
4B	Identify and spin-up all drives
4C	Detect Secondary IRQ, if VL/AT-Bus IDE exists but its IRQ not known yet, then autodetect it
4D	Detect/log 32-bit I/O ATA devices
4E	Atapi drive M/S bitmap to Shadow-RAM, Set INT13 Vector
4F	Finalize Shadow-RAM variables
50	Chain INT 13
51	Load PnP, Processor Vector init'd, BIOS Vector init'd, OEM Vector init'd

Appendix A: BIOS Information

Code (hex)	Description
52	Scan PLUGnPLAY, update PnP Device Count
53	Supplement IRQ usage — AT IRQs
54	Conditionally assign everything PnP wants
58	Perform OEM Custom boot sequence just prior to INT 19 boot
59	Return from OEM custom boot sequence. Pass control to 1NT 19 boot
5A	Display MR BIOS logo
88	Dead motherboard and/or CPU and/or BIOS ROM.
FF	BIOS POST Finished

Appendix B:
Glossary

There are a great many terms having to do with BIOS. To give you some guidance in your studies of user manuals, & allow you to find what you need without reading through all the chapters of the manual, we have given you a quick overview here with brief, meaningful explanations of the terms.

(E)CHS

(E)CHS (Extended CHS) mode is an extended mode that also supports hard drives above 528 Megs. However, it only works with DOS.

32 bit mode

With 32-bit mode the data are transferred from the EIDE controller to the hard drive at 32-bit bandwidth.

ACPI

The new power management is called ACPI (**A**dvanced **C**onfiguration and **P**ower **I**nterface) and has an enhanced energy management compared to the API.

AGP

The AGP is the new slot for video cards (**A**ccelerated **G**raphics **P**ort).

APM

The APM (**A**dvanced **P**ower **M**anagment) is a power management for the PC that lets you put various components into hibernation/sleep mode.

ATA

ATA (**AT** **A**ttachment) is a standard for the attachment of hard drives and CD-ROM drives.

Benchmark

This is a test procedure in which the performance of the PC is determined using readings of the individual components

BIOS

The BIOS (**B**asic **I**nput/**O**utput **S**ystem) is a part of the operating system that is permanently stored in the ROM of the PC.

Appendix B: Glossary

BIOS-ID-Codes

Each BIOS displays a BIOS Ident-Line on the screen after power-up. It is a combination of letters and numbers that can also be used as an identification string.

Bit

The bit is the smallest information unit in computer technology. It consists of a binary number that can either accept 0 or 1.

Boot

Booting means starting the PC.

Boot sector

The boot sector is the first sector of the hard drive, where a program code for starting the operating system is located.

Bootstrap-Loader

This is a small program that knows the file structure of the storage medium and thus is able to call the start routine of the operating system.

Burst

With burst access lots of data is transferred as quickly as possible in one block. This saves time and resources in addressing.

Byte

The byte is a combination of 8 bits.

Cache

The cache is a fast buffer for components that only have a slow RAM.

CAS

CAS (**C**olumn **A**ddress **S**trobe) is a control signal for the column address in the memory chip.

Checksum

The checksum is added in the storage of data and later used as a comparison data in a change.

Chipset

The motherboard chipset consists of a variable number of chips which control all components such as memory, controller, ports and the bus system on the motherboard.

CHS

Only old IDE hard drives use CHS mode (**C**ylinders-**H**eads-**S**ectors). It addresses the hard drive through cylinders, heads and sectors and thus cannot manage more than 528 Megs.

Appendix B: Glossary

CMOS

The CMOS (**C**omplementary **M**etal **O**xide **S**emiconductor) RAM is the memory in which the data of the BIOS are permanently kept by a battery.

Controller

The controller is the control electronics of the drive, which is directly integrated into the hard drives, CD-ROM drives, CD burners or ZIP drives etc.

CPU

The CPU (**C**entral **P**rocessing **U**nit) is the main processor in the PC.

CPU-SOFT-MENU

The CPU-SOFT-MENU allows you to install the used processor directly in BIOS Setup without setting jumpers on the motherboard.

DIMM

The DIMM (**D**ual **I**nline **M**emory **M**odule) is used as main memory and consists of SDRAM chips (**S**ynchronous **DRAM**). They run stably with the external system bus clock up to 100 MHz. They also have a real internal 2K cache.

Disabled

The Disabled setting turns off the selected option.

DMA

The DMA (**D**irect **M**emory **A**ccess) is a direct transfer of data of the components to the main memory that occurs without the processor.

DPMS

Newer monitors and video cards support DPMS (**D**isplay **P**ower **M**anagment **S**ignaling-Standard). With DPMS the monitor can be switched off through a signal from the video card.

DRAM

DRAM (**D**ynamic **RAM**) is used on FP and EDO memory modules. It consists chiefly of integrated circuits containing capacitors. However, the capacitors lose their charge after a time and along with it, their stored information. For this reason, they need a refresh at regular intervals.

ECC

Some of the new SDRAM modules have an automatic error correction code, ECC (**E**rror **C**orrection **C**ode). If it is integrated in the chip the corresponding option can be enabled in the BIOS.

ECP

ECP (**E**xtended **C**apabilities **P**ort) mode is an extended mode for the parallel printer port. It has a 16K FIFO buffer similar to the serial port. In addition, data compression is used.

Appendix B: Glossary

EDTP

An EDTP (**E**nhance-**D**rive-**P**arameter-**T**able) is necessary for LBA translation. The POST routine creates this special hard drive parameter table, which contains two records with the information of the cylinders, heads and sectors. The hard drive parameters are converted with this table.

EEPROM

The EEPROM (**E**lectrically **E**rasable **P**rogrammable **ROM**) is a memory chip that can be written and erased electronically without additional devices.

EIDE

With EIDE (**E**nhance **I**ntegrated **D**rive **E**lectronics) the controller is directly integrated in the drive, and no longer as a separate expansion card in the PC. What is incorrectly termed "controller" in the PC is only an adapter for connection of the EIDE components.

Enabled

The Enabled setting turns on the selected option.

EPA

The American environmental authority, the EPA (**E**nvironmental **P**rotection **A**gency), sees to it that users can voluntarily save power. For this purpose, the necessary devices are built into the corresponding machine.

EPP mode

EPP (**E**nhance **P**arallel **P**ort) mode is an enhanced mode for the parallel port. It is mainly intended for devices that are not printers (e.g. scanners) that support EPP.

EPROM

The EPROM (**E**rasable **P**rogrammable **ROM**) is a memory chip that can be electronically written to with an EPROM burner and completely erased with an EPROM eraser.

ESCD

In ESCD (**E**xtended **S**ystem **C**onfiguration **D**ata) the data is saved by the Plug & Play system.

External clock

The external clock is generated by the clock on the motherboard. It provides the processor as well as the RAM modules and a few other components on the board with a settable clock frequency.

FAT

The FAT (**F**ile **A**llocation **T**able) is the hard drive's table of contents. The addresses of the allocation units (clusters) are stored in it, which in turn, contain your data.

FIFO

The FIFO (**F**ile **I**nput **F**ile **O**utput) is a buffer for the data input and the data output. For example, it is used for the serial and parallel port to speed up data transfer.

Appendix B: Glossary

Firewire

Firewire or IEEE 1934 (**I**nstitute of **E**lectrical and **E**lectronics **E**ngineers) is a new inteface which can establish a digital connection for 63 devices and a data transfer rate of up to 400 Mbit/s. Adapters with a rate of 1.2 Gbit/s are currently in development.

Firmware

Hardware with integrated software is also called firmware.

Flash ROM

The BIOS is termed flash ROM when it can get an update by software.

Flasher

The program with which the update file is written to the BIOS is referred to as a flasher.

Gate A20

The A20 signal is used to switch from Real mode of the processor, which uses the memory area to 1,024K, to Protect mode, which uses the memory above 1,024K.

Hardcopy

A printout of the screen contents is referred to as hard copy. You start hard copy by pressing the [Print] key.

I/O Address

The input/output address for add-on cards. For communication, each card needs an I/O address in memory for buffering the data.

ICU

The ICU (**ISA C**onfiguration Utility) first determines the hardware equipment of the PC and then the individual parameters of the plug-in card. Then the utility, which simulates a PnP BIOS, lets you assign the resources for the card.

IDE

IDE (**I**ntegrated **D**rive **E**lectronics) is structured like EIDE.

INT

INT refers to the variable interrupts A - D of the PCI components.

Integrated Peripherals

The onboard interfaces of the PC.

Internal clock

The internal clock is generated by a circuit in the processor. It can be determined by a multiplier, that multiplies the external clock.

Appendix B: Glossary

IrDa Port

The IrDa (Infrared Data) port is an infrared interface used for a cable-free transfer of data, e.g. from a desktop to a laptop.

IRQ

The IRQ (**I**nterrupt **Req**uest) is an interruption that takes place in program execution. The interruption is conducted to the processor through an IRQ channel, which then executes a different task and then returns to its original program execution.

IRQ Sharing

With IRQ sharing two compatible PC cards share one interrupt.

ISA bus

The ISA (Industry Standard Architecture) bus is, like other bus systems, a line system that is used for data transfer to the individual system components.

Jumper

Jumpers are small lengths of conductor for hardware configuration.

LBA

LBA (**L**ogical **B**lock **A**dressing) refers to the translation mode for the data blocks through the BIOS. It is the best mode for addressing hard drives larger than 528 Megs.

Master

The master is the first hard drive on the (E)IDE port.

MBR

The MBR (**M**aster **B**oot **R**ecord) is a small program (bootstrap loader) that loads the system components. It is located in the first sector of the boot drive and is executed by the BIOS.

NMI

The NMI (**N**on **M**askable **I**nterrupt) is a non maskable hardware interrupt that cannot be interrupted by the processor through a bit and must be executed immediately. The NMI has absolute priority over all other interrupts.

Operating system software

The operating system software is the program code in the BIOS that executes the self test and starts the PC.

Overclocking

Overclocking means clocking the processor beyond its specifications.

PCI bus

The PCI (**P**eripheral **C**omponent **I**nterconnect) bus is, like other bus variants, a line system used for data transfer to the individual system components.

Performance

The ability of a PC to perform tasks.

PIO Mode

PIO (**P**rogrammed **I**nput/**O**utput) mode is an industrial standard and determines the data transfer method between the controller and the hard drive.

Plug & Play

PnP refers to the automatic configuration of the IRQs and DMAs of plug-in cards through the system BIOS.

Port

A port is the connection for a device (hard drive, CD-ROM, floppy drive, printer, mouse, modem).

POST

The PC runs a self test right after you power it up. This test is called POST (**P**ower **O**n **S**elf **T**est).

RAS

RAS (**R**ow **A**ddress **S**trobe) is a control signal for the row address in the memory chip.

Refresh

The refresh itself is a short surge of current, which can charge the capacitors in the RAM module back up in a specified period of time in the µs (microseconds) range.

Register

The registers are located in the chipset of the motherboard and control various components such as the memory, controller, ports and the bus system. They are evaluated and set by the operating system software in the BIOS.

ROM

The ROM memory chip (**R**ead **O**nly **M**emory) is a read-only memory. It is programmed for good after chip production and cannot be erased.

SCSI Host Adapter

The SCSI host adapter is the controller of the SCSI system.

SCSI-ID

The SCSI-ID is the identity for a SCSI device, which can be set by jumpers or a switch. Each ID can only be assigned once.

Appendix B: Glossary

Shadow RAM

The system and video ROM of the BIOS are shadowed to RAM. The RAM chips are much faster than the ROM. As a result, program flow speeds up.

SIMMs

The SIMM (**S**ingle **I**nline **M**emory **M**odule) is used as main memory and consists of DRAM (**D**ynamic **RAM**) chips. Most SIMMs have nine chips on the 30-pin SIMM or 72-pin PS/2 module.

SIP Module

The SIP (**S**ingle **I**nline **P**ackage) module is used as main memory and consists of DRAM chips (**D**ynamic **RAM**). They are identical to SIMMs in structure, but have small legs soldered onto the contacts.

Slave

The slave is the second hard drive on the (E)IDE port.

SMB (**S**ystem **M**anagment **B**us)

A simple two-wire bus used for communication with low-bandwidth devices on a motherboard, especially power related chips. Other devices might include temperature sensors and lid switches.

SPP

The SPP (**S**tandard **P**arallel **P**ort) is the conventional printer port without extensions.

Terminator

The terminator is an active or passive terminal resistance for SCSI systems, with which the last component on the cable must be equipped.

Timing

Timing refers to the timing between several executions.

UART

The UART (**U**niversal **A**synchronous **R**eceiver **T**ransmitter) chip is responsible for the transfer of data from and to the port. The new 16550 UART chip has a significantly higher data transfer rate compared to the old 8250, as a result of its 16 byte cache, the FIFO (**F**ile **I**nput **F**ile **O**utput) for buffering data.

UDMA

Like normal DMA mode, UDMA (**U**ltra **DMA**) mode also transports the data from the hard drive to the main memory, without burdening the CPU. In addition, it has a new protocol with automatic error correction.

USB

The USB (**U**niversal **S**erial **B**us) is a new bus system that makes possible the connection of 128 devices with a maximum data transfer of 12 MBit/s. However, it requires a suitable operating system such as Windows 95/98.

Waitstates (WS)

Since the processor and the system bus usually work more quickly than the DRAMs respond, the processor has to execute some waitstates while it waits for the memory return.

Y2K

Y stands for year, 2 is 2 and K stands for Kilo, often used to mean 1000. Put them together and you've got, year 2000.

Z Buffer

Auxiliary memory for the 3D video card. The depth information of a pixel of the Z axis from the three-dimensional coordinate system is stored here. In some BIOS versions the size of the memory can be defined.

Index

Books from Abacus

Easy Digital Video

A "How-To" Guide that makes digital video for the PC Easy, Practical, Affordable and Fun!

Today the industry spotlight is shining on PC video. Thanks to less expensive and more powerful PCs, inexpensive video editors and video capture cards, consumers are looking for ways to use this exciting technology. *Easy Digital Photo* teaches how to produce videos quickly and inexpensively.

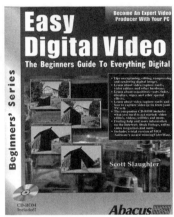

Easy Digital Video uses today's hardware and software to "produce" and "tweak" your videos on your PC. *Easy Digital Video* is for digital "producers" who want to dig into this enjoyable, user-friendly technology.

Author Scott Slaughter introduces basic concepts (video formats, capture cards, streaming video, hardware requirements, bandwidth and more) in an easy-to-digest format. *Easy Digital Video* includes useful descriptions of video editors and video capture cards as well as expert advice on what to look for when buying them.

Learn about today's popular video editors from major manufacturers: Asymetrix, MGI Software, Corel, Adobe Systems, NewSoft, In:sync, Ulead Systems and others. Learn when and how to use transitions (cuts, dissolves, fades, wipes and digital video effects), simple special effects (including advanced) and other tasks previously meant only for professionals. Learn to do more with your videos than you ever thought possible.

The companion CD-ROM includes evaluations and demonstrations of software, sample video clips, pictures, sounds and utilities.

Suggested Retail Price $29.95 US/$39.95 CAN	Shipping and Handling
Author: Scott Slaughter	In US & Canada Add $5.00
Order Item #B340	Foreign Orders Add $13.00 per item
ISBN: 1-55755-340-8	**To order direct call toll free**
Michigan residents add 6% sales tax	**1-800-451-4319**

Books from Abacus

Building A Pentium Server

Building A Powerful Server With Confidence

Servers are now at the heart of many businesses. Operating systems today are very capable with powerful computers that secure, validate, and control the critical data and applications of a business.

Prices for personal computers are very attractive compared to the sky high prices for servers. *Building A Pentium Server* takes aim at these high prices and shows how to plan your system, select and buy components, assemble the computer and install the operating system.

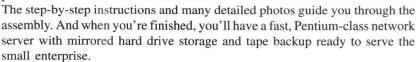

This book shows you how to build a quality, performance-oriented server at the least cost. The step-by-step instructions and many detailed photos guide you through the assembly. And when you're finished, you'll have a fast, Pentium-class network server with mirrored hard drive storage and tape backup ready to serve the small enterprise.

Topics include:

- Pentium, Pentium Pro, and other chip decisions

- Motherboard considerations

- Hard drive mirroring — SCSI vs. IDE

- Selection & purchase of components

- Assembling the server

- Installing the operating system

Suggested Retail Price: $34.95 US/$46.95 CAN
Author: Nate Vandershaaf
Order Item #B328
ISBN: 1-55755-328-9
UPC 0 90869 55378 6
Michigan residents add 6% sales tax

Shipping and Handling
In US & Canada Add $5.00
Foreign Orders Add $13.00 per item
To order direct call toll free
1-800-451-4319

Books from Abacus

Your Family Tree

Your Family Tree is a beginner's guide to researching, organizing and sharing your family's heritage with relatives and friends. If you want to trace your family roots, get started by using this book and companion CD-ROM.

Author Jim Oldfield, Jr., shows how to get started tracing your roots using his expert, easy-to-follow steps and your personal computer. An experienced genealogist, Jim has produced three family history books of his own, and now you can too. You'll learn how to gather facts and information, transfer them to popular genealogy programs, add illustrations, use your word processor or desktop publisher to produce reports, share the info in a meaningful way and keep up with "newer" family additions.

Topics discussed include:

- Researching on the Internet

- Creating a Web site for your family pages

- Starting your own newsletter or association

CD-ROM INCLUDED!

- Adding photos and sound to your family tree

- Using conversion programs to publish data on the Web

- Using software like- Family Tree Maker, Family Origins and more

The companion CD-ROM has various family pedigree forms for collecting family information, sample family data that shows you "hands-on" how to get started, family photos and a collection of the most popular shareware for genealogy and illustrations.

Suggested Retail Price $25.95 US/$34.95
Author: Jim Oldfield, Jr.
Order Item #B310
ISBN: 1-55755-310-6
Michigan residents add 6% sales tax

Shipping and Handling
In US & Canada Add $5.00
Foreign Orders Add $13.00 per item
To order direct call toll free
1-800-451-4319

Books from Abacus

Win98 Rx

Solve Your PC Problems Easily!

The installed base for Windows 95 reached millions of PC users. Windows 98 is expected to reach 220 million by the end of the decade! Making the transition to Windows 98 will not be any easier than it was to upgrade to Windows 95. There will be a tremendous demand for customer support and remedies for their problems. *Win98 Rx* is just the prescription for Windows problems.

Win98 Rx is a troubleshooting handbook and complete first-aid kit for the Windows 98 PC. Windows 98 users will learn to troubleshoot all types of problems and errors,

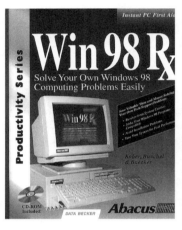

from maintenance and configuration, to recovering from total system crashes! Preventive as well as corrective, *Win98 Rx* will teach you how to avoid most problems you could expect to encounter as well as how to prepare for emergencies. Learn how to make backups, maintain your hard drive, create a startup disk and determine tools for use in each situation. Learn to recognize and remove viruses.

CD-ROM
INCLUDED!

Taking a "what do I do when?" approach to correcting both minor and major problems, this book clearly and extensively describes what to do when your PC won't boot, if you can't access your hard drive, when devices such as your mouse or keyboard don't respond, or when your printer simply won't work. All real life and common system failures that can interrupt your productivity or fun are addressed in *Win98 Rx*.

Suggested Retail Price $34.95 US/$46.95
Author: Kober, Bueche, Baecker
Order Item #B349
ISBN: 1-55755-349-1
Michigan residents add 6% sales tax

Shipping and Handling
In US & Canada Add $5.00
Foreign Orders Add $13.00 per item
To order direct call toll free
1-800-451-4319

Books from Abacus

Building Your Own PC

Buying And Assembling With Confidence

Written for the novice, this step-by-step book helps the average consumer confidently select and buy the right components and assemble them into a high-performance Pentium II PC.

For some consumers, the thought of building a personal computer is just too much to contemplate. However, building a PC is really much easier than it might appear. This book strips away the mystery and fear most people have about the internals of a PC. If you can follow a recipe or build a *Lego* toy, you can build your own PC and save money as well.

Based on personal experience and knowledge of the industry, the author gives you specific advice on what components you'll need to buy — from the right motherboard and chipset, to memory and the correct video board. It covers all the important considerations. The book's step-by-step instructions and many detailed photos will walk you through assembly.

With realworld examples, the author looks at well-known national retail chains as sources for hardware components to help you make informed buying decisions. You'll learn how to shop the many nontraditional outlets for all of the same brandname components. The detailed "Shopping CheckList" helps you buy with confidence.

- Selecting the Right Components
- Sources and Suppliers
- Assembling the Computer
- Installing your Operating System
- Shopping Check List

Suggested Retail Price: $24.95 US/$34.95 CAN
Author: Arnie Lee
Order Item #B355
ISBN: 1-55755-355-6
Michigan residents add 6% sales tax

Shipping and Handling
In US & Canada Add $5.00
Foreign Orders Add $13.00 per item
To order direct call toll free
1-800-451-4319

Books from Abacus

Easy Digital Photography

Beginners Guide to Everything Digital
New 2nd Edition

Have you noticed that the whole world is going digital? And it's not only your cell phone or music appliances, but the whole spectrum of digital images.

Yes, photography is well on it's way to becoming digital. This brand new book introduces you to this mighty new force that is just now taking over the consumer landscape.

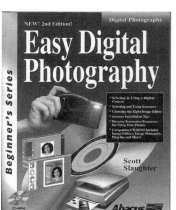

Easy Digital Photography packs the lastest, up-to-date information on using digital cameras, scanners and image editors.

Find out how they work. Read the buying tips. Tweak your photos. Retouch your prized snapshots. Unleash those powerful darkroom techniques on your desktop.

The companion CD-ROM includes evaluation and demonstration versions of some of the most popular commercial software, such as "Eye Candy" from Alien Software, New Soft, Arriba Soft and many more. It also includes a wealth of sample images and selected image conversion programs to use and evaluate.

You'll see how you can use the World Wide Web as a film developer or distributor.

Make the new digital photography a part of your personal computing life.

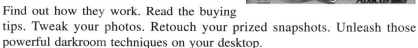

Suggested Retail Price: $29.95 US/$39.95 CAN
Author: Scott Slaughter
Order Item #B364
ISBN: 1-55755-364-5
Michigan residents add 6% sales tax

Shipping and Handling
In US & Canada Add $5.00
Foreign Orders Add $13.00 per item
To order direct call toll free
1-800-451-4319

Books from Abacus

WinZip for Beginners

WinZip is one of those programs that nearly everyone uses. Thanks to the Internet, WinZip is even more popular today. Almost all files that users download are in a compressed or "zipped" format. WinZip is the program of choice for handling these files.

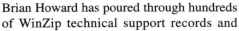

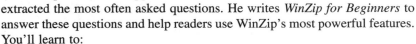

The genius behind WinZip is Nico Mak. Nico has strived to keep his classic WinZip program easy to use. However, he has added so many new and creative features that users always have questions.

Brian Howard has poured through hundreds of WinZip technical support records and extracted the most often asked questions. He writes *WinZip for Beginners* to answer these questions and help readers use WinZip's most powerful features. You'll learn to:

- Zip (compress a file)

- Unzip (decompress a file)

- View the contents of a zipped file

- Create a self-extracting archive

- Create a "spanned" archive — a large compressed file covering more than one diskette

WinZip for Beginners' clear, illustrated, step-by-step instructions walk you through the exact keystrokes so you can become an expert "zipper."

The companion CD-ROM contains a fully functional evaluation copy of WinZip 6.3.

Suggested Retail Price $19.95 US/$29.95 CAN
Author: Brian Howard
Order Item #B339
ISBN: 1-55755-3339-4
Michigan residents add 6% sales tax

Shipping and Handling
In US & Canada Add $5.00
Foreign Orders Add $13.00 per item
To order direct call toll free
1-800-451-4319

Visit our website

Make certain to visit and bookmark the Abacus website (www.abacuspub.com) for the latest information on products, specials, FAQs and mc

www.abacuspub.com